The Farnes & Holy Island

THE FARNES & HOLY ISLAND

A COMPREHENSIVE NEW DIVE GUIDE

RON YOUNG

Whittles Publishing

Published by
Whittles Publishing Ltd.,
Dunbeath,
Caithness, KW6 6EG,
Scotland, UK

www.whittlespublishing.com

ISBN 978-184995-041-1

Printed in India by Imprint Digital

CONTENTS

A PERSONAL INTRODUCTION

Ever since I was a lad, I've been fascinated by the sea: I used to dream about the world beneath the waves and what it must be like. In the real world, though, it was World War Two and its aftermath which dominated my early years. I spent the early 1950s serving an apprenticeship as a fitter and turner, deferring my two years of compulsory National Service until I was 21, but, bored with the tedium of my job and of my life in general, I decided – after some considerable thought – to join the army as a regular. This freed me from the dreaded National Service and allowed me to take advantage of a regular soldier's higher wages, better postings and more exciting opportunities: in those days, the three arms of the British forces had postings in almost every corner of the globe.

After my initial training and a few months assigned to a transport company in Blighty, I applied for a posting to Malaya, a decision that was to shape my destiny.

For a young and adventurous man, free of the caution and fear that come only with age, life was, at first, very exciting. I made many friends while working with the Iban and Dyak scouts, jungle trackers from the elite Sarawak Rangers, who led many of our patrols and whose fathers had been fearsome, blowpipe-wielding headhunters in Borneo. They taught me many of their jungle skills and I learned other forms of survival technique with the now famous special forces. I could have done without the hard, miserable weeks spent soaking wet on secret patrols, hacking through jungle or thorn swamps infested with blood-sucking leeches, insects, giant spiders, snakes and armies of huge, biting red ants, searching for C.T.s (Communist Terrorists). I began seriously to wonder what I had done to deserve such misery and very quickly learnt not to volunteer for anything. Life was really hard and everyone lost weight through sweat and the miserable damp jungle conditions. We relished any break from patrol duties, so on return to HQ in Kuala Lumpur, with the opportunity to take time off, I would head for the lovely tropical beach resort at Port Dickson on the Straits of Malacca, a place also very popular with local people.

It was there that I discovered a different and fascinating new world, away from the biting creepy crawlies of the jungle. The wide sandy beaches below the high water mark swarmed with countless millions of little red fiddler crabs. If anyone approached, the whole beach seemed to move, as the mass of tiny crabs darted in unison to the safety of their sandy burrows while waving their relatively large single claws menacingly towards the sky. At the southern end of the beach, around the headland and separating it from a beautiful blue lagoon, a small mangrove forest jutted out into the shallow green-blue sea. Here, the muddy bottom among the mangrove roots was a kindergarten for multitudes of young fish of every description. The overhanging branches in the mangrove were lined with dozens of brilliant metallic-green and brown-and-white kingfishers that were always on the lookout for an easy meal. When the tide receded, hundreds of quaint little mudskippers emerged from the salty pools to search for insects and the invertebrates that swarmed over the oozy, muddy surface. By flexing their hind end they could move by giving a little skipping jump and the specially-adapted pectoral fin 'fingers' enabled them to waddle over the mud. They breathed by means of water trapped in little gill cover sacs, giving them a few precious minutes when out of the water. Occasionally, troupes of macaque monkeys slipped cheekily down from the forest canopy to forage for their favourite crabs among the mangrove roots while, in the sky, majestic white-breasted fish eagles gracefully swirled high over the palm-lined tropical sea, sometimes sweeping down to grab fish in their razor-sharp talons.

Surprisingly, visibility underwater was never very good, only two or three metres thanks to a large number of working tin mines and heavy rainfall, which turned the jungle rivers pouring into the shallow Malacca Straits a peaty-brown in colour. One thing, though, made up for the inconvenience and hardship of a jungle existence: the coral reefs within snorkelling distance of the beach still teemed with the variety and abundance of marine life that you only read about in books. I had caught the snorkelling bug and purchased a full-face mask, complete with integrated snorkel and ping-pong ball valve, a set of fins (which I still have) and a small single rubber-powered harpoon gun, for protection against the tiger sharks which, I'd been told, cruised the coastline of Malaya. From a friendly local fisherman I learned what was dangerous in the sea and what not to touch on the reefs, and his advice almost certainly saved me from countless stings and bites during my snorkelling adventures. I later disposed of the harpoon gun after my snorkelling buddy Dennis, a Scouser, accidentally stabbed himself in the leg while paddling backwards over a large coral head. He required hospital treatment to remove the one-inch double-edged barb and took some stick from the British Army hospital doctor. I never did see any sharks, but maybe only because of the poor visibility. And when I look back, I often think how futile that little rubber powered gun would have been against a five-metre tiger shark.

From that time on I was well and truly hooked and spent every spare minute snorkelling over the reefs around Port Dickson. Frogman's gear was in its infancy and far beyond my pocket, but the excitement of those coral reef sorties and the underwater environment lived with me long after I came home.

In the early 1960s, still hankering for the underwater life, I visited a local sub-aqua club on Tyneside. With a very young family to look after and mediocre wages, the cost of joining the club and then of buying the equipment I'd need was seriously prohibitive.

In 1973, with a little more money at my disposal, I joined Durham British Sub-Aqua Club and embarked on a long course of lectures and intensive pool-training. After nearly six months of two bath sessions and three lectures a week, I progressed to the 'F' test. The training was extremely difficult, because the tests were all performed with faulty equipment, twin-hose regulators with the return valves removed and bottles which were usually less than half full. Even if you were intending to purchase one of the new single-hose demand valves after qualifying, you were still forced to use the club's faulty twin-hose regulators for training. Very often, as a test drew to a close, the air would run out or the faulty gear would pack up completely, leaving no alternative but to begin the whole rigmarole again the following week. And then again the week after, more often than not.

Over the Easter Bank Holiday in 1974, the club were to make their annual pilgrimage to Oban. I had been really looking forward to this trip because I had heard so much about the fabulous diving there and the great club get-together in the evenings.

When the day came to leave, eight of us crammed into two half-ton vans, lying on top of diving equipment and a folded inflatable dinghy, complete with outboard engine and fuel tank. It certainly wasn't the most comfortable eight-hour journey I have ever experienced but I had been promised a dive or two, so the discomfort seemed worth it at the time. Although I should officially have been onto my 'G' test before going on a sea dive, the Diving Officer said I could go ahead because I had reached a good standard in the pool – which wasn't surprising, given the number of repeated tests and training I had endured. For £40 I had acquired a Spartan 55-cubic ft. bottle and twin-hose Siebe Heinke demand valve, and over some four months I had made myself a Long John wetsuit, making the most of quiet periods on nightshift in the ambulance station where I worked as an ambulanceman. My wetsuit was bought as a kit from Aquaquipment at St Albans for about £20. I had no lifejacket, but then only two of the eight members of the party did.

I made my first three sea dives over that long weekend, and learned a lot of valuable lessons.

For the first dive, we drove down to Easdale Island and motored out to some rocks in the middle, just past Cuan Sound between Luing and Torsa islands. The water was crystal clear and there was a four-knot current running, with the depth showing just five metres. To my dismay, though, nobody wanted to dive as the boozy evening entertainment seemed more important. I moaned on so much that the Diving Officer said I could go in by myself, on condition that I held onto the anchor rope. With no hesitation I quickly donned my gear and went down the line and was happy just sitting on the bottom amongst some huge, waving kelp fronds, watching some little spider crabs ambling around. The 'dive', though, was short-lived: the anchor line was dragged out of my hand and one of the guys came down and told me to get up.

On the next two dives I was taken to depths of over 35 metres and on the third dive found myself abandoned when one of the most experienced club members twice lost consciousness during the ascent. I surfaced far too fast from 30 metres and was left with air bubbles crackling in my neck. They lasted for many weeks and the memories have haunted me ever since, but the intensive training to which I was subjected in that club certainly never did me any lasting harm. In fact, it probably helped me out of one or two tricky situations over the next 30 years.

After those frightening first diving experiences and the bickering in Durham BSAC, I decided that enough was enough. I joined the Burnside Sub-Aqua Club, a new independent club which was also much closer to home. I re-sat my exams and re-did my training, but this time with some half-decent gear and a totally different club atmosphere. I never looked back, and was eventually elected Diving Officer at the Burnside, which later became Sub-Aqua Association 23. Diving had well and truly taken over my life.

For about ten years as Diving Officer I organised club diving holidays around the world. Even my own holidays with my wife Rose have always been planned round diving and we have visited Sardinia, Minorca, Cyprus, Crete, Sri Lanka, Peninsular Malaysia, Singapore, Penang Island, Baros in the Maldives, Kapos in the South China Sea, Sharm, Bali and Lombok in Indonesia, Koh Samui in the Gulf of Siam, Phuket, the Phi Phi Islands and the Similan Islands in the Andaman Sea. My favourite destination, though, was still always the Farne Islands, even though the visibility is far better and the marine life much more prolific in many of the more far-flung places we have visited.

From 1975, my buddy Trevor and I completed over 3,700 dives and, weather permitting, took every opportunity, in every season, to dive around the islands until they became like a second home. I have been lucky to have had, for 52 years, a very understanding wife, which has definitely been a help.

I first began writing letters to the diving magazines in the mid-1970s and pro-gressed to writing monthly articles for *Underwater World* and *Sub-Aqua Scene*, for which I was even presented with the 'Golden Writer of the Year' award at the

London Boat Show. Then, after doing a series for *Sub-Aqua Scene* about diving around the Farnes, I was deluged with letters from people asking for more information. Unfortunately, the magazine had left out some of the numbered maps, or printed them so small that they were unreadable. After that, I was continually asked to share our knowledge of the diving sites around the Farne Islands but it was at that time an impossible task as I only used an ordinary typewriter. The word processor bought for me by my wife Rose for Christmas 1997 solved those problems and now, of course, I use a computer.

My diving days are now long gone, my health may be failing, but at 73 my memories and dreams of the world beneath the waves are as vivid as ever.

Ron Young

Unlike many divers' guide books, where the information on divesites has been acquired from second-hand sources, every numbered site in this book (with the exception of the deep wrecks and their positions, which came courtesy of the UK Hydrographic Office and Meridian Chartware at Norwich) has been personally dived by the author. The information should therefore be accurate, unless the site has been altered in some way by the elements.

The book, first written on a font writer and published by me in 1998, is an honest and truthful account of my years spent diving around the Farnes. I know that diving solo is a very controversial issue, leaving my buddy and me open to criticism from certain quarters, and that some club divers may even be appalled at the very idea. Rightly or wrongly, it was a system that we adopted due to the pressures of shift work and our lives in general: it was a matter of diving solo or not diving at all, meaning we would miss out on many hundreds of dives. Although I am certainly not recommending it for everyone, I feel that as long as a diver is totally aware of their environment, feels confident and knows their own capabilities, diving solo in reasonably shallow water is sometimes acceptable and often more interesting.

This book includes many wrecks that are much deeper than I could have ever dived to, but times have changed. In the 1970s, 50 metres was a very deep dive, but with the array of technical gear now on sale and the availability of re-breathing courses, the world of deep wrecks appears to be at anyone's disposal.

I sincerely hope that you enjoy reading this book and that it will be of real help on any future diving trips to this fantastic area off the northeast coast of England.

ACKNOWLEDGEMENTS

The author owes his thanks and appreciation to the following people and organisations for all of their help and support, without which this book could never have been written:

Nelson McEachan, June Dillon, Glynis Furse and the staff at the UK Hydrographic Office; Michael Lowrey, lecturer, author, naval historian and researcher of World War One U-boats; Dr. Axel Niestlé, naval historian, author and researcher; the World Ship Society; Terry Whalebone, maritime researcher; Billy McGee, author of *Ropner's Navy*, maritime historian and researcher of merchant crews; Roger Jordan, author and maritime researcher; Pamela Armstrong, author and submarine researcher; Allan Lopez, skipper/owner of the Tyne-based charter-boat *Spellbinder*; Andy Anderson, technical diver, and his wife Moira; technical diver Ian Wright, his wife Barbara and her sister; Roy Martin, author of *Salvors Risdon Beazley*; Jeff Morris, Honorary Archivist of the Lifeboat Enthusiasts' Society; Sue Satterthwaite, author of *Gus Bonner V.C.*; Sgt Scott of 'A' Flight, 202 Squadron and his C.O. at RAF Boulmer, Northumberland for aerial views of the Farne Islands; Siri Holm Lawson, author/owner of www.warsailors.com; the Commonwealth War Graves Commission; Rolf Kristensen; Walter Bulmer, Director of the Northern Optical Company; Torsten Hagnéus; Oliver Lörscher, U-boat researcher and maritime historian; Trevor Hallifax; Andy Hall, trawler enthusiast; and Jan-Olof Hendig, ship researcher. The author also remembers with gratitude the work of the late Steve Cheshire, sports diver and researcher.

To Rose Young, my long-suffering wife of 52 years, I owe thanks for her proof reading and her patience.

And last, but not least, I must acknowledge the help and co-operation of my long-time diving buddy Trevor Corner. He must share the credit for most of the dive sites listed in this book as, over more than 30 years, we systematically searched every underwater rock, islet, island and seabed around the Farnes and Holy Island.

Thank you, too, to those people who preferred not to be mentioned. My sincere apologies go to anyone whom I have inadvertently missed out.

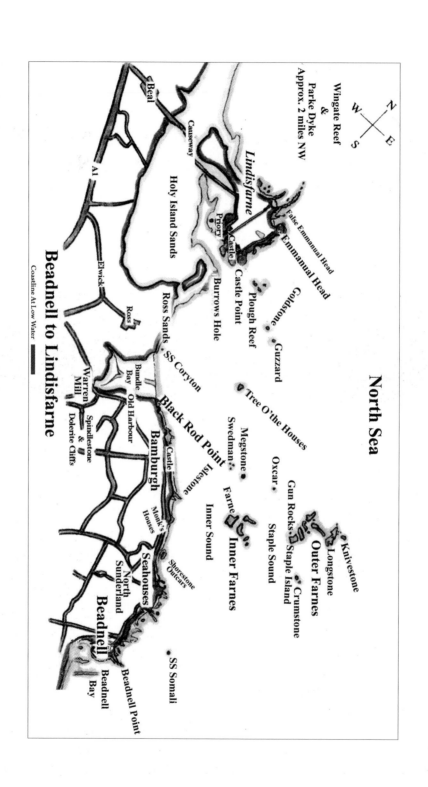

North Sea

Wingate Reef
&
Parke Dyke
Approx. 2 miles NW

N
W — E
S

Beal

Causeway

Lindisfarne

False Emmanual Head

Priory

Castle

Castle Point

A1

Holy Island Sands

Burrows Hole

Emmanual Head

Castle Point

Plough Reef

Goldstone

Guzzard

Tree O'the Houses

Knivestone

Longstone

Outer Farnes

Crumstone

Gun Rocks · Staple Island

Staple Sound

Elwick

Ross

Ross Sands · SS Coryton

Black Rod Point

Islestone

Megstone

Swedman ·

Oxcar ·

Farne

Inner Farnes

Inner Sound

Beadnell to Lindisfarne

Coastline At Low Water

Warren
Mill

Spindlestone
&
Dolerite Cliffs

Bundle
Bay

Old Harbour

Bamburgh

Castle

Monk's
Houses

Seahouses

North
Sunderland

Shorestone
Outcars

Shorestone Outcars

Beadnell

SS Somali

Beadnell Point

Beadnell
Bay

The coastal villages of Bamburgh, Seahouses and Beadnell

Aerial view of the Farnes by Sgt Scott RAF

Bamburgh

The Farne Islands lie between 1¼ and 4 miles off the north Northumberland coast and, at low tide, consist of 33 islands, islets or rocks, although at high tide this number is reduced to only 23. They are mainly divided into two major groups, the Inner and Outer Farnes The island of Farne, or House Island, situated in the Inner Farnes, is the largest and highest in either group and lies almost directly two miles due east of the pretty little historic village of Bamburgh. A magnificent medieval castle towers majestically over the village on one side and dominates the beautiful long sandy beach with its high rolling dunes on the other. The castle is built on a huge mound of black igneous rock and its walls and ramparts combine with this to form a precipitous 50-metre cliff wall on the seaward side, making the castle a virtually impregnable fortress during the Middle Ages.

Founded in 547 A.D., during the reign of Ida, Bamburgh Castle was the ancient residence of the Northumbrian kings. Oswald, a seventh-century Anglo-Saxon king, was the greatest and kindest of all the Northumbrian kings and the first Christian ruler to live there, from the year 605 until 642. He took over the throne from his uncle, Edwin, a Christian, later made a saint, who had been killed in battle on Hatfield Moor in Yorkshire just the previous year. After Edwin's death, the people reverted to paganism, so when Oswald came to power, his first serious task was to re-establish the Christian faith in his kingdom. He employed the help of Aidan, a well-known monk from the island of Iona and also later canonised, who quickly converted the people from their heathen ways. To show his gratitude, Oswald appointed Aidan the first Bishop of Lindisfarne and the pair became good friends. One Easter Sunday, while they were sitting down to dinner, word was brought to the king that many poor and hungry people had gathered outside his palace. Oswald immediately ordered that all the food prepared for him should be sent out to them and that the silver dish on which it was served should be cut up and divided among the poor. The king's kindness impressed Aidan so much that he grasped his hand and blessed him, saying, 'Never let this hand consume or wither!'

Oswald reigned for only eight years because at the age of 37, on 5 August 641 or 642, he was killed in the Battle of Maserfield fighting King Penda of Mercia. Penda ordered that Oswald's head and hand be hacked off his corpse but St Aidan's blessing appears to have been a powerful one: the hand was taken away to be enclosed in a silver casket and placed in Bamburgh Castle, where it remained for 400 years until, in the 11th century, the casket was stolen and taken to Peterborough. When it was opened, the hand was found to be in perfect condition. It was then decided that King Oswald should be made a saint.

Bamburgh Castle from seaward side

Above: Rough sea and high tide at Longstone from the air

Below: Spring tide at Longstone

In 1757, the east turret of Bamburgh Castle was used as an observatory to watch for shipwrecks, while a cannon gun was used to summon helpers from the nearby village. The cannon used had been taken from the armed Dutch vessel that came to grief on Gun Rocks in the Outer Farnes around 1650.

Up until 1898, the Lord Crewe Trustees awarded one pound sterling – a small fortune for the local villagers – to the crew of the first boat to arrive at the scene of a shipwreck. It served as a real incentive to them to take to the sea in their small boats, while wrecksites themselves were also a very lucrative source of revenue.

The castle, with its dungeon and medieval torture chamber, has now been adapted to give off the realistically terrifying screams of tortured prisoners and is well worth a visit. You can spend at least a couple of interesting hours just wandering around, taking in all the sights and sounds.

Bamburgh village really consists of just one small main street, although as well as the castle, it does have another couple of sites worth seeing, such as the Grace Darling museum, which is on the left-hand side of the main road going west, 200 m out of the village towards Budle Bay. Here you can see relics from the SS *Forfarshire*, to which William Darling and Grace, keepers of the lighthouse, launched their heroic rescue from the Longstone Lighthouse (featured later in this book). Also at the museum is the local *Lizzie Porter* self-righting lifeboat that was once stationed at Holy Island. Just across the road from the little museum is the cemetery where the Darling family were laid to rest: here you can see the elaborate monument erected to Grace Darling's memory. The poor lass did not really live long enough to enjoy her Farne, as she died of consumption (tuberculosis) at the early age of 27. The cemetery serves as a history book in itself and the old inscriptions make interesting reading. Some bear witness to the many shipwrecks and to the dreaded diseases that ravaged the area in the 18th and 19th centuries. The historic church of St Aidan, with its beautiful stained glass windows, stands a few metres away in the same grounds.

Bamburgh also has a few decent pubs, one or two shops and a golf course, but its main outstanding features, apart from the castle, are the magnificent sand dunes and beach which are equal to, if not better than, any in Britain.

SEAHOUSES

Half a mile south of Bamburgh, on the seaward (eastern) side of the road, standing high up on top of the giant sand dunes, is the part-time coastguard station, Half a mile further on, and on the same side of the road, stand three very old stone houses, called 'Monkshouses' or 'Brockshouse', reputed to be St Cuthbert's Inn, his storehouse and chapel. Considering, though, that the buildings were only granted to the Farne Island monks in the year 1257, they are highly unlikely to have actually belonged to Cuthbert nearly 600 years earlier. The beach area between the rocks at the rear of the houses is the site of the old North Sunderland harbour that was used by the monks going to and from Farne Island.

Proceeding further south for another mile will bring you to one of the main access points to the Farne Islands, the picturesque and busy little fishing village of Seahouses.

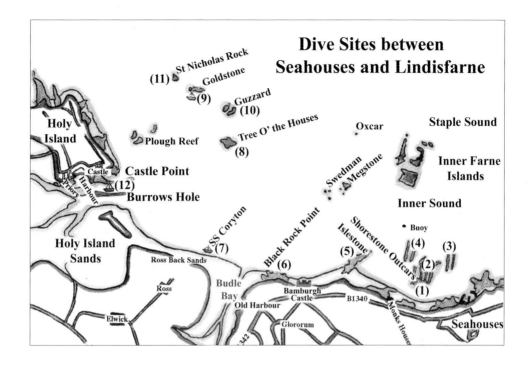

Seahouses harbour

The Olde Ship hotel at Seahouses

There are actually two separate villages, Seahouses and North Sunderland, but because they are interlinked, most visitors think that they are one long village.

In the Dark Ages, when the Norsemen and Vikings came from Scandinavia in their longships to pillage and plunder the Northumbrian coast, there were very few houses near what is now the main harbour. It was for this very reason that North Sunderland village is located about one mile inland, away from the coast; any approaching marauders would have been seen by the people overlooking the cliffs

Aerial view of Beadnell Point (Courtesy David Brown)

who acted as runners, warning the North Sunderland villagers of an impending attack. Today, while it is difficult to tell where one village starts and the other ends, the houses on both sides of the main road at North Sunderland look much older. The harbour was built to serve the fisherfolk living at North Sunderland but Seahouses village, as we know it today, developed only from the late 19th century.

A must for all divers should be a visit to the Ship Inn, overlooking the harbour in Seahouses. Here, the bar area is crammed with hundreds of ship's artefacts, leaving hardly a square inch of space on the walls and ceilings between steam horns, divers' helmets, the top of a submarine periscope, ships' wheels, the bell from the MV *Yewglen*, wrecked on Beadnell Point, and a steam whistle from the paddle steamer *Pegasus*, which was wrecked on the Goldstone off Holy Island in 1843. Incidentally, the whistle was donated to the Ship Inn by Brian Pouting, a former diver of the old school, who once owned The Lodge at North Sunderland and who sadly died in the early 1990s. Everything in this pub has been collected over the past 60 years or so by the landlord and owner, Alan Glenn, and his father before him. The bar is always full during the summer months and on Bank Holidays but it is worth squeezing in for a time just to sample the huge range of real ales on offer, some of them local to the area.

At weekends during the summer months, the picturesque little harbour hums to the sound of marine engines as trip boats, diving and pleasure craft run to and from the islands. Every day between Easter and October, the trip boats ferry many hundreds of visitors out to the Farne Islands, including large parties of ornithologists and groups of school children.

Over the years, a considerable degree of ill feeling has developed between some trip boat skippers and the general diving fraternity at Seahouses. Surprisingly, very little of it has come from full-time fishermen, although they certainly resent divers removing shellfish from the sea. A change in the law, preventing divers from removing more than one lobster per boat, has finally eased the situation.

Attempts have been made in the past to ban visitors, and divers in particular, from launching their boats from the privately-owned harbour at Seahouses, but the revenue they bring in helps towards its upkeep. The slipway offered at the harbour is concrete but runs onto a small sandy beach. Most of the sand is usually firm but at low tide and especially spring tides, the sand bottom gives way to horrible, gooey, foul-smelling mud, in which trailers and cars can sink down to their axles and from which suction makes it impossible to extract anything.

On most evenings during the summer, Seahouses harbour is full of fishing boats, trip boats and pleasure craft, making it a very picturesque and photogenic scene.

The slipway in Seahouses harbour is closed during the winter months and re-opens at Easter until October. It is also closed at the discretion of the Harbour Master during periods of bad weather.

It is important to have permission and to pay the appropriate launching fee before taking your boat onto the harbour beach. Once the boat is launched, both car and trailer must be removed to the nearby car park, which quickly gets very full at weekends and during Bank Holidays, so it is important to get there early. There are also a number of rules to abide by around the harbour:

- It is forbidden to change into and out of dive suits at the slipway, because it quickly brings complaints from the nearby residents

- Do not moor craft near the landing steps from which trip boats operate (this could probably result in a damaged craft)

- There is a strict three-knot speed limit

- It is forbidden to enter the inner harbour, even just to look around, as this will bring the Harbour Master out of his office in double quick time

- Clear the slipway as quickly as possible

- The landing of shellfish is seriously frowned upon. Whatever you might think of the argument, the local fisheries committee contends that 'lobsters are not forced into the fishermen's creels and only go in of their own free will, while divers take them against their will'.

Surprisingly, until only a few years ago, Stan Hall, who runs the dive centre at Beadnell, was the only person operating a diving charter boat along this stretch of coast, Now, though, there are many to choose from at Seahouses.

For a fairly small village, Seahouses has plenty of pubs and good bed and breakfasts to choose from, along with lots of more upmarket accommodation for those with a bit of extra cash to spare. Near the harbour, there are amusement arcades, fish and chip shops, ice cream parlours, gift shops and cafés and a Chinese takeaway further up the village. There are two garages selling petrol and two-stroke oil, one on the road into Seahouses from Beadnell and one just after the Seafield restaurant on the seafront going north towards Bamburgh. Seahouses also has an excellent and inexpensive golf course on the road south towards Beadnell. The Lodge at North Sunderland used to be a dive centre but was sold a few years ago. Divers requiring compressed air or/and diving equipment can find it at Toby Douglas' dive shop in a unit in the industrial estate at North Sunderland; this is now the only place in the area that sells air. Toby and his brother Andrew run the Sovereign charter boats out of Seahouses harbour.

BEADNELL

From Seahouses, the open, windswept coast road winds its way south for three miles before arriving at the pretty little village of Beadnell. The journey takes you past Seahouses golf course with its streams and ponds, and then the Camping Club site on the right-hand side of the road just before Beadnell village. This is the only organised campsite for tents and campervans within a 15-mile radius of Beadnell, the next nearest being at Waren Mill, two miles north of Bamburgh. It is, though, sometimes possible to seek permission to pitch a tent in the field next to the Links caravan site. Fortunately for divers, they are now able to camp in the sheltered grounds of Stan Hall's land behind the Beadnell Hotel. The camping site on the seafront, run by the Camping Club of Great Britain, has good access to the beach, exceptionally clean toilets and hot showers, with attached ironing rooms and washrooms, but the site is not cheap compared with many others around the country. Opposite the Camping Club entrance and across the road, a concrete slipway leads onto soft sand, but it is still a long, hard haul launching a boat without the use of a four-wheel drive vehicle, while the sandy channel between the rocks at low tide is strewn with large boulders on which many a lower leg or propeller has

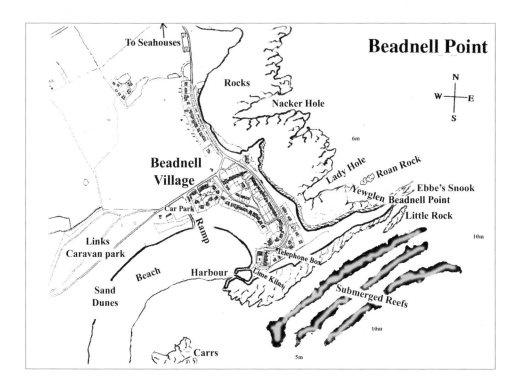

Church of Saint Ebba at Beadnell, circa 1900

been damaged. The National Trust owns the slipway and surrounding land giving access to the beach and they have some sort of agreement with the Camping Club, who charge campers a small fee to launch a boat.

Camping is a favourite economical leisure activity for many thousands of people and because of its location, the Beadnell campsite attracts large numbers of divers from all over the country. Although this particular site might be rather expensive, it is still a cheaper proposition for a family, or a large group of divers, than staying in a hotel or bed and breakfast. Beadnell is spread out over half a mile, from the harbour to the village centre, and although the actual village is tiny, there are still a couple of good watering holes which also sell excellent food. There are only two shops to serve the local community, one at each end of the village: The Village Shop, as it is called, stands in front of the quaint old church of St Ebba and directly opposite the Craster Arms public house, while the post office-cum-general dealers on the seafront has a fish and chip shop attached to it.

The nearby garage closed down in 1997, so divers and anglers now have to travel to Seahouses to refuel their cars and boats.

A must for anyone with an interest in history is a visit to the old three-storey Preston Pele tower, located about two miles to the southwest of Beadnell and on the way to the A1 Newcastle- Berwick main road. The tower, which has walls six feet thick and a huge bronze bell at the top, was built to protect the villagers from marauding Border reivers, English and Scottish raiders or bandits who made a living from pillaging and plundering along the Anglo-Scottish border from the 13th to the 16th century.

The Preston tower is free to visit and is open to the public most of the year, although it relies on small donations for its upkeep. You can climb the wooden stairs and see how people lived during a siege: it is all very realistically set out with straw beds and artificial fires. From the fish and chip shop at Beadnell and heading inland (west) for about 300 metres, you arrive at the big old stone house called St. Ebba in the middle of the village, on the left-hand side of the road. This is the base for the diving business operated by Stan Hall and his son Lee. They used to fill diving bottles, but the compressor is no longer in use. Stan is a great local character with a strong Northumbrian accent, Breton cap, beard and never-changing age. In his younger days, what he calls his 'prehistoric' era, Stan says he was so fascinated with diving that he acquired some basic gear and taught himself the rudiments the hard way. His diving days are now long gone, but he is the original charter boat skipper and has been taking divers out to favourite dive sites, like his very own wreck, the SS *Somali*, for so long now that he can almost go blindfold. I'm sure his boats know their own way there. Stan now operates at least three dive boats and during the summer months they are usually booked up well in advance at weekends and especially over Bank Holidays. Accommodation on offer at the dive centre ranges from a six-bed bunkhouse with bath, toilet and huge English breakfast for as little as you will pay anywhere, to twelve double and twin en suite facilities, three self-catering cottages and now a sheltered campsite.

Driving south from the post office for about half a mile along the coast brings you to a fork in the road. The main road swings right and ends after 200 metres at the public car park and the entrance to the Links caravan site. Although this is a static caravan site, they do allow a few touring caravans during the summer. The car park has its own toilet and shower block, which is a real bonus when returning from a dive. At weekends during the summer and especially on Sundays and Bank Holidays, the car park gets really crammed with divers' and anglers' cars and boats, often queuing up to get in, because it is the best launching site in the area. There is ample space for changing without the danger of people complaining, although discretion is still called for because it is a public place. There is also no need to take your car and trailer somewhere else after launching, as you do at Seahouses. The real bonus with this site is that there is a tractor and full-time driver (paid for by Berwick Council) to launch and recover the boat, for a fee, between 0900 hrs and 1800 hrs, although you used to be able – and may still be able – to push your boat down to the beach free of charge. Anyone arriving back after 1800 hrs will either have to go to Seahouses or wait until the next morning, because the barrier is locked. The total cost of launching with the tractor used to be quite reasonable, but is less so now. Season tickets are available for anyone who is likely to use the launching site more than about ten times and this will save a lot of money over the season, but the price of these has also spiralled. Local bye-laws prohibit four-wheel vehicles on the beach and there is a six-knot speed limit in the harbour and beach area. Season tickets are also available for Berwick area car parks, covering all the public car parks from Beadnell to Berwick and allowing another good saving. There are two drawbacks to launching from Beadnell rather than Seahouses, but they are still both worth it in the end:

- The distance involved adds an extra six miles to the return journey to the Farne Islands

- During strong southeast winds there can be a few rollers breaking in the bay, making it difficult to get the boat back onto the trailer. Beadnell, though, has the only west-facing harbour on the east coast and it usually gives excellent shelter in most weather

- During thick fog and occasionally on stormy days the launch site may be closed on advice from HM Coastguard

Going straight on at the fork in the road will take you past a lot of mostly holiday homes and down to the picturesque little harbour, with ancient lime kilns towering above it and where a few local fishing cobles are still in use.

On the way down to the harbour, a telephone box stands on the left-hand side of the road and here a pathway leads onto the 500-metre long wedge-shaped reef called Beadnell Point. The Point is an excellent shore dive for both novice and experienced divers, but it entails a long hike lugging diving gear. Unfortunately there are also double yellow lines on both sides of the road and the nearest car park is 500 metres away, over the beach. The easiest way is to take the car and drop the equipment off at the telephone box, leaving someone with it, and then return the car to the public car park.

On the south side of Beadnell Point the reef slopes down to the water and three excellent reefs of three or four metres run parallel with it, well within swimming distance. The northern edge is a cliff face all the way along, with its highest point being a sheer 8-metre drop into the water, and over about 400 metres it gradually slopes down, disappearing under the sea, which makes entry and exit fairly easy. The north side of the Point takes a tremendous battering from the winter storms and here the jagged underwater cliff face is indented with many crevices, slots and overhangs, providing ideal cover for many species of marine life. The submerged part of the reef runs a long way out underwater and on the surface there can be a very strong current running, either north or south, so it is always best to make the

*Above: Beadnell harbour
and lime kilns*

*Left: Towers Hotel in
Beadnell, circa 1900*

return journey along the bottom. Many divers have been caught out by attempting
to swim back on the surface without any boat cover.

MV *YEWGLEN*

Halfway along the north side of Beadnell Point are the battered remains of the MV
Yewglen, which came to grief on 29 February 1960. She was a vessel of 1,018 tons
and yet there is now very little left of her, apart from some broken spars and twisted
steel framework and the occasional bit of non-ferrous metal lying amongst the rocks
under a thick carpet of kelp. The *Yewglen* was a steel-hulled, diesel-powered motor
vessel that was completed as Yard No.372 by Jas Lamont and Co. at Port Glasgow in
October 1952 and was launched on 9 May 1952 for J. Stewart and Co. She measured
67.4 m in length, with a 10.8-m beam and a 4.26-m draught.

At 2100 hrs on 27 February 1960 the *Yewglen* left London, en route for Leith,
with 1,000 tons of bagged cement and lime. She was making a steady ten knots when,
about two miles abeam of Flamborough Head at 1950 hrs on 28 February, the master
altered course with a view to passing three miles off the Longstone light on the Outer
Farnes. It appears that from this point in her journey to disaster, the ship was handled

Above: MV Yewglen *in happier days*

Right: MV Yewglen *two days after she ran aground*

Below: MV Yewglen *wrecked at Beadnell Point*

negligently by her master and certain members of her crew. After changing course, the master left the bridge with instructions to the second mate that he was only to be called every four hours to take medication, unless there was a problem or the weather became foggy. The first and second mates took charge of the ship, only taking rough estimates of their position as it was recorded off Coquet Island Light.

The second mate estimated their position to be six or seven miles offshore, yet had the vessel been on its proper course, it would have been twice that distance. The ship went through one or two fog patches and the second mate decided to call the master at 0500 hrs on 29 February, but a moment later he noticed something on the port bow that looked like foam. He went to get his binoculars and was returning to the controls when he heard the distinct sound of breakers. There was nothing he could do because, before he could get to the telegraph to stop her, the *Yewglen* ground up onto the reef with her bows high and dry. The master took command and attempted to pull the ship off with her own power and then with the help of a tug, all to no avail. Seahouses lifeboat came alongside and a breeches buoy was rigged up, but neither was needed, because the crew literally walked along the reef top to safety. The ship stood on the reef for about six weeks, sometimes almost high and dry, while the insurance company and salvage people argued about money, until one day she broke her back and had to be partly salvaged where she stood. At the court of inquiry the master was found guilty of negligence along with the first and second mate (the latter was very inexperienced) and the master also had to pay the nominal sum of £100 towards the costs of the court.

REEF DIVING BETWEEN BEADNELL AND SEAHOUSES

The rocky shoreline at low tide between Beadnell and Seahouses provides some excellent dive sites with some first-class reefs at almost every access point to the sea: Lady Hole, just before Beadnell Point; Nacker Hole at the fork in the road leading to the car park; down over the rocky bit of headland, close to and behind the fishermen's huts, while in front of the camping site there are a few separate little sandy bays between the rocks from which to swim out, leading to a number of different reefs. From Seahouses, below the golf course, there are numerous reefs leading out and away from the shore all along this stretch of coast, right up to Seahouses harbour. To the seaward side of the harbour wall there is a nice rocky cove with lovely high reefs sheltered from the tide and good, easy access. The only problem with most of these sites is the long swim involved and having to hike with heavy diving equipment across often slippery rocks. Sadly, there are not the same numbers of crustaceans on the shore sites now compared with some twenty years ago, yet for those divers without a boat or needing a good second dive, the diving here is still first class.

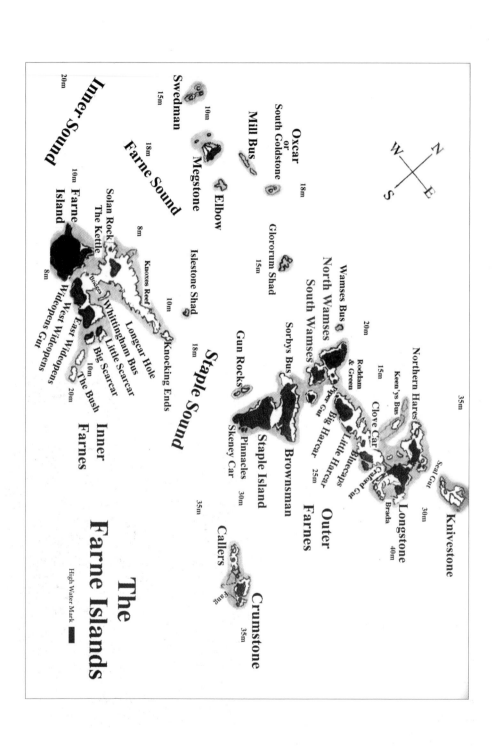

The Farne Islands

Inner Sound

20m

Swedman 15m

Oxcar
or
South Goldstone

Mill Bus 10m

18m

Farne Sound

18m

Megstone

Elbow

Farne Island 10m

Solan Rock
The Kettle

8m

Glororum Shad 15m

Knoxes Reef

Islestone Shad 10m

Longcar Hole

Whittingham Bus

Bridges

West Wideopens Gut

West Wideopens 8m

East Wideopens 20m

Little Scarcar

Big Scarcar

The Bush 10m

Knocking Ends 18m

Staple Sound

Wamses Bus
North Wamses

South Wamses

Sorbys Bus

Gun Rocks

Staple Island

Pinnacles

Skeney Car 30m

Brownsman

20m

Roddam
& Green

15m

Fire Gut

Big Harcar

Little Harcar 25m

Bluecaps

Clove Car

Crafod Gun

Brada 40m

Outer Farnes

Northern Hares

Keen'ys Bus

35m

Seal Gut

Longstone 30m

Knivestone

Inner Farnes

35m

Callers

Crumstone 35m

Fang

High Water Mark ▬

N
W — E
S

THE FARNE ISLANDS

THE NATURAL AND GEOGRAPHICAL HISTORY

The strange names given to the individual Farne Islands date back to the Dark Ages of the 6th and 7th centuries and many remain almost unchanged even to this day: Swedman, Wamses, Knavestone, The Wedums, Megstone, Crumstone and Glororum Shad, to mention just a few. The ancient Celtic influence is most obviously seen in the name Farne itself, which is a derivation of 'ferann', their word for land.

The Farne Islands are the most easterly part of what is known as the Great Whin Sill, a 30-metre seam of igneous rock, mainly hard black dolerite stretching from High Force and Cauldron Snout in Teesdale, some 80 miles to the south. The Whin Sill was formed in recent geological history when streams of molten rock were forced up from the earth's core like a fast-flowing river. It travelled over 100 miles before cooling down, to leave an almost diamond-hard layer of dolerite rock. The seam stretches right through Durham and Northumberland until it reaches the coast at Cullernose Point, where it can then be seen as vertical cliffs. From here it forms the coastal rocks as far as Dunstanburgh Castle. The igneous rocks of the Great Whin Sill also surface on the

'Heroe's Halt' near Bamburgh

17

mainland at Embleton and two miles west of Bamburgh, where it forms into precipitous 30-metre cliffs. In places, it is hugely fissured and columnar and at the base of the cliffs near Bambugh, this shows in a peculiarly-shaped whinstone pillar called the Spindlestone or Hero's Halt. Legend has it that the pillar was the place where the Childe of Wynde, the son of the King of Bamburgh, tethered his horse before going off to fight the infamous monster, the Laidley Worm. The fearsome creature was in fact his own sister, who had been turned into the dragon by a wicked witch. The Childe delivered his sister from the evil spell, which then resulted in the witch being transformed into a toad.

Some of the most spectacular columnar and fissured characteristics of the Whin Sill are to be seen at the Farne Islands. Standing out from the cliffs at the southern end of Farne Island is a 20-metre high pillar of rock, standing like a huge monolith, called The Stack. Some more fine examples can be seen off the southwestern corner of Staple Island. Here, three large pillars, aptly named The Pinnacles, rise vertically from the seabed, making a very convenient home for many hundreds of seabirds. At low tide and just visible are the remains of a fourth pinnacle, called Broken Branch, to the north of the other group. This is said to have been destroyed during the Great Storm of 1783, along with the old tower lighthouse on Staple Island.

Farne Island, often referred to as House Island, also has some interesting large rock fissures in the seacliffs at St Cuthbert's Gut and at The Churn. When there is a heavy northerly swell, water funnels up the channel through a blowhole at The Churn and causes spectacular geysers up to 30 metres high.

During the last Ice Age, the islands were severely scoured and ground down by glacial action, rounding off much of the rock and leaving deposits of boulder clay on Farne Island, West Wideopen, North and South Wamses, Staple and Brownsman. Then, gradually, over thousands of years, a layer of peaty soil was formed which has been enriched by many centuries of bird droppings. Although the area of soil is rather small, there is a surprising amount and variety of vegetation growing on it and during the summer months the islands bloom like a flower garden. More than 125 plant species have been recorded, the majority of these being found on Farne Island; they include nettles, bugloss, ragwort, silverweed, dock, thrift, scurvy grass, lichens and mosses, Yorkshire fog and various other grasses, although the most common and characteristic plant to be seen during the summer is the white sea campion, which blooms very profusely. Another interesting species is the orange flowering borage, *Amsinckia intermedia*, a native of southern California. This was accidentally introduced by the island's keepers many years ago through the poultry feed. This pretty flower can be seen all around the old buildings on Farne Island and with some unwitting help from the birds it is very likely, sooner or later, to spread to other islands.

The islands were first inhabited by St Aidan who went to live and meditate there as a hermit in 635, before he became Bishop of Lindisfarne. An ancient legend about St Aidan has it that in 651, the village of Bamburgh was set on fire by Penga, the pagan king of Mercia, and that when Aidan saw the flames from the Farne Island, 'he went down and prayed in earnest'. In reply to the holy man's prayers, the wind is said to have changed direction and the flames swept back onto the besiegers and their wicked king, making them flee for their lives.

St Cuthbert arrived on Farne Island in the year 676, also to live as a hermit, and it was he who made the island famous. He built himself a cell, dug a well for fresh water, made a cross and then later built a guesthouse for any visiting monks. The cell was reputed to have had no windows and instead had a large square hole in the roof so that Cuthbert could see heaven. Unfortunately nothing of them exists today, except possibly the well, as there is one inside the Prior Castell's Tower and no other well has ever been found. If this is correct, then it is very likely that Cuthbert's cell would also have been positioned inside the Pele tower. It is also possible that the old stone remains of what is thought to be the 'fishe-house', located near the trip boat landing, are those of the monk's guesthouse or *hospitium*.

Legends dating back to this period claim that spirits and demons frequented the islands but that when Cuthbert arrived, he put them to flight from Farne Island. They only retreated to the outer islands, however, where their haunting

Thomas Castell's Pele tower on Farne Island

screams could still be heard. The haunting wailing sounds were probably made by grey seals, but people of the day believed that they were the ghosts of drowned sailors.

St Cuthbert was born in Lauderdale, Berwickshire in around 635, where as a young man he worked as a shepherd. One night, when he was attending his sheep, he saw a company of angels coming down from heaven along a bright ray of light. While he watched, a human spirit approached them and was taken into the heavenly band before the apparition disappeared. The following day he discovered that St Aidan had died at the same moment as his vision had appeared and it persuaded him to become a monk. He spent the next 13 years in Melrose Abbey in Roxburghshire, where he eventually became bishop; he often roamed the Northumbrian hills teaching the gospel. He became famous across the land for his 'good worldly deeds' and for working dozens of miracles. One of his penances and self-disciplines was to spend the night in prayer, standing in the sea. One story says that one morning, after his prayers were ended, as he came out of the sea and knelt down, two seals came up to him and began to warm and dry his feet with their breath. They stayed with him until he had blessed them and they returned to the sea.

Cuthbert lived on Farne Island for 12 years and was persuaded to take the post of Bishop of Lindisfarne, but he resigned within two years. Then, on 20 March 687, only three months after returning from Lindisfarne to his beloved Farne Island, Cuthbert died. He was buried on Lindisfarne, but his remains were eventually taken from the island by the monks and placed in a crypt in Durham Cathedral. It is claimed that centuries later, in 1104 and again in 1537, his body was exhumed and found still to be in perfect condition, yet when his grave was reopened in 1827 only the bones were found. The story persists, however, because the bones were claimed to be that of another monk and Cuthbert's body, it is said, had been reburied elsewhere, centuries earlier.

During the period before Cuthbert went to the islands, he lived as a hermit in the Northumbrian hills and a Pictish king's daughter falsely accused him of fathering her child. The story goes on to say that Cuthbert prayed aloud to prove his innocence, and that the ground opened up and swallowed the princess. Her father hastily forgave him and begged for his daughter's return. Cuthbert agreed on condition that no woman should ever be allowed to approach him again. The king then decreed that no woman must ever enter any church dedicated to Cuthbert. This legend lasted long after his body had been moved to Durham Cathedral from Lindisfarne and he became known as 'the saint who hated women'.

The presence of the eider duck was first recorded as early as the 7th century when Cuthbert laid down the rules for the bird's safety and protection, so he became known as the first person in the country officially to protect wild birds.

Cuthbert was succeeded by a monk from Ripon called Ethelwald who lived on Farne from 687 to the year 699. He was followed by other hermit monks, Felgeld and Elwin, but very little is known about their lives; the next hermit monk, Bartholomew, though, was fairly well documented in a book called *Life of Bartholomew*. He was joined by the prior of Durham, Thomas de Melonsby, who had to take refuge on the Farne in fear of his life from Henry III, because the king objected to his promotion to prior. The documents about Bartholomew's life make interesting reference to the islands surrounding Farne. It says that one adjacent island was used to supply hay, another to supply fuel and another, the nearest, served as a burial place for drowned mariners. This last island is obviously West Wideopen or West Widum, because it is the only one which has any depth of soil and shingle on it and it is only about 200 metres away across the shallow stretch of water called Wideopen Gut. It then mentions ghosts and hideous demons referred to by Cuthbert many years earlier. Apparently they had returned to Farne after Cuthbert died and were once again plaguing the hermit monks. It is said that 'they were clad in black, were hideously deformed, short in stature with long heads and the whole troop was horrible as they rode upon goats while brandishing hand lances'. Apparently the goat was the beast favoured by the devil himself. At first sight the cross would drive them away, but eventually the only protection was a 'circumvallation of straws, signed with a cross and fixed in the sand around which the demons galloped until they tired themselves out'. Demonology was rife during the Dark Ages and it is more likely that these ghosts and hideous demons were just very poor humans scratching a meagre living around the shoreline.

After Bartholomew died, the Convent of Durham made the Farne hermitage a proper permanent institution. Two monks called Magister and Socius were sent there and the hermitage was renamed the House of Farne. The house became wealthy and flourished, according to the records, with the monks exploiting the fishing and agricultural wealth around them. They collected and sold birds' eggs, grew crops, kept cattle, caught fish and hunted the plentiful supply of grey seals. The celys, as they were known in medieval times, attracted a good price: in 1371, six seals would bring in £1.7s.4d. Shipwrecks were another regular and valuable source of income which made the monks very rich. In 1364 they received £4.5s.7d from the salvage of a wreck and by the year 1371, they had enough spare cash to be able to buy a clock – an extremely rare and valuable item – for £2.5s.0d.

By the 15th century, many of the monks had become no more than scruffy tramps, beggars wandering the countryside in torn and dirty clothes, but it was their habit of using women of ill-repute which eventually lost them the respect of the common people. Then, in 1443, even the head monk on Farne was dismissed for pawning the most excellent chalice and an assortment of the best spoons in the house.

Farne Lighthouse with white carbide coating

In 1538 Henry VIII ordered the religious corporations on the Farne Islands to be closed down and the monks no longer had a presence there. The islands were then handed over to the Dean and Chapter of Durham in which they remained until the 18th century, when they were sold into private hands. In 1861 the Inner group of the islands were sold to Archdeacon Thorpe and in 1894 the Outer group went to Lord Armstrong. In 1925, however, all the islands were bought by public subscription and passed over to the National Trust, in whose hands they have remained ever since for the enjoyment of all.

During the late 16th and 17th centuries the pele-type tower on Farne Island, built by Thomas Castell, the prior of Durham, was used by the government as a fort. The Pele towers were built like small castles and were quite self-sufficient. They usually incorporated a drinking well and had walls six feet thick to keep out the enemy, usually the Border rievers, Inside the Pele tower on Farne was a vaulted under-storey and stone part-spiral staircase. During the reign of Charles II, a coal-fired lighthouse was established, with the fire being lit on the top of Prior Castell's tower every night. It may have been very basic but it nevertheless saved many people during its working life. It was not until 1809 that a 'modern' lighthouse with an oil light was built. The present lighthouse, which stands at the southwest corner of Farne, overlooking the high cliffs and The Stack, is now fully automatic. The light was provided by acetylene gas produced by carbide, and the white coating covering the cliff face here, which can be seen from Seahouses, is not caused by bird droppings, as many people think, but by waste carbide. Like most of the lighthouses around Britain, including the Longstone Lighthouse on the Outer Farnes, it is more than probable that the power source has just recently been changed again, making them even more reliable.

THE BIRDS OF THE FARNE ISLANDS

The Farne Islands are a nature reserve and world-famous bird sanctuary, owned and administered by the National Trust. They have laid down rules to protect the birds, animals and flora and fauna on all of the islands and have made it illegal to land on them, except in an emergency, although landing on Farne and Staple is permitted at certain times of the year for a fee payable to the National Trust. This can be made either to the wardens at the boat-landing sites or be pre-paid at the Information Centre at Seahouses. Further inquiries can be made through the warden/naturalist in Seahouses. After paying the admission fee, there are still some strict guidelines to be followed when visiting the islands.

The Farne Islands are an absolute dream for visiting ornithologists, being one of the very few places where you can get extremely close to all kinds of breeding, nesting seabirds, normally only to be seen through the lenses of powerful binoculars.

Although the vast majority of divers do not go to the Farne Islands just to look at the birds, there cannot be many who are not fascinated and impressed by their diving abilities, the speed at which they can travel underwater and the depths they can reach in search of food. Near their nesting colonies on Staple Island and the Pinnacles, the birds sometimes cover the sea in huge flocks. Very often, many hundreds of guillemots, puffins and cormorants will skim across the surface, ducking and diving in front of an approaching dive boat. Thankfully, the majority of boats cut their speed to avoid unnecessary collisions or injury to the birds, although it is also worth remembering that it is an offence to frighten or harrass the Farnes' bird population.

Guillemot (*Uria aalge*)

By far the most common birds in the summer months are the guillemots and puffins which make up 80% of the total number of breeding birds. Each breeding pair of guillemots will lay one large egg, the contents of which would make three or four normal hen's eggs. It is laid on bare rock and often in a very precarious position. The egg is pyriform, or pear-shaped, a design which helps to minimise rolling; and if the egg does happen to roll, it will just roll in a very tight circle, usually enough to stop it from falling off the ledge. The eggs can be any shade of brown, green, yellow or nearly white, with or without blotches or brown marks. The guillemot is about 16 in. (41 cm) in length, is darkish brown in colour, has a white chest and underbelly and is a member of the auk family. It swims by using its wings and dives for sand eels and other small fish to depths of between 30 and 60 metres, but can go deeper.

Puffin with fish

Razorbill

Gannet in flight

Fulmar in flight

Arctic Skua in flight

Seabirds of the Farne Islands

Recently, the staff manning a remotely-controlled camera on an oil rig in the North Sea were amazed to see one swim past their camera at well over 100 metres.

Eggs of the guillemot, along with the eggs of many other birds, formed part of a very lucrative trade in the 1800s, when people from the coastal villages collected them in their thousands. Some were kept for local consumption, but the vast majority were sent down to London to be sold in gentlemen's clubs for a lot of money. They were often used to make puddings while the eggs of the gulls were boiled and eaten cold for breakfast. Many wealthy families considered them a luxury when eaten like that. They are said to taste very nice when eaten cold, but have a very strong tangy flavour when they are still warm. The fowlers used to place narrow planks of wood from Staple Island across to the Pinnacles, then more planks from one rock to another, before clambering around precariously with their baskets, collecting the eggs. The Pinnacles are a major breeding area where at least a thousand pairs of guillemots cram together with hardly a body's length between them, so the collectors must have had a field day. The guillemot is the most sociable of the auk family and unlike most birds, is tolerant of its neighbours, in spite of the vocal uproar and gesticulatory movements in the densely-packed colonies. It is surprising that the chicks, which take around 16 days to fledge, are able to breathe, let alone be reared successfully.

Guillemots also breed on Farne, West and East Wideopens, Staple, Brownsman, North and South Wamses (600–800 breed here) and a few on Megstone. It is a true seabird, catching all of its food under the water and spending the winter months well out at sea, although it is sometimes driven inshore by easterly gales. This means that as well as having some very rewarding times, feeding on the huge shoals of prey such as sand eels, it can also have some desperately poor times, especially during the winter months. Months of gale-force easterly winds in 1990, for example, caused mountainous seas and destroyed the underwater visibility. This seriously affected the guillemot's feeding habits, along with the razorbills, puffins and cormorants. My colleagues found thousands of these birds dead in the narrow underwater gullies at the Outer Farnes.

Guillemots, like all the members of the auk family, fly more or less in a straight line and, unlike many other seabirds, do not have the ability to manoeuvre in flight. The rapid beating of their short, narrow wings make a bee-like whirring noise which gives the impression of power and speed, but they are very easily outpaced by the predatory gulls and skuas. Their only avenue of escape is often to plunge into the sea and swim underwater where the attackers cannot follow. All of the auks have great difficulty in taking off from a flat surface on land or sea, because their whole body structure is better adapted to swimming underwater. The feet are used to steer the bird both in the water and in the air, but are not used as propulsion, except when they are moving slowly in search of fish or first diving down or coming up to the surface. If they have fed well, they look really comical, skimming and bouncing over the sea from wave to wave, like a flat stone that has been thrown along the water's surface.

Razorbill (*Alca torda*)

The razorbill is a very similar bird to the guillemot in size, shape and colour, but its plumage is more of a chocolate-brown than black. The beak of the razorbill is also shorter and more flattened with a white, grooved line across it and there is a white bar running along its wing tip. It too is a member of the auk family and there are some 50–60 pairs nesting on the islands, with most of them on Farne.

All of the auk family are constantly menaced by predatory gulls so the most successful razorbills and guillemot chicks are those that are hatched and fledged in the shortest possible time. Herring gulls are normally the biggest egg thieves, but the black-backed gull causes the biggest mortality rate among fledglings.

The one egg laid by a breeding pair of razorbills is similar in shape and size to that of the guillemot, but the colour is a buffish white or pale greenish-blue, with blotches of dark brown. The egg takes about 34 days to incubate and the chick about another 15 or 16 days to fledge. The nestlings are fed on fish, small crustaceans and large planktonic creatures of varying species, with the size of the fish depending on the age of the chick. The chicks will often wander around the colony when they are hungry and are sometimes temporarily adopted by other birds while their mother is away looking for food. When a chick squeaks and cries because it has been orphaned or it is cold or hungry, another bird will usually adopt it as its own. They very often even pirate the egg of another razorbill and guillemot of the same species and adopt that as their own.

The razorbill dives to similar depths as the guillemot and can carry up to seven or eight fish, usually holding them across the bill.

Puffin (*Fratercula artica*)

The puffin is often referred to as a 'sea parrot' but its local name is the 'tommie noddie'.

It nests on all of the islands which earth deep enough to build a burrow. There are about 3,000 pairs nesting on the bigger islands of Farne, Brownsman, Staple and the Wideopens. They are a strange-looking bird: thickset and squat, they stand upright and are about twelve inches (30 cm) high. Their legs and feet are bright orange, while the massive coloured bill is striped with grey-blue scarlet and yellow. During flight, which is usually more or less in a straight line, the short wings flap so fast they remind you of the hummingbird, but like the other members of the auk family, the wings are designed mainly for swimming underwater. Their nests are in deep burrows, which they either excavate themselves or borrow from rabbits, while the one egg laid is nearly white with a few greyish spots. This takes about 42 days to incubate, but the chick doe not fledge for a further 49 or 50 days. After around the 40th day, the young bird is entirely deserted and its parents retire to the open sea to begin their autumn moult of body feathers. The chick will remain in the burrow for a further week, during which time the last of its soft down disappears and its full flight plumage is completed. Then hunger and nature drive it out of the burrow to make its first flight out to sea, which is always at night, reducing the risk of attack by predatory gulls. The parent birds take no interest whatsoever in their newly-fledged youngsters and they in turn do not acknowledge their parents. The burrows where the puffin chicks live all their young lives are usually so dark that the birds recognise each other by voice alone and seldom, if ever, see one another. Puffins dive to great depths in search of their main diet of sand eels and the huge parrot-like bill can hold as many as 30 fish at one time. They are seriously harassed by gulls when returning with food for their chicks, but the worst threat is from the great black-backed gull, which attacks puffins in flight and swallows them whole. The puffin's only avenue of escape is by diving under water, where the gulls cannot reach them.

The puffin, being a member of the auk family, is also related to the now extinct flightless dodo.

Cormorant (*Phalacrocorax carbo*)

The cormorant is a large bird measuring around 36 in. (91 cm) in length, with webbed feet and a long beak with the upper mandible sharp and hooked. It is related to the tropical pelican, Its plumage is black and very dark brown with a green-and-purple sheen but in spring it has a white patch across the thigh, while immature birds are dark brown and whitish underneath the chest. They lay between three and five nearly-white, chalky-coloured eggs in April or May and build their nest of seaweed, sticks, twigs, flotsam and jetsam on rocky cliffs and ridges on the islands. When they dive, both cormorant and shag can sink below the surface without causing a ripple, but their usual habit is to leap up in a semi-circular movement and 'duck dive' back down, gaining some momentum for swimming underwater. When travelling fast underwater, the bird keeps its wings folded flat to its body and propels itself simultaneously with strokes of its feet, only using the wings when it searches for fish on the seabed. Both birds usually fly low over the water's surface but settle onto it before diving for food. The cormorant eats fish of all kinds, including coley, pollack, codling, wrasse, whiting, herring, mackerel, sand eels, plaice and even sticklebacks, but 40% of the cormorant's main diet is flatfish, with the other favourite being the common eel. Feeding usually takes place in reasonably shallow water, at least compared with members of the auk family, and

Nesting Puffins

the cormorant stays down for as long as seventy seconds. Beneath the surface, both the cormorant and shag look like silver darts as they flash past, air trapped in their feathers. When the sun shines on its feathers in the breeding season, it is at close range a surprisingly colourful bird.

There are a considerable number of breeding cormorants on the Farne Islands with over 300 counted in one season. They are usually seen flying low as individuals, but tend to like company and collect in colonies on the rock ledges. The young birds group together in crèches, sometimes numbering 50, and they swim and dive in unison. Along with the related shag, they are present all the year round and can often be seen with outstretched wings standing on rocky islets or lined up like soldiers on parade on the tops and upper rocks of islands. The chief areas to see them are Staple, Brownsman, East and West Wideopens, Megstone, Little and Big Scarcar and Crumstone, but the main concentration is on North and South Wamses. Here the guano (bird droppings) stands inches deep and has coloured the rock faces white, while the smell from it is overpowering when the wind is in the wrong direction.

Shag (*Phalacrocorax aristotelis*)

The shag or green cormorant is very similar to the cormorant in looks, but is slightly smaller in size, measuring only 30 in. (76 cm) with no white on its chin and thighs. The adult birds are a glossy metallic green in colour. The shag can stay underwater for up to 170 seconds, more than twice the time of the cormorant, but they normally average about 50 seconds. The eggs are very similar but the shag nests on individual ledges on rocky cliffs at the coast, unlike the cormorant which builds its nest close to others in clusters on flattish rocky islands. Most of the shags around the Farne Islands have moved down from Bass Rock in the Firth of Forth or from the Isle of May, and the shag is very seldom seen inland.

Eider duck (*Somateria mollissima*)

Eider ducks are on record as having been around the Farne Islands since the days of St Cuthbert and are present all the year round. They are very tame during the nesting season and will stay at the nest no matter how close you approach them. They are about 24 in. long (61 cm) and are very seldom found inland on the mainland. The females are a mottled brown in colour, while the drake has a magnificent and distinctive velvety-black underside and a glistening white top half, a pink flushed chest and emerald green nape. In both birds, the head and bill form a heavy wedge shape. After the breeding season is finished at the end of June, the drakes moult and become almost indistinguishable from the females. The eider duck lays up to six pale olive eggs in a sumptuous nest made of her own soft down plucked from her chest, while the base of her nest is made of seaweed, coarse grass and bits of twig. Over the centuries, eiders have been one of the most important birds on the Farnes, because their soft down has been collected from the nests to make eiderdown quilts. There are about 700–800 nesting pairs, mainly on Farne, Brownsman, Longstone and Staple Islands. When the ducklings hatch they congregate in large crèches and cross over to the inshore waters around Seahouses and Bamburgh accompanied by at least one devoted mother, but very often by two or three, just like devoted aunts, while the drakes take no part in rearing the young birds. Their main diet consists mostly of crustaceans and shellfish.

Other ducks such as widgeon, scoters and mallards have been recorded on the islands but only the mallard and shelducks have bred there.

Fulmar (*Fulmarus gladalis*)

The fulmar is an ocean bird of the *Procellariidae* family and usually only comes ashore to breed. It seems a friendly bird and one which divers see regularly on a trip to the Farne Islands. Fulmars will often follow a RIB for miles, criss-crossing and gliding just above the waves in front of and behind the dive boat. Legends say they are the souls of dead mariners, so they may be trying to tell us something. Fulmars were first seen on the Farnes in 1919, but there are still only a dozen or so pairs breeding on the Inner Farnes and Staple. They are 18 in. (46 cm) long and the plumage is white with a grey mantle (back) and tail and no black. They are a very quiet bird, except in colonies, when they will then really let you know they are there. Having no nesting material, the pair lays one large white egg on a rocky ledge or in a slight hollow in turf. Their food is fish, oily offal and refuse and the parents protect their young by projecting a foul-smelling oily liquid at any intruders. Anybody who has been boat-angling at sea will have noticed that the fulmar is one of the first birds to come to the boat and, once you start gutting fish, is cheeky enough to waddle right up to the anglers to grab the first morsels.

Terns

Four out of five of the species of tern that visit the British Isles breed on the Farne Islands. The most numerous species is the Arctic tern (*Sterna paradisaea*), not the common tern (*Sterna hirundo*) as might be expected. There are normally around 4,000 breeding pairs of Arctic, 2,000–3,000 sandwich terns (*Sterna sandvicensis*), but only 200–300 pairs common terns and 100 pairs of roseate terns (*Sterna dougallii*). The tern family are all very similar in appearance and have only slight technical differences in colour variations which probably only a dedicated bird enthusiast would recognise, with the possible exception of the roseate tern, which has a soft pink blush on its underparts and a blackish-grey bill with scarlet at the base. The tern family in general are between 14 and 16 in. (36–41 cm) in length and are easily recognised by their fine sleek lines and long, deeply-forked streamer-like tails. Often referred to as the sea swallow, they are a very dainty bird. Their plumage is white and they have a grey mantle and a black nape. Terns usually live in large colonies on rocky islands or sandy, shingle dunes and lay between one and three eggs, coloured buff or pale green, blotched with brown. The incubation and fledging period varies between the different species: the sandwich terns take 21–24 days incubation and 35 days to fledging, Arctic terns 21–22 days incubation and 21–28 to fledging, roseate terns 23–25 days incubation and 28 to fledging and the common terns 22–26 incubation and 28 to fledging. In cold stormy summers the mortality rate among chicks can be devastating, with sometimes whole colonies being wiped out due to lack of food, cold, rain or the danger of shifting sand which can easily bury them, but when conditions are decent and they are left undisturbed, the young chicks stay close to the nest and grow very quickly.

Flocks of terns can often be seen diving like bullets into shoals of small fish just beneath the surface and making quite a racket with their cries of 'krik... tre-wit'. Small fish are their main diet, but they will catch insects when the opportunity arises. Terns are constantly harrassed by gulls when returning to the nest with small fish for their chicks but unfortunately, unlike some other birds, cannot dive underwater to escape and have to use their agility in flight by ducking and weaving to avoid the repeated attacks. During normal flight their bodies tend to dip as their long streamlined wings flap, making them rather comical, but they are extremely fast and agile.

All terns fly south to winter in the southern hemisphere, as far as South Africa and even islands in the Antarctic Ocean. The Arctic tern even returns each year to its place of birth and can live to a ripe old age, given the chance by man and nature; one such bird on Farne Island was recorded as being 27 years old. The sandwich tern, however, often moves around and although it usually returns to the north of England, it may change its area. Some have even changed countries and ended up in Holland, Germany, Denmark, and Northern Ireland. One four-month-old tern from the Farne Islands was recorded in Melbourne, Australia, and it returned home that summer, covering 17,509 km. The black tern, the fifth species of tern to nest in Britain, occasionally calls in to rest on the islands, as do two other species, the sooty tern and the little tern. The most exciting visitor for birdwatchers, though, was the Aleutian tern in 1979, the first time a North Pacific bird had ever been seen in Europe.

Kittiwake (*Rissa tridactyla*)

The kittiwake resembles a herring gull but can be distinguished by its yellow bill, smaller size (16 in. or 41 cm) and its continuous shrieking cries of 'kitti-w-a-ke' from where its name originated. It is a delightful little bird, visiting every summer in increasing numbers with more than 4,000 pairs now nesting. Kittiwakes travel far and wide after leaving our shores late in the summer and some have even been found in the USA and Newfoundland. Their cup-shaped nest of seaweed and grass is literally glued into narrow clefts or ledges on precipitous cliffs and rocky promontories. The pair lay two or three pale buff or grey, blotched with grey or brown eggs, forming a band chiefly around the larger end. The adult bird is about 16 inches long and has a dark blue-grey back, white head and pale greenish-yellow beak, but young birds, or 'tarrocks', are totally different from their parents, having a black ring round the back of the neck, a broad black band down the inner edge of the folded wing and a black beak.

The kittiwake makes a delightful photographic subject and Kittiwake Gully at the southern end of Staple Island is the ideal place to view or photograph them.

Gulls

Apart from kittiwakes and terns, there are three other types of gull which nest on the Farne Islands: the herring gull (*Laras argentatus*) at 22 in. (56 cm), the lesser black-backed gull (*Larus fuscus*) at 21 in. (53 cm) and the black-headed gull (*Larus ridiundus*) at 15 in.(38 cm). Occasionally the common gull (*Larus canus*) at 16 in. (41 cm) and the great black-backed gull (*Larus marinus*) at a massive 27 in. (68 cm) have also managed to nest on the islands but they are still always present with the other predatory gulls in the large flocks during the winter. They are scavenging predators which prey on the eggs and fledglings of all the birds and, unfortunately, most of them stay all of the year round, much to the dismay of the other birdlife. All the large gulls cause mayhem amongst the Farnes' bird population, but the worst are the great black-backed gulls, which not only devour the young and eggs, but kill and eats whole adult puffins and terns. The wardens collect as many of the gulls' eggs as they can possibly find, in an attempt to keep their numbers down, but with over 1,000 pairs breeding and thousands more just visiting the islands looking for food, it is an endless task. The larger gulls can be found nesting on most of the Farne Islands. The only good news is that gulls' eggs still fetch a good price on the London market and so put more money into the National Trust's coffers.

Waders

Waders are so called because they have long legs to walk in the shallow water searching out tiny crustaceans and worms. There are a number of waders that visit the islands, such as dunlins, redshanks, turnstones and purple sandpipers, but only two species breed on them: the ringed plover (*Charadrius hiaticula*), a small bird of 7½ in. (19 cm) of which there are up to 24 pairs, and the oystercatcher (*Haemmatopus ostralegus*) at 17 in. (43 cm), with up to 40 breeding pairs. The oystercatcher sports a bright scarlet bill and is glossy black on its head, back and upper breast, with a white underneath. The 3–4 yellowish eggs, blotched with dark brown, are simply laid in the shingle. The bird's main diet consists of lugworm, limpets, small shellfish and shrimps.

The ringed plover's food, eggs and nest are very much the same, while the main islands they visit are the Inner Farnes, Brownsman and Staple Island.

OTHER VISITING SEABIRDS

Gannet (*Sula bassana*)

The sleek and majestic gannet is part of the *Sulidae* or pelican family and can be seen on a daily basis all around the Farne Islands. They make regular forays down from their huge colonies, high up on Bass Rock in the Firth of Forth, about 50 miles to the north of the Farne Islands. This magnificent bird, with a two-m wingspan and standing 36 in.(91 cm) high, is the largest seabird in the northern hemisphere. The plumage of the adult gannet is white with a tinge of yellow on the head and neck and dark brown wing tips. Young birds are a dusty light brown colour all over, which gradually changes to a kind of freckled white as they start to mature. The gannet is

Black Headed
Gull

Guillemot

Cormorant

Shag

Tern
in flight

Seabirds of the Farne Islands

a true seabird because it hunts and catches its own fish. It glides about 5–10 metres above the water's surface, using its binocular vision to help it to see the fish prey, then drops into the sea like a dart, its wings stretched back behind the body. The wings are not used underwater until it has either caught its prey or finished the dive: they are then half-opened in typical flight motion ready for take off, even before it reaches the surface. The bird is very fast, whether paddling on the surface or swimming underneath, and the only time it uses its wings is to prolong a dive when it beats along the seabed. Most of the gannet's prey is found near to the surface, so it rarely exceeds about ten seconds underwater, but it has been found caught in nets at a depth of 55 metres. The gannet is naturally buoyant due to the subcutaneous cellular tissues of the upper neck and breast which automatically fill up with air just before diving. The gannet is much more buoyant than the cormorant and it cannot dive from a floating position. It spends the winter well out to sea and can often be seen following ships.

A line of these beautiful, graceful birds, flying and gliding in formation just above the waves, is a lovely sight and they make an excellent picture.

Arctic skua (*Stercorarius parasiticus*)

Although not seen in any great numbers, the Arctic skua is another seabird seen regularly around the peripheries of the Farne Islands. The Arctic skua, at 18 in. (46 cm), is a member of the *Stercorariidae* family of birds which are generally parasitic, preying on other birds to get their food. They have plumage which ranges from light to dark brown or any shade in between, a black bill and legs, short tail and a thickset body. The Arctic skua is a true pirate of the sky because it will attack and terrorise any bird seen carrying fish: even the big gannet is not immune to its parasitic, predatory attacks. The skua is an expert aerial acrobat and has been said to chase birds 'like a Spitfire harrassing a bomber' until they regurgitate or drop their fish. It will then accelerate down and catch the food before it even hits the water. They have been known to relentlessly pursue smaller birds to the point of exhaustion before swooping in for the kill.

The Arctic skua, along with its bigger brother, the great skua, usually breeds in the Orkneys and Shetland, building its nest in grass and heather on the moors. It migrates south in the autumn, feeding on stolen food including carrion, eggs, nestlings and small birds. It makes a harsh, deep, barking type of cry and its colour, size, short tail and antics make it stand out from its fellow seabirds.

Passerine (perching) birds

During their migratory journeys, many thousands of passerine (perching) birds pass through the Farne Islands, many of them resting for days, but only a few stay for any length of time before moving on to their final destinations. A small number of local birds come over from the mainland and make the Farne Islands their permanent home: blackbirds, jackdaws, crows, meadow pipits, pied wagtails, sparrows and starlings, the last two nesting in old buildings. Up to 40 pairs of rock pipits also nest on the largest of the islands.

GREY SEALS

The grey seal, also commonly referred to as the Atlantic seal, is one of the main attractions at the Farne Islands and every year thousands of visitors wanting to see them make the journey over in one of the many trip boats which operate from Seahouses harbour. The seals have now become accustomed to the visitors who mean them no harm, a far cry from days gone by when they were hunted relentlessly by the Farne Island monks and fishermen from the coastal villages who made lucrative profits from hunting the 'celys'. Trip boats can now get as close to the seal colonies as is practically possible but divers are at an advantage because they can meet the seals in their own underwater environment. Grey seal pups are very curious, playful creatures and can even become a nuisance when they sneak up and tug at your fins, often when you are least expecting it. They will swim underneath you to pop up close in front of your mask, which can be quite unnerving, to say the least. Pups regularly come right up to the boat but we have twice been amazed to have a young seal actually climb over the side of the RIB and look curiously around at the diving equipment before slipping back over the side again.

It is common, when swimming through the narrow gullies on the east side of Crumstone and in Brada off Longstone, to see seals lying fast asleep on the bottom, looking very much as if they were dead. A little tap on the rump usually sends them off like a Polaris missile – sometimes, though, in the wrong direction. I'm sure there must be dozens of unsuspecting divers who have thought they had found a dead seal, only to get the shock of their lives when the seal came back to life. Like most people, I always believed that seals clambered out onto rocks when they needed to sleep, and they do obviously rest on them: they can be seen with their eyes closed, their head poking out of the water, as if looking up at the sky. In fact, seals sleep quite comfortably on the water surface by automatically closing their nostrils and keeping enough air in their lungs to stay buoyant, while to stay on the sea floor they have to be less buoyant so automatically reduce the amount of air in their lungs. When a seal needs to return to the surface to replenish the air supply, it will somewhat lazily and slowly swim to the surface, still with its eyes tightly closed and fast asleep. Its body functions tell it what to do, again automatically, just like someone sleepwalking. As its head breaks the surface, still with the eyes closed, the tightly- closed nostrils open wide and it breathes in and out a dozen or more times, exhaling the stale air from its lungs and breathing in fresh oxygen. Once this is done, the nostrils close and the seal turns and sinks head first below the surface, giving a flip with its forelimbs to take it down to the bottom again, or sometimes just drifting downwards until it touches the seabed. This behaviour has been recorded on various occasions in seal colonies, when they appear like yo-yos bobbing up and down.

Grey seals, like humans, are warm-blooded mammals, but they also have a thick layer of blubber which insulates them from the cold waters of the North Sea and acts as an energy store when food is scarce. The Farne Island seals were hunted and killed for their skins and blubber for oil lamps and other purposes for over 800 years and by the beginning of the 20th century, the colonies were down to only about 100 animals. In 1932 the Grey Seal Act was passed, which gave them almost complete protection, resulting in an explosion of the seal population. By 1966 there were so many seals that it was decided that a cull was necessary to protect the vegetation and topsoil of the islands, which was being slowly destroyed. In 1970 nearly 2,000 pups were born and the colony expanded to well over 9,000 once again. Many of the seals were dying or suffering bad health and the main nurseries on Brownsman and Staple had become so cramped and overcrowded that by the end of December, virtually all of the plant life and a large part of the topsoil had disappeared. This also had a devastating affect on birds like the puffin, which needed the soil to dig their burrows. The National Trust realised that urgent steps had to be taken to curb the seal population and they decided that the best way to do this was to reduce the number of births on the most vulnerable islands. Fortunately, today, with increased staffing, along with added expenditure, this method has been a great success. The vegetation and soil on the islands of Brownsman and Staple is back to normal and the numbers of seal pups is strictly controlled without the need for culls. Today there are probably about 6,000 seals in the Farne colonies, with nearly 2,000 breeding cows, which give birth to some 1,200 pups annually.

There are about 110,000 grey seals around the UK and most of them are born in Scotland, but the Farne Islands are the most important site in England and the only breeding place on the east coast of Britain. On land, grey seals are for the most part ungainly and awkward, but in the water they are in their element, with fish-like movement of the limbs designed for an aquatic life. The limb bones are similar to those of land carnivores, but the upper parts are much shorter and each forearm is fixed direct to the skeleton because there is no shoulder or collarbone. This allows the forelimbs to lay flush with the body and give virtually no resistance to the water, while the hindlimbs extend straight to the rear. Only the hands and feet protrude from the body; the remainder of the limb is internal. The forearms are buried in blubber and are used for slow paddling and changing direction, while the hindlimbs are used for sculling and rapid propulsion. All four limbs have five fingers and no thumb but they cannot be opened separately, as we open our fingers, because they close together and have to be used as one to open, close or hold. The forelimbs can also be used for gripping objects or prey, but the hindlimbs cannot grip or hold. There is webbing between the fingers which turns them into very efficient fin-like flippers for swimming.

On the surface, the heartbeat of the seal can be as high as 120 beats per minute but when they submerge, this drops to fewer than ten beats and sometimes the heartbeat is no more than just a flutter, which gives the seal its remarkable ability to stay underwater over such long periods. Just prior to the point of diving, it will breathe in and out several times and then exhale, leaving the lungs almost empty of oxygen while it is below the surface. The nostrils close completely, and muscles prevent them from being forced open by the pressure of water. As there is little or no oxygen in the lungs to be passed by circulating blood, the heartbeat rate is low, but it is enough to keep blood flowing to the brain, a sphincter muscle near the heart reducing the blood flow to the kidneys, intestines and extremities of the body, starving these of blood, while the vital organs, heart, lungs and brain still receive blood and oxygen. There are airlocks in the lungs too, which are intended to stop any air getting into the respiratory cells and in turn preventing nitrogen being absorbed under pressure into the blood. If this did happen as the seal rose to the surface, bubbles of gas would form in the small blood vessels as pressure reduced and cause the bends, which would prove fatal for the seal as it would for a man. With the circulation slowed down in this way, the seal's body temperature falls, especially in the flippers and extremities, so that when it comes to the surface it shivers for a short while, but after a couple of deep breaths, it very quickly returns to normal without coming to any harm.

Bull grey seals are dark grey-brown in colour and fairly large, measuring almost three metres in length and weighing as much as 285 kilos. It is always wise to be wary of bull seals, especially during the breeding season. Never get between one and its only route to the sea and do not block its way in a dead-end space such as a cave, as it may possibly lash out with its head and bite the nearest part of your body. The breeding season is the time when they are at their rattiest and it is during this time that many savage fights break out among rival bulls vying for females. They inflict some devastatingly nasty wounds on each other.

A grey seal cow is almost half the size of the bull and is coloured grey on the upper parts with creamy patches underneath. They are ready to breed after three or four years and have a gestation period of eleven and a half months, usually giving birth to one pup. The pups are born creamy white and weigh something like 15 kilos. Seal's milk contains 50% fat and is extremely nutritious, so as a result the pups put on weight rapidly at something like 1.7 kilos a day. After weaning, at about three weeks and weighing around 40 kilos, they are abandoned by the mother and have to live on their fat reserves for a couple of weeks, but remain in the nursery. During this period they lose the nourishing fat at the rate of half a kilo a day and may even lose a third of their bodyweight until hunger drives them into the sea, where they have to learn survival skills on their own. Only about half of the pups born will live to see their first birthday. The adults will mate as soon as the pups are weaned and the cycle starts again.

In the USA, all seals are protected by the US Marine Mammal Protection Act 1972, but they have not been as lucky in Europe so far. Even though most people love their doleful, dog-like faces, most commercial fishermen partly blame the seals for the serious decline in fish stocks, even though seals have been fishing for much longer than man. It is only since trawlers began to use new, sophisticated equipment and intensified their methods that the stocks have been so severely depleted. The grey seal's diet consists mostly of fish, and sand eels make up more than half of its quarry. By tracking the animals with special radio transmitters, the Sea Mammal Research Unit in Fife, Scotland has discovered that the specific feeding areas of the Farnes grey seals are at depths of 50–70 metres, down to a flat seabed of sand and gravel, and this is also the terrain of the sand eel shoals. Grey seals can dive to depths of well over 250 metres and stay down for more than five minutes, but that is nothing compared with their cousin, the Southern elephant seal, which dives to a record 2,000 metres and can stay down for two hours. Seals will also eat squid, octopus and other cephalopods, as well as crustaceans, marine organisms and even small quantities of molluscs when they can find them. Octopus also eat crustaceans and one small octopus can wipe out a whole reef of shellfish in no time at all. In recent years there has been a huge increase in octopus numbers: ten years ago a diver might only see about three octopus in something like 200 dives in a year, but these days they may see three on every dive, and creel fishermen were actually catching up to ten in a string of pots every day. That really should put the creel fisherman on good terms with the seal. In the past, I have seen seals chomping into octopus on the surface, surrounded by squawking flocks of seagulls trying to grab titbits that had broken off. Another seal we saw looked really comical as an octopus had wrapped its tentacles around the seal's head and it was shaking it vigorously from side to side in an attempt to loosen the octopus's grip. On other occasions I have seen them violently beating an octopus off the rocks before eating it. It was also amusing to watch a seal deliberately stalking two lobsters underneath an overhanging rock ledge off Knavestone: sadly for the seal, both lobsters escaped.

The teeth of the seal consist of long canines to catch prey, incisors to cut off flesh and molars with cusps which are used to hold struggling prey. They catch, tear and swallow their diet in lumps, rather than hold, bite and chew, but when they feed on hard-shelled crustaceans, the points of their teeth wear away and the animal eventually dies of starvation.

One interesting point to note is that even though there are something like 6,000 seals (or maybe more) around the Farne Islands, there are still huge, dense shoals of saithe, plenty of cod and individual pollack weighing up to four kilos swimming with the seals over places like Whirl Rocks.

The trip boats miss some of the best places where seals congregate on a regular basis and anyone with a boat can visit them privately. By approaching slowly and quietly, it is quite easy to get very close to the colonies without scattering them in every direction. The best time is at the bottom of the tide, when the small islets and rocks are showing, because most of the seals will have hauled themselves out to rest. The favourite sites with resident seals are the east side of Crumstone and the Callers, the north side of Knavestone, the small islets on the east side of Longstone near the lighthouse, the southeast end of Longstone, the south side of the Wamses, South Goldstone, the south corner of Megstone, around the Bush and inside Knoxes Reef. Late in the summer the seals come in large numbers from the other areas to rest on the north side of Little and Big Harcars.

The best areas to snorkel or to encounter seals underwater at low tide are north of Knavestone, the narrow little lagoon on the east side of Longstone where the three little islets are, in the horseshoe-shaped bay called Brada, the southwest corner of Megstone, the east side of Crumstone, the V-shaped gully at the north end of North Wamses and, late in summer, the north side of Little Harcar and South Wamses.

There are many diving clubs that go to the Farne Islands just to dive or swim with the seals and while it can be a very satisfying experience to have half a dozen or more youngsters playing around you like puppies, seals do sometimes bite. It may only be a playful puppy-like nip but it could be for real, so it is worth remembering that they have needle-sharp teeth which can easily penetrate a thin neoprene glove. Apart from the immediate pain, it could turn out to be a nasty experience because seals carry some very serious and potentially lethal diseases. A couple of years ago, tests carried out on one young seal showed it to be riddled with six diseases which can be fatal to humans, including tetanus. Since then, though, I have on six occasions witnessed divers, both male and female, placing their hands or fingers in a seal's mouth. Enjoy the experiences seals can offer, but do be careful.

RABBITS

Surprisingly, there are still a few rabbits on the islands of Farne, Brownsman, Staple and the Wamses. Over the centuries the monks and island keepers bred domestic rabbits as a regular source of meat. Some either escaped or were set free and then interbred with the wild rabbits already on the islands, which has resulted in various colour combinations in today's population.

Having done a little research in Seahouses, I was informed that after the National Trust took over ownership of the Farne Islands they believed that the puffins should have priority over the rabbits' honeycomb of burrows and had many of the rabbits exterminated. The rabbits had been responsible for curtailing the height of the grass and vegetation which, when they were removed, grew out of control and caused great difficulty for birds wanting to land or take off. In an effort to keep the grass down and solve the birds' problem, the National Trust decided, in their wisdom, to introduce goats to the islands. The goats were certainly very efficient in eating the vegetation but they also trampled everything else into the ground, including many of the birds' nests and eggs. More decisions were required to put things right, so they removed the goats and tried lawnmowers instead. These succeeded in frightening the birds away. A request was put out for rabbits and they were once again reintroduced to the islands.

DIVING AROUND THE FARNE ISLANDS

The dive sites in this book have been given a star rating of between 1 and 6: the higher the number, the better the dive site. This is to give those readers who are unfamiliar with the islands and their tides, currents, general depths, wrecks and marine life a better and more reliable chance of selecting the right dive site for what they wish to experience. It should also greatly reduce the risk of wasting valuable time on uninteresting dive sites.

    ✳   A totally uninteresting area: you may as well have gone home

    ✳ ✳   A rather poor area with not much going for it

    ✳ ✳ ✳   A fairly average site but still worth visiting

    ✳ ✳ ✳ ✳   An above-average site with lots of interest

    ✳ ✳ ✳ ✳ ✳   Exciting, first-class site and not to be missed

    ✳ ✳ ✳ ✳ ✳ ✳   A fantastic dive

To help divers locate the dive sites when the islands and rocks are under water, the author has provided some GPS co-ordinates taken from his Meridian electronic chart plotter, so the positions should be fairly accurate. The positions offered for the dive sites and wrecks are WGS84 and the wrecks have all been surveyed by the Hydrographic Department's survey vessel. The position of the wreck is accurate to within 13 metres.

The tidal run varies around nearly all of the islands to such an extent that you can be at one place where there is slack water and yet watch the current running only 100 metres away. By far the best way of organising a dive is to arrive at your chosen site at least half an hour before the tide is expected to go slack. The size of the tide (neap or springs) has an effect on the actual amount of slack water you can expect on the dive, so a spring tide at places like Whirl Rocks or Seal Gut, where the current is very strong, means that will you get little, if any, slack water at all. A neap tide over Whirl Rocks takes place approximately 1¾ hours after bottom of the tide at Seahouses harbour, giving you around 20 minutes of slack water, but within another 20 minutes the tide will be running like an express train again. On a spring tide over Whirl Rocks, the slack period is so small that the current seems simply to change direction almost at once. Each small group of islands may have different slack water times at anything between 1½ and 2½ hours after bottom (or top) of the tide at Seahouses, depending also on the size of the tide, so make sure you get there early.

The slack water period is an unusual phenomenon to watch when close to the islands like Knavestone and The Callers. Watch as the tide recedes on the ebb at low water and the rocks appear above the surface until they are at their highest point; that is the time when you would expect the tide to have turned, but the rocks submerge again, with the current still ebbing. Then, after about 1¾ hours, the tide goes slack and soon begins to flow in the opposite direction, on the flood.

THE CRUMSTONE AND CALLERS

Crumstone: 55 37'.640 N 001 35'.921 W

1st Caller, nearest to Crumstone: 55 37'.701 N 001 36'.041 W
2nd Caller, northwest of Crumstone: 55 37'.689 N 001 36'.108 W
3rd Caller, northwest of Crumstone: 55 37'.701 N 001 36'.181 W
4th Caller, furthest northwest of Crumstone: 55 37'.708N 001 36'.261W

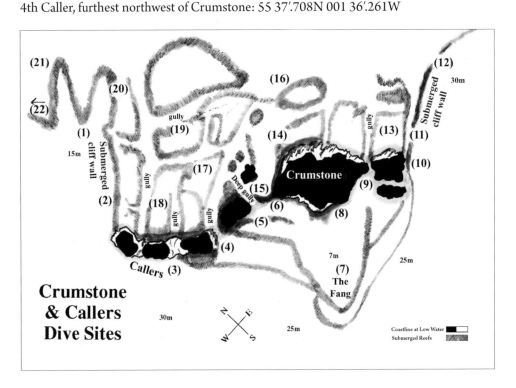

Crumstone and the Callers are the most southerly group of islands, islets and rocks in the Farnes, with Crumstone situated 0.88 miles ESE of Brownsman and 3.63 miles NNE of Seahouses. The Crumstone is actually three bare rocky islands, divided by narrow channels, which give the impression from a distance of being one island. The highest part of Crumstone can be seen at all states of the tide and is home to a large colony of grey seals. It is, though, so exposed to the elements that birds seldom, if ever, nest there. The Callers, which are no more than four weed-covered rocks or islets, are dry to 2.3 metres on a low spring tide. They are the highest point of a reef which curves out from Crumstone for some 338 metres to the WNW; the reef, however, is broken by narrow channels between the four islets.

All of the Farne Islands have been potential death traps to shipping, especially during the age of sail, but because of their rather remote location and surrounding depths, Crumstone and the Callers are among the most lethal. Since 1795, at least 12 known vessels have been wrecked on the three combined islets of Crumstone. A brig called *Britannia* (not to be confused with the steamers) was the earliest recorded vessel to come to an untimely end on 3 April 1795. That was followed by the 300-ton Hull-registered barque *Thomas Jackson* on 18 March 1825; she was on passage from Hull for Leith and Miramichi in Canada when she struck the Crumstone and was lost along with five of her crew. There followed another nine sloops, schooners, keel ships, brigs and one tug up to 1892. The last to be wrecked on Crumstone was as late as 1939, when the SS *Helmsdale* came to grief.

Since 1836, a further eight known vessels have ran aground on the jagged rocks of the Callers but, unlike the Crumstone, which was responsible for the sinking of mainly sailing vessels, all but one of the wrecks on the Callers were steam powered and did not rely entirely on the wind: on 7 October 1875, the 323-ton schooner *Courier* (built in 1850), on 25 September 1915, the 727-ton steamer *Britannia IIII* (1885 – Leith, Hull and Hamburg Steam Packet Co. Ltd, Leith); on 27 January 1917, *Skovdal* of Christiania; in 1920, the 3,356-ton steamer *Graciana* (1903 - Furness, Withy and Co. Ltd, West Hartlepool) ran aground but was able to re-float and sustained very little damage and, on 24 January 1924, the steam trawler *Saint Louis* of Hull suffered the same fate when it too ran aground. The last known wreck on the Callers was on 9 January 1975 when the 44-ton MFV *Sedulous II* of Pittenweem, Fife, tore her bottom out and became a total loss. Fortunately, my records show that from all the ships mentioned on both Crumstone and the Callers, only five people lost their lives, possibly thanks to the proximity and number of local lifeboat stations. The most vulnerable vessels these days seems to be diving craft, because every weekend during the summer months sees dozens of rigid-hulled inflatable boats (RHIBs), with their unsuspecting occupants, fly out to the Outer Farnes from Beadnell. The route to Longstone takes them right over, or very close to, the Callers

Velvet crab scurrying for cover off Crumstone

and every year a small number fail to realise how close the reefs are to the surface. This often results in a broken outboard leg or bent propeller, and sometimes in something much worse.

Currents can be vicious and confusing around the Callers because they tend to run in various directions, taking the deepest route around the islets and reefs. Although you can dive most of the sites, especially the kelp-filled gullies, at any state of the tide, by far the best time is at low slack water. Surfacing close to the Callers on the top half of the tide may result in the diver being swept over the reef through swirling water, which will cause both the diver and boat handler some anxious moments. During an easterly swell, large breakers crash over the Callers reef, so it is very wise to stay well clear of the eastern side.

Dive sites

(1) ✫ ✫ ✫ ✫

55 37ʹ.769 N 001 36ʹ.327 W

This is a gully that funnels in from a depth of 20 metres to around 5 metres, so when the tide is running on the ebb there is a lot of water going into it. This is an excellent dive site, with a maximum depth of about 15 metres, and high reef walls with the sides and gully bottom covered in a profusion of various types of anemone and other species. The reef top, at about 6 metres, is covered in short kelp fronds with lots of urchins and is where, very often, you can pick up a large edible crab sheltering in one of the crevices. There are lots of nooks and crannies in the reef walls with a couple of interesting small caves to poke around in, where shellfish are not uncommon. The currents can be very strong, especially over the reef wall and above the kelp line, while on spring tides it is impossible to stay on the bottom. The best time to dive is at low slack water.

(2) ★ ★ ★ ★

55 37'.731 N 001 36'.301 W

This is another very good dive site, with an 8-metre cliff wall going down to 15 metres onto a stony bottom. Again, the current is very strong as it runs east–west along the curving wall face and into the narrow gully on dive site (1) on the ebb. At the base of the cliff wall there are the remains of an old ship's boiler. Over the years we have found quite a number of small artefacts among the stones and close to the boiler. Most of them are half-buried and difficult to notice without a close inspection; there are locks, keys, hinges, broken cups and we even found a whole sugar basin stamped 'Hull, Leith, Hamburg Steam Package Company'. Who knows what else may lie buried around the boilers? The top of the reef has lots of little gullies and crevices under the dense kelp forest on the seaward side of the Callers. A fair number of grey seals swim around the surface and there is a good selection of marine life to be found on the bottom. Visibility is usually very good in the summer months after a few days of westerly winds and dry weather. Large shoals of coley and individual large pollack are common in this vicinity too.

SS *Britannia* IIII

(3) ★ ★ ★

55 37'.663 N 001 36'.148 W

SS Britannia, circa 1910

A decent dive leading onto the very broken remains of the SS *Britannia*. The ship ran aground and was wrecked in thick fog on 25 September 1915, while on passage from Newcastle upon Tyne for Leith with a general cargo. The *Forster Fawsett* from Seahouses, a self-righting 10.7-m oared lifeboat, was launched at 0620 hrs and rescued seven of her crew of nineteen. Unfortunately, two men had already drowned, while the other ten had succeeded in getting ashore in one of the ship's boats.

The *Britannia IIII* (Official No. 91078) was an iron-hulled 727-ton steam passenger/cargo vessel measuring 64.10 m in length, with an 8.24-m beam and a 4.57-m draught. S. and H. Morton and Co. Leith built and completed her as Yard No. 46 in April 1885; she was launched on 28 February 1885 for the Leith, Hull and Hamburg Steam Packet Co. Ltd, Leith with J. Currie and Co. the manager. The single iron screw was powered by a 122-nhp, two-cylinder compound steam engine that used two (OBS) single-ended boilers working at a pressure of 65 psi, with six corrugated furnaces, 6.50 sq.m (70 sq. ft) of grate surface and 197.88 sq. m (2,130 sq. ft) of heating surface. The cylinders measured 76.2 cm and 132.08 cm with a 91.44-cm stroke (30 in. and 52 in. with a 36-in. stroke). S. and H. Morton and Co. manufactured the machinery at Leith. She had two decks.

Interestingly, the *Britannia IIII* had left Leith for passage to Newcastle on the evening of Saturday, 10 January 1891 with a general cargo and 43 passengers. However, at around 0330 hrs on Sunday the 11th, she was involved in a collision off St. Abb's Head with the steamer *Bear*; the incident happened in position 55 55'.360N 002 07'.596W and resulted in the loss of 13 people. The *Bear* was a 593-ton cargo vessel built and completed by Raylton Dixon and Co. of Middlesbrough as Yard No.137 in March 1877 for J. Watson and Co. of Middlesbrough; she was bound from Middlesbrough to Grangemouth with a deadweight cargo of pig iron. The *Britannia IIII*, which had reversed her engines, struck the *Bear* amidships with her bow and the Middlesbrough vessel immediately began to founder. A boat was quickly lowered from the *Britannia* and, with the aid of a lamp, two men were rescued, the second mate A. J. Anderson and the lamp trimmer A. Ireland, both of whom were in an exhausted state. Twelve other men, though, went down with the ship. It was the middle of the night and so dark at the time, but the weather was described as 'dark but clear', with a WSW force 5 wind blowing. David Wilson, the first mate on the *Britannia IIII*, alleged that the helm of the *Bear* was put starboard to cross the bow of the Leith steamer, yet two survivors from the *Bear* asserted that by blowing the whistle, they gave the *Britannia IIII* warning that they were going starboard. By all accounts, on sighting each other, it appears that *Britannia IIII* gave one single blast of her whistle to warn the *Bear* to port, while the latter gave two blasts indicating the *Britannia IIII* to steer to starboard, but it resulted in a huge amount of confusion between both crews, leading, it would seem, to the collision. The *Britannia IIII* had her bows stove in and water began to pour into the vessel, so the officers sent out distress signals, firing a number of rockets. Two vessels passed by without offering assistance, but the Carron Company steamer *Thames* of Grangemouth, which was en route to London, came to her aid. As it was clear that the *Britannia IIII* was in poor condition, the 45 passengers were immediately transferred to the *Thames*, unfortunately without their effects. A hawser was quickly passed between the two ships and the *Britannia IIII* was towed slowly stern-foremost up the Firth, her crew remaining on board. Gradually, and with the utmost care, the towing proceeded until about 1500 hrs. The vessels were two miles to the west of Fidra Island when the hawser snapped and the *Britannia IIII* foundered. Captain Robinson and the eight crewmen were thrown into the sea but, fortunately, all of the men except for the captain were wearing lifebelts. The Alloa tug *Yorkshire Lass* quickly arrived on the scene and succeeded in rescuing seven of the men including the captain, although sadly the chief engineer, Mr David Ettershanks, was drowned.

The *Thames* and *Yorkshire Lass* returned to Leith Roads. The 45 passengers were then transferred from the *Thames* to the *Yorkshire Lass*, which sailed for Leith harbour with Captain Robinson, the two survivors from the *Bear* and the crew of the *Britannia IIII,* arriving there just after 1900 hrs. From there they were taken to the Sailors' Home, where refreshments were offered. It was later stated that when the vessels were opposite St. Abb's Head, the officers of both vessels had observed the lights of the other ship and orders were given on each vessel to ensure that a collision be avoided.

The *Britannia IIII* was later salvaged, overhauled and put back into regular service.

Her final wreckage near the Callers is now well spread about on the steep slope from 3 metres down to 28 metres. The engine lies partly buried on the bottom close to the upright boiler/condenser in a gully at 10 metres, while the winch and bows are some way out from the reef in 25–28 metres. Currents are very strong and it is a slack water dive. This is not a particularly good wreck dive to see marine life. Visibility varies greatly but can at times be exceptional.

Starke/Schell Registers; BoT Wreck Return WWI, p.18 (2); *The History of the Seahouses Lifeboats* by J. Morris; *The Times*: Monday, 27 September, 1915, p.12; *The Times*, Monday, 12 January, 1891, p. 7.

(4) ✮ ✮ ✮

55 37'.674 N 001 36'.074 W

A shallow area, where lots of small marine life can be found amongst the short seaweed. There are also plenty of crevices, gullies and small boulders hiding crustaceans.

A surprising sight to behold is the long lost cargo of 'green slate', which is actually black Norwegian riverbed slate and worth a small fortune. It is stacked up neatly and looks like concrete paving slabs, just the way it was when the vessel sank. The slate lies in 8 metres and about 50 metres out from the Callers reef. Most of the slate is intact and the 7.6 cm-thick slabs are about a metre square. The cargo obviously comes from a sailing vessel but nothing at all of that remains. There is no doubt that this could be a profitable project for some enterprising club willing to put a bit of hard graft into their diving. Visibility is usually fairly good, but currents are very strong on the ebb tide because it sweeps around the steep wall of the reef and runs through the channel between the two Callers islets.

At bottom of the tide, on the flood, this area is fairly sheltered until the water washes over the reef top, so this would be the best time to do any salvaging.

SS Skovdal

(5) ★ ★ ★ ★

55 37'.629 N 001 35'.989 W

At this site lie the skeletal remains of an old steamer, most probably that of the Norwegian steamer *Skovdal*. The *Skovdal* was wrecked on the Crumstone Rock on 27 January 1917, while on a voyage from Middlesbrough to Skien with a cargo of salt. Nothing is known about her crew or if they survived.

The *Skovdal* was a 607-ton wooden-hulled steam cargo vessel, completed by R. O. Hærem, Stavanger and launched in 1891 for E. Berentsen, Stavanger as the *Sjøgutten*. She measured 50.3-m in length, with a 7.69-m beam and 4.92-m draught. The single screw was powered by a 52-nhp, three-cylinder triple expansion steam engine that used one boiler. The cylinders measured 30.48 cm, 50.8 cm and 81.28 cm with a 66.04-cm stroke (12 in., 20 in. and 32 in. with a 26-in. stroke). Akers Mek Verk at Christiania manufactured the machinery. She also had a 43-ton quarterdeck, a 64-ton bridge deck, 5-ton deck housing and 19-ton forecastle. The designated code recognition signal letters were: JWQM.

In 1892 the registered owner was Sigval Bergesen, Stavanger.

On 2 February 1905, following grounding in Moldøsundet, she sank, while voyaging from Fredrikstad to Ålesund. The vessel was refloated and sold to Brødrene Anda of Stavanger for scrapping; however they re-sold and repaired her. In 1905 the registered owners were Aksjeselskap Sjøgutten, Kragerø with A. O. Lindvig the managers. In 1907 she was owned by Aksjeselskap Sjøgutten, Stavanger and L. Kloster was the manager.

A/S D/S Sjøgutten, Bergen was the owner in 1912 and A. Anderssen the manager.

In 1915 she was renamed *Lars Lea* by new owners A/S D/S Lars Lea, Bergen and E. Grant Lea became the manager. In early 1916 she was renamed *Skovda* when sold to Aksjeselskap Skovdal, Stavanger and Brødr. Olsen became the manager. Later in 1916, the registered owner was Aksjeselskap Skovdal, Christiania, and P. Ant. Larsen became the manager.

The wreck lies well broken up about 25 metres out from the Callers' reef wall, across a 15-metre stony basin. The remains lie on the opposite sloping bank of a submerged boulder-strewn reef and is orientated in a north to south direction. Although the wreckage is very decayed and scattered around, it is still an interesting sight, especially to the underwater photographer.

The engine frame and boiler stand fairly high and look very photogenic when the light shines through them. Very often crabs and lobsters can be found hiding among the pile of debris and, surprisingly, there is still the glint of the odd copper pipe concreted into the pile. An anchor and chain, an iron propeller, a prop shaft and lots of rusting metal and two big winches lie close by on the sloping bank. Anemones, which are attracted by the strong currents, cover the side of the rocks and walls of the Callers. The current runs around the inside of the Crumstone and then sweeps through the gullies between the Callers; sometimes it is strong enough to purge your demand valve. Slack low water is the best time to dive and the visibility is usually good.

(6) ✭✭✭

Down the western corner of Crumstone, there are lots of rusting plates and girders in depths ranging from only 5–8 metres, where the occasional lobster and cod can sometimes be found. The sloping bottom is a mass of rocks and boulders, all covered in small marine growth, and it then gives way to sand, lower down at about 15 metres. Many young seal pups frolic around in this area but the current is very strong on the top half of the tide.

(7) ✭✭

55 37′.519 N 001 35′.972 W

This area, called the Fang, is a V-shaped shallow stretch of ground reaching out from the western side of Crumstone and the second Caller islets for about 250 metres. There are lots of creeks and gullies but very few holes and crevices, and for some reason not much marine life, despite being constantly swept by strong currents from both sides on the flood and ebb tides. The reef top is covered in heavy kelp and there are sheer 20-metre drop-offs to a sand/stony seabed on both the north and south sides.

(8) ✶ ✶

This is not a very interesting dive site, amongst thick kelp and in a maximum depth of 7 metres, but there are a few boulders and rocks here, so a careful poke around may result in a crustacean for lunch. The area is rather more sheltered from the currents than most of the inside of Crumstone. With a little careful planning it is possible to combine this dive with the next.

(9) ✶ ✶

This is the position where the three islands of Crumstone are divided by narrow channels. The one which leads to the eastern side of Crumstone is rather shallow and has bits of wreckage strewn about on the bottom; care should be taken because of the moderate to strong current that often sweeps through it. The other gully/channel to the south is a little deeper and leads out to the drop-off a few metres out. Any swell from the south or southeast creates a surge through the channel and it is best to avoid it during these periods.

(10) ✶ ✶ ✶ ✶

55 37'.632 N 001 35'.668 W

This is a first-class dive with a drop-off to 25 metres where the cliff walls are absolutely carpeted in colourful anemones, including jewel anemones, Devonshire cup corals and soft corals. There are overhanging ledges with crevices covered in marine life and it is a great experience to glide down the cliff walls to 20–25 metres, feeling free as a bird, especially when the visibility is good. The only drawback is the ferocious current near the reef top on the ebb or spring tides where the force of water is strong enough to purge your valve and pull your mask off. Obviously it is best dived at low slack water but it is possible to dive on the flood as there are no down-sweeping currents to worry about. Once over the edge of the wall, the strength of the current dies off and you can literally go anywhere. The ebb tide, though, is different: because there is so much water welling up over the reef from the deep water, it is impossible to move against it. It is also at this point that the ebb flow hits the Crumstone and swings seaward (northeast) along the reef wall for about 500 metres before turning north again. The bottom of the reef wall is a collection of boulders leading onto stony seabed.

It was from this position that two Seaham divers went adrift during heavy weather in the 1980s. Any surface swell combined with a big tide causes the sea literally to boil just after the drop-off and it was these same conditions in which the pair went missing. A full-scale search and rescue operation was launched, involving RAF helicopters and RNLI lifeboats. They had almost given up all hope when, two days later, the two divers just wandered ashore at Boulmer, ten miles down the coast, and alerted the authorities. Even to this day, very few local people, including some of the rescue crews, believe their story of having swum for two days without being spotted, especially after such an intensive search. The guys were both wearing Northern Diver neoprene drysuits, which obviously kept them warm and saved their lives; for the publicity received, Northern Diver presented them with brand new £600 drysuits.

(11) ✮ ✮ ✮ ✮

An echo sounder is required to pick up the reef wall. A similar dive to site (10) but the drop-off is broken into wide steps and ledges in the first 10 metres before dropping away to the sand and stone seabed at 30 metres. The reef has lots of marine life on it, including Devonshire cup corals and jewel anemones, which are not seen in many other areas around the Farne Islands, apart from at Whirl Rocks. The tidal streams and currents are the same as the last dive site (10).

(12) ✮ ✮

55 37'.662 N 001 35'.614 W

Marine life is a bit sparse here compared with at the last two sites, with the shallowest point at 16 metres and dropping away to the flat stony bottom at 30 metres. The strong currents still prevail but the rocks are fairly bare. Again, the echo sounder is required to locate the reef should anyone be interested enough to want to dive at this site.

(13) ✮ ✮ ✮ ✮

55 37'.685 N 001 35'.754 W

A shallow plateau with dense kelp and tangleweed and depths ranging between 5 and 10 metres; the plateau is also broken by a few deep narrow gullies. This is a very good dive with lots of marine life among the deep crevices, slots and gullies, including velvet swimming crabs, edible brown crabs and lobsters. The problem is finding them under the fine dense weed which now covers most of the holes during the summer months. This fine lace-like weed is a new phenomenon which has appeared during the summer over the last ten years or so. It is gradually spreading everywhere throughout the Farne Islands. Currents are also on the strong side, especially near the southern end of the plateau, making it difficult to stay put; the effort, though, can be very rewarding. Very often the whole grey seal colony will leave the island and come over to inspect any visiting divers underwater. If seals are what you are looking for, this could be the ideal site, but sometimes they can be a real nuisance, pulling and biting your fins.

SS *Helmsdale*

(14) ✭ ✭ ✭

55 37'.689 N 001 35'.914 W

Thick kelp jungle with lots of crevices and deep channels but there is not quite as much life about on this dive. You do, though, have the bonus of diving among the smashed-up remains of a wreck, or wrecks, including that of the SS *Helmsdale*.

The *Helmsdale* foundered after striking the Crumstone during thick fog on 19 July 1939 while transporting a cargo of cement from Ipswich to Aberdeen. Fortunately all of her crew were rescued by the Holy Island lifeboat.

The *Helmsdale* was a 717-ton steam cargo vessel, completed by J. Chambers Ltd, Lowestoft in October 1921 and launched as the *Marjorie Mellonie* (Official No.145831) for Mellonie and Goulder Ltd, Ipswich. The single screw was powered by an aft-positioned 107-nhp, three-cylinder triple expansion steam engine that used one boiler. The cylinders measured 38.1 cm, 63.5 cm and 104.14 cm with a 68.58-cm stroke (15 in., 25 in. and 41 in. with a 27-in. stroke). Yeaman and Baggesen manufactured the machinery at King George Wharf, Dundee. The vessel measured 54.6 m in length and had an 8.7-m beam. She was fitted with electric lights and had a well deck, one steel deck, three bulkheads cemented, a 35.35-m quarter deck, a 6.70-m forecastle and a cellular double bottom. The designated code recognition signal letters were: MVKC.

In 1930 she was registered to Sam Robford and Co. Ltd, Ipswich with W. G. Penman the managers. In 1932 she was renamed *Helmsdale* by G. Couper and Co. Ltd, of Ipswich.

Large lumps of lead can be found spread around under the thick bed of kelp, but very little else remains of the steamer, not even the boiler, so she has obviously been salvaged at some time..

Another twelve vessels are recorded as having foundered on Crumstone in the last hundred years, so it is possible that part of the wreckage in this area may be from some of the other wrecks, nearly all wooden ones.

(15) ✭ ✭ ✭

A narrow underwater 'bridge' links the Crumstone with the first of the Callers' islets at the southwest corner of Crumstone, but the tide races over the top of it. On its seaward side is an eight metre channel fanning out in two directions, full of debris from a wreck or possibly even part of the *Helmsdale*. There are rusting steel plates and lots of framework under which lobsters and cod can often be found, while the glint of brass among the brown weed makes it a good rummage dive.

Anyone interested in having a close encounter with grey seals should be quite happy in this vicinity, as the young pups often frequent the area, especially when divers are around. If you stay close to the bottom in the channel, which is covered in short brown seaweed, the current is fairly mild and even more so on the ebb tide.

(16) ✶✶

Two hundred metres seaward of the channel in the last dive (15) are huge rounded, weed-less boulders split by deep gullies with depths of around 15 metres plus. The current increases significantly the further east you travel and it turns to a NE direction towards the Longstone on the ebb tide. Dense shoals of coley very often patrol around the reef perimeters but otherwise it is not a very interesting dive.

(17) ✶✶

This is shallow, 'hilly' ground covered in thick kelp although there are some massive rocks and boulders up to 8 metres high just to the south of Crumstone. There are plenty of gullies with loads of sea urchins, and a few decent edible crabs and velvet crabs can be found, but generally it is rather boring. Beneath the kelp bed it is fairly sheltered, especially at low water, but the current builds up considerably on the flood tide once the Callers are covered; it then runs in three directions, which can be very confusing when looking at your compass.

(18) ✶✶✶

55 37'.737 N 001 36'.174 W

Again, this is 'hilly' undulating type of ground covered by the dense kelp forest with wide deep gullies and a few decent crevices to poke around in for those elusive lobsters. One bonus (and they are a firm favourite of mine) are the large numbers of buckies or buck whelks to be found, usually on the bottom of the rock-strewn channels and gullies. There is plenty of shelter staying close to the bottom in the gullies, but the current runs fast in a NW direction on the flood and then it turns south after about 100 metres and goes down over into deep water (25 metres plus). Divers are well advised to moor the boat well away from the most northerly Callers rock, especially during periods when there is an easterly ground swell.

On the top half of the tide, divers should take note of their position in conjunction with the boat and observe which way the tide is running before they surface; it often pays to try and make your way back to the anchor line too.

(19) ✶ ✶

Rather flat rock with some wide deep gullies and a scattering of short kelp on top of the rocks. Again, there is a good picking of whelks to be had, if you look hard and close enough. Dense shoals of coley and large individual pollack are common at certain times of the year; it is worth doing a spot of fly fishing after the dive. Both these fish are part of the cod family and although their meat is softer, they are very sweet and tasty. A string of mackerel feathers will bag you four or five fish at a time when you hit the big shoals. The depth drops away quickly out here from 15 metres plus and the tidal strength increase significantly the further away from the Callers you travel.

(20) ✶ ✶ ✶ ✶ ✶

Nice dive with strong currents and lots of marine life about everywhere. Deep valleys, crevices, caves and holes all around, with the gully bottom covered in anemones. Depths range between 8 and 15 metres, while the current runs to the northeast or southwest, depending on the ebb or flood tides.

(21) ✶ ✶ ✶

Depths are in the region of between 15 and 20 metres, with the reef top criss-crossed with narrow gullies, but it is a wee bit drab. The reef top slopes away down to the bottom at 25 metres some 200 metres northwards. Due to the depth there is very little marine growth, but you can still find a few buckies on the reef top. The more adventurous divers who don't mind taking a risk can take a dive to the bottom at 25 to 30 metres, where they may be rewarded with a bag of queenies or greater scallops. There definitely are scallops out there, because some of the boats from Seahouses trawl to the east and south of the islands and make a lot of money out of it.

(22) Unknown star rating

Who knows? This could be a six-star site! About 400 metres to the north of dive site (21), my colleague and I picked up a good magnetometer and echo sounder reading but had run out of dive time and air. The weather then changed for the worse for three months and we never did get back to see what it was. Maybe one day somebody will hit the jackpot on this site.

THE OUTER FARNE ISLANDS

Knavestone Rocks

55 38'.993 N 001 36'.103 W

The Knavestone is the most easterly and seaward of all the Farne Islands that are visible at low tide. It dries to 3.6 metres and consists of one large island and four

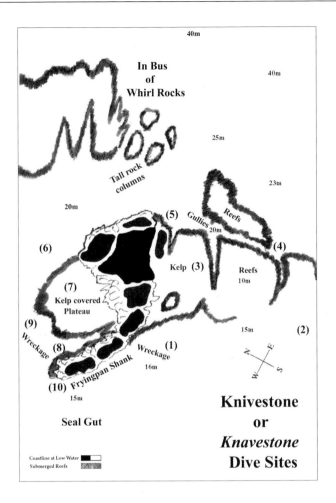

In Bus of Whirl Rocks

40m

40m

Tall rock columns

25m

23m

20m

(5) Gullies Reefs
20m

(6) (4)

Kelp (3) Reefs
10m

(7)
Kelp covered Plateau

(9)
Wreckage (8) Wreckage (1)
15m 16m (2)

(10) Fryingpan Shank
15m

Seal Gut

Coastline at Low Water
Submerged Reefs

Knivestone
or
Knavestone
Dive Sites

tangleweed-covered rocks which reach out from the island's western corner, earning themselves the name of Frying Pan Shank, due to their overall shape. Knavestone is 4.98 miles NNE of Seahouses, 4.63 miles from the nearest part of the mainland coast and about 600 metres seaward of Longstone. The island also has a large colony of grey seals that live on and around it. The medieval name of Knavestone dates back to the time of St Cuthbert and is still sometimes used by the people of the coastal villages.

With its surrounding reefs, the Knavestone has presented a serious hazard to shipping over the centuries and many dozens of people have perished in the swirling riptides surrounding it. The very sight of it must have struck terror into the hearts of those poor mariners as they struggled against the walls of pounding white water, especially during a storm. The combination of low water temperatures, even in the middle of summer, and the powerful swirling currents must have left them with very little chance of survival. The tide runs in a north–south direction, so even the strongest of swimmers could not have managed to swim to the nearest dry land, the craggy rocks of Longstone over 600 metres away, across the swirling waters of Seal Gut. More than sixty known vessels have come to grief here since the year 1800, but many more unrecorded ones must have vanished without trace. The following records are just a little sample of those unfortunate vessels that have come to grief on the Knavestone Rocks:

In 1805 the sailing vessel *Glasgow Packet* foundered in heavy weather after striking the rocks and her crew was lost.

The wooden sloop *Sarah* was en route to London from Leith with a cargo of beef, pork and wine when, at midday on 15 August 1815, she struck the Knavestone. The vessel sat on top of the rocks for three days in good weather, but because of a dispute about the salvage arrangements with local fishermen, the ship and its cargo were eventually lost.

On 15 September 1815, the wooden sailing vessel *Hazard* struck the rocks and foundered and all hands perished.

On 31 October 1933 the wooden brig *Fame* foundered during a storm after grounding on the rocks of Knavestone and her crew was lost.

On 27 December 1834 the wooden sloop *Autumn* was heading for Peterhead from Sunderland with a cargo of coal when she smashed into the eastern corner of the Knavestone and sank almost immediately. Two of her crew of three were lost, but the third man, called James Logan, hung onto the masthead and a partly-submerged rock for nearly ten hours before being rescued. William Darling, the keeper of the Longstone Lighthouse, famed for the rescue of people from the ill-fated paddle steamer *Forfarshire* soon after, said that it was the biggest risk he had ever undertaken in his life, rowing across the treacherous channel to rescue a cold and weary Mr Logan. Apparently Grace Darling had heard Mr Logan's cries and she alerted her two brothers and her father who then performed the heroic deed.

The British schooner *Alexander* perished with her crew after striking the Knavestone rocks on 24 March 1845.

The *Countess of Mar* was wrecked and smashed to pieces on Knavestone on 6 August 1847.

On 14 March 1847, the *Lady Ross* came to grief and foundered after running onto the rocks.

On 4 January 1850, the British schooner *Brave* of Inverness was lost to the Knavestone and all hands were lost.

The sailing vessel *Plough* struck the Knavestone and sank with all hands on 12 December 1850.

Early in the morning of 18 February 1908, the Norwegian iron steamer *Geir*, with Captain Johannes Bru in command, ran aground on the Knavestone Rock during a snowstorm and a NNE force 8 gale; the vessel was in ballast and on passage from Bergen for Blyth. At 1200 hrs, the master had Bell Rock lighthouse in a WNW direction and about 10 nautical miles distant. At 1600 hrs, he reckoned that St. Abb's Head Lighthouse was in a WSW direction and approximately 10 nautical miles away. From that point the course was set: SSW, about ¼ E, to get clear of the Longstone light. However at 1815 hrs, the master had the lighthouse on the starboard side, approximately in southwest to west and the ship was quite close to land. Before he started the hard starboard turn of the rudder, the ship ran aground on Knavestone Rocks. The North Sunderland (Seahouses) self-righting lifeboat *Forster Fawsett* was launched in pitch darkness at 1900 hrs and went to her aid. It proved impossible, however, for the lifeboat to get alongside the stricken steamer because of the powerful swirling white water and the number of large rocks in the area. After carefully considering the situation, the boat's 28-year-old coxswain, James Robson, took the lifeboat to a small rock nearby, where he landed with a lifebuoy and ropes before the lifeboat moved off to a safer distance. With the use of lines and the lifebuoy, Coxswain Robson brought the crew of fourteen off the stranded ship and onto the Knavestone; they were then hauled one by one over to the lifeboat. With everyone safely on board, the *Forster Fawsett* returned to North Sunderland harbour to be greeted by a large crowd of cheering people who had gathered on the harbour pier. The *Geir* gradually slipped back off the Knavestone and sank, where she quickly broke up.

The Maritime Examinations in Oath took place at Berwick-on-Tweed on 19 February 1908 with the Declarations in Newcastle upon Tyne on 25 February. During the examinations at the inquiries, the inspector said that the reason for running aground was, without doubt, bad navigation. The master did not use the line and he did not assure himself that the distance to St. Abb's Head was safe before he turned for Longstone. In addition there were no lookouts and the speed of the vessel was too fast. The captain was therefore found guilty and fined 200 Norwegian kroner.

For outstanding gallantry, Coxswain James Robson was awarded the Royal National Lifeboat Institute's Silver Medal at a public meeting on 12 March 1908, the chairman of North Sunderland Lifeboat Station, Lt. Col. Marshal, presenting it on behalf of the RNLI. James' father, a former coxswain, was also presented with a framed certificate to mark his years of dedication to the service. The King of Norway presented James Robson with a silver medal for 'His Noble Deeds' in rescuing the crew of the *Geir*.

The *Geir* (Official No.84946) was an iron-hulled 848-ton Norwegian steam cargo vessel measuring 61.13 m in length, with a 9.60-m beam and a 3.75-m draught. Workman, Clark and Co. Belfast built and completed her in July 1882 as Yard No.11; she was launched on 17 July 1882 as the *Newhaven* for R. Mackie and

Co. Leith. The single iron screw was powered by a 94-nhp, two-cylinder compound steam engine that used one boiler. Lees, Anderson and Co. manufactured the engine and ancillary machinery in Glasgow. Her designated code recognition signal letters were: WMPD.

In 1895–1896 she was still called *Newhaven*, but the designated code recognition signal letters were MBJN and the tonnage was also increased to 909 gross.

In 1901, New Line Steamship Co. Ltd was the registered owner and R. Mackie and Co. became the manager. From 1904, Halfdan Kuhnle in Bergen, Norway was the registered owner and she was renamed *Geir*, with the designated code recognition signal letters MBJN.

BoT Wreck Return 1908, Appendix C, Table 1, p. 128 (332); LCR 1908 p. 8 (h); *The History of the Seahouses Lifeboats* by J. Morris.

Another ship that came to grief on the Knavestone was the Gefle-registered steamer *Emma* which stranded there on Wednesday, 9 December 1914, while carrying a cargo of wood pulp and pig iron from Sundsvall to Manchester. The *Emma*, however, drifted off the Knavestone unseen and during the next few days disappeared, after being blown away in gale-force winds and heavy weather. It is very probable that the wreck now lies in 61 metres at position: 55 41'.045 N 001 34'.986 W (UK Hydrographic Wreck No. 60564.)

Two years later, on 4 September 1916, the Norwegian steamer *Gustav Vigeland* was wrecked on the Knavestone while on passage from the Russian port of Archangelsk to London with a cargo of timber; soon after striking the rocks she began breaking up, so the crew of 21 took to the boats and landed at Seahouses.

The *Gustav Vigeland* was a 2,185-ton steam cargo ship completed as Yard No.104 at the North Hylton shipyard of Osbourne, Graham and Co, Sunderland in October 1897; she was launched as the *Rustington* (Official No.108258) on 28 August 1897 for Southdown Steam Ship Co. Ltd, London, with Bell, Symondson and Co. as the manager. She measured 87.8 m in length and had a 12.8-m beam. The single screw was powered by a three-cylinder triple expansion steam engine that used two boilers. In 1906 she was renamed *Portsmouth* by Portsea S.S. Co. Ltd, Cardiff, and McNeil, Hinde and Co. were the managers. In 1912 she was renamed *William* (Official No.5395) by the new owners Trelleborgs Ångfartygs Nya A/B., Trelleborg, Sweden and F. D. Malmros became the manager. In 1916 she was registered to Olaf Ørvig, Bergen, who renamed her *Gustav Vigeland*.

On 2 December 1916 the steam trawler *Queenstown* was wrecked on Knavestone while en route to the fishing grounds from Grimsby. She was skippered by Captain T. Hoult and was carrying a crew of ten when she stranded on the northeastern side of the rocks and became a total loss. The crew all took to the boat.

The *Queenstown* was a steel-hulled 161-ton steam trawler completed as Yard No.137 by Mackie and Thomson at Govan, near Glasgow; she was launched on 16 February 1898 for Consolidated Steam Fishing and Ice Co. Grimsby. She measured: 31.75 m in length, with a 6.22-m beam and 3.22-m draught. The single steel screw was powered by a 41-hp three-cylinder triple expansion steam engine that used one boiler. Muir and Houston manufactured the machinery at Glasgow. She had a superstructure that consisted of a 5.15-m quarter deck and a 5.77-m forecastle. The bell from the *Queenstown* was located by divers some fifteen years ago.

HM tug *George R. Gray* ran aground on the Knavestone Rock on 27 October 1918.

Commanded by Lieutenant George Beckett RNVR, the tug was bound for Leith, but at 2240 hrs, in dark and foggy weather, she ran onto the Knavestone. The local lifeboat was called out and took off the crew. When inspected the following day, she was shown to have had a heavy list and her back was broken. The *George R. Gray* disappeared during the night of 30–31 October 1918 and was presumed to have slipped off the rock and foundered.

The *George R. Gray* was a wooden-hulled 268-ton British steam tug completed by Robert J. Morrill at Collingwood, Ontario in 1917 and delivered in 1917 to Lake Superior Paper Co. Ltd at Saulte Ste-Marie. She measured: 35.25m in length with a 7.54-m beam and a 3.81-m draught. The single screw was powered by a 56.5-nhp (380-ihp) two-cylinder compound steam engine that used one boiler and gave ten knots. The machinery was manufactured by John Doty Engine Co. at Toronto, Canada. On 29 November 1917 she was towed to Britain and hired for service with the Royal Navy. The tug was registered as *G. R Gray*: Official No.134620.

Probably the largest and best known of the ships to be wrecked on Knavestone was the German steamer *Abessinia* on 3 September 1920. The *Abessinia*'s maiden voyage was acting as a troopship during the Boxer uprising in China. The ship also served as a supply collier to the Kaiserliche Deutsche Marine's surface warship, SMS *Leipzig*. In 1901, the *Abessinia* made her first merchant voyage from Hamburg to New Orleans.

German steamer Abessinia, *wrecked on Knavestone*

When war broke out in 1914, the *Abessinia* was at anchor, sheltering in the Chilean port of Pisagua, and was immediately interned. At the end of 1918 she was released, but the crew were unhappy about returning to Germany so they evidently sabotaged the machinery. When the problems were solved in 1920, she was towed to Hamburg for repairs and then delivered on reparations account to a British company. However on 3 September 1921 the ship ran onto the Knavestone rocks; motor boats went out from Seahouses to help but assistance was refused. The crew of seven were saved. The ship later toppled over and became a total wreck.

The *Abessinia* was a steel-hulled 5,753-ton four-masted German passenger-cargo steamer measuring 137.76 m in length, with a 15.89-m beam and an 8.53-m draught. Palmer's Ship Building and Iron Co. Ltd, Jarrow-on-Tyne, built and completed her as Yard No.746 in August 1900; she was launched on 16 June 1900 for the Hamburg-Amerika Line, Hamburg. The single screw was powered by a 642-hp, three-cylinder triple expansion steam engine that used three boilers and gave 11.5 knots. She also had two decks and seven bulkheads.

The wreck lies on the southwest side of the rocks in depths from 8 metres to about 16 metres and, although now well broken up, is still very substantial and a good dive. There are in fact two wrecks, the other one being on the north side of the reef. There is still some dispute over which is which, although the one on the southwest side is more likely to be that of the *Abessinia*.

At 0400 hrs on 29 August 1922, the 311-ton steamer *Horley* was on passage from Aberdeen for Whitstable with a cargo of stones when, in dense fog, she stranded in the shallow gully on the north side of the Knavestone and became a total loss.

The *Horley* (Official No.144322) was a steel-hulled 311-ton steam cargo vessel completed by E. and M. Coops, Hoogezand, Netherlands in 1919 and launched as the *Waterweg* for N.V. Hollandsche Algemeene Atlantische Scheepv. Mij., Amsterdam; N. Haas was the manager. She measured 37 m in length with a 6.9-m beam and a 3.07-m draught. The single steel screw was powered by an aft positioned three-cylinder triple expansion steam engine that used one boiler.

In 1920 she was renamed *Horley* by new owners J. Harrison, Ltd of London.

In the last 20 years, two lovely ship's bells have been found at the base of the Knavestone reef in 18 metres and there must be many more just waiting to be discovered by some lucky diver.

The orca

Occasionally orcas, or killer whales, make visits to the waters around the Outer Farnes, and about 25 years ago I had the privilege of seeing one quite close up. I was in 15 metres of water on the south side of Knavestone when one of these beautiful creatures swam right over the top of me. I happened to be looking in a crevice when suddenly it went very dark, as if someone had switched off the light. I thought a cloud must have blocked out the sun, but when I looked up and saw the orca, my heart skipped more than a few beats. I lay motionless on the bottom, like an ostrich burying its head in the sand. The orca must have been about seven or eight metres in length and was so close to me as it passed by that I could have reached out and touched it. Then – within a few seconds, but what seemed like minutes – it was gone. The experience caused a massive surge of adrenaline throughout my system but I felt like a great bag of nerves and could not relax until I was safely in the boat. Later that day, I thought about the documentary I had seen some time before, showing the creatures to be friendly towards humans. These days, with far more experience and understanding of nature, I very much regret not having made the most of that unique and once-in-a-lifetime encounter with that beautiful, majestic animal.

Donald the dolphin

In the late 1970s, I also had the privilege of spending two whole dives with a 3.8-m bottle-nosed dolphin called Donald at Lamorna Cove in Cornwall. I was on a two-week camping holiday at Newquay with my wife and three children and we visited the cove, where I intended to have a shallow dive. I put my gear on and was hoping to join two divers who were already in the water, but before I could reach them they had disappeared from view, so I decided to carry on by myself. I snorkelled out into the bay for about 100 metres before diving to the bottom and was peering into a hole containing a large conger eel, a novelty for me at the time, when I had the uncanny feeling that something was watching me. I looked to my right and then my left and nearly fainted when I saw a huge eye staring at me. It belonged to a gigantic grey-blue creature, only inches away from my face; it was actually looking in the hole with me. I got such a shock in those first few seconds that I couldn't comprehend what it was: was it a shark? A whale? It then pulled back quickly and made some squeaking noises while nodding its head and I realised that I was looking at the eye and snout of a large dolphin. I was so shocked that I just stayed still while it swam around me making these squeaking noises. Then, to my horror, it came up and took hold of my arm in its mouth. I had visions of my arm being chewed off but, amazingly, the dolphin started to clasp my arm gently, then my hand, as a friendly dog does when it shows its master affection. I began to relax and stroked it each time it came to me. I became engrossed in this unique experience and spent my whole dive playing with it, until I suddenly realised that I was a long way out from the harbour. I surfaced and began my return journey. I was beginning to get concerned at the distance I was from the harbour when Donald suddenly came alongside and more or less offered me a tow. I held onto his dorsal fin and he towed me to within fifty metres of Lamorna Cove harbour and then disappeared. Unknown to me, crowds of holidaymakers had gathered on the harbour wall and had been watching me being towed in by the dolphin. When I waded out of the sea, some people asked if I had been attacked by a shark.

The next day I was invited out for a dive by some guys from Stevenage BSAC who were down in Cornwall on a diving trip. On the return journey in one of their inflatable boats, Donald appeared alongside the boat and followed us all the way back to the harbour where he submerged again. Then, after about 20 minutes, much to the horror of my seven-year-old daughter Diane and her friend, who were playing in the water up to their chests, the dolphin surfaced right between them. The scene was reminiscent of the film *Jaws*, as everyone began screaming 'Shark!' and there was an almighty scramble out of the sea. Of course the guys I had been on the diving trip with were ecstatic and all jumped into the sea. I think the dolphin was in its element too as they all played together around the harbour. They were an unforgettable couple of days.

I remember being told by a fisherman friend of mine, Ron Eglinton, who operated a shark- and deep-sea angling boat out of Newquay at the time, that during the winter he used to hand-line for mackerel out of Fowey on the Channel side of Cornwall. His boat was moored a little offshore and he and his son Garry had to cross over to it in a little fibreglass dinghy. Ron said that Donald would very often come up out of the water, propelling himself along while standing on his tail, right alongside his little boat; almost swamping it. Ron said that he knew the dolphin was just being playful but that it was extremely frightening because the water was icy cold and deep! Sadly, I was told some years later that the playful animal had been shot by fishermen.

But back to the Knavestone…

Dive sites

SS *Abessinia*

(1) ★★★★

55 38'.950 N 001 36'.049 W

This is the wreck of the German steamer *Abessinia*, which lies in 16 metres on a sloping stony bank about 10 m west from the northwestern corner of Knavestone. The boilers are fairly close to the reef wall of Knavestone and stand proud of the rocky seabed amidst a huge jumble of wreckage that extends all the way along to the large Seal Gut reef. If you look hard enough there are still a few goodies to be found: brass valves, brass shell casings, the odd porthole and the huge winches still have signs of copper pipe on them. This is an excellent dive with lots of marine life about, both swimming and crawling. On one of my last dives, a very large wolf fish had taken up residence in a boiler, willing to defend itself at any cost and there were four lobsters (albeit small ones) within five square metres of the boiler. Although it is possible to dive on neap tides with care, it really is a slack water dive. The position of the wreck puts it slap-bang in the main tidal flow of Seal Gut, right where the water is funnelled up and over the huge reef on the ebb tide. To the north of the wreck are some medium-sized boulders and a collection of old and broken lobster pots which appear still to be roped together.

The best time to dive this site is just before low slack water and if the tide has started to run on the flood, it is best to moor the boat close in, behind the island, to avoid the strong tidal stream. On spring tides there can be some nasty overfalls making it quite uncomfortable and even dangerous for a small craft.

G. R. *Gray,* HM Tug

(2) ✶ ✶

The wreckage from the tug G. R. *Gray* is spread out on the sloping seabed in 16–18 metres on the southwest side of Knavestone, about 75 metres south from the main rock. The vessel's bronze screw was salvaged from the wreck in the 1970s by a local diver and charter boat skipper. The little boiler, the remains of her engine and a few steel plates and frames can still be seen but these are gradually concreting into the stone- and rock-strewn seabed, although the site is a worthwhile second dive if only for a rummage around. The tidal current is fierce in both directions and there is no protection from it, making this a definite slack water dive. The poisonous, trailing, stinging cells (nematocyst) of the lion's mane jellyfish that flow along in the strong currents can be a real nuisance during July and August. The surrounding seabed consists of small rocks and boulders, covered in anemones, on a sloping bank that drops away down from 16 metres to over 25 metres.

About 200 metres southwest of the Knavestone, the stony bottom slopes gradually away to 20 metres plus. There is a profusion of small marine life: various kinds of anemones covering the bottom, along with some decent-sized edible brown crabs and lobsters which hide under the small boulders and low reefs. The vicious tidal streams, however, make it a slack water dive as there are very few rocks to shelter behind. This is probably a site best left to the dedicated marine biologist or close-up underwater photographer who needs to look more closely at the flora and fauna at slack water.

(3) ✶ ✶ ✶ ✶

This is a shallow sloping plateau between 5 and 15 metres deep, with numerous ledges, channels and mounds covering an area of around 150 metres. About 25 metres or so out from the centre and south side of the Knavestone is a 20-metre funnel-shaped submarine canyon cut deep into the plateau, running parallel to Knavestone. It begins at the submerged cliffs at the eastern edge and terminates at a cave halfway across the plateau. I must admit that I have never had any inclination to enter the cave, chiefly because there has always been a surge pushing me towards it and I have never fancied the idea of being wedged in a submarine cave at 20 metres! The canyon bottom is mostly coarse sand and fine stones and there is a pronounced downward current on the ebb tide. The reef top is heavy with kelp and young seal pups zip around every-where. The surrounding cliff walls of the plateau are covered in anemones and soft cor-als and dense shoals of coley (*Pollachius virens*) often swarm around the reef top, while large cod, conger and ling can be found under the overhanging ledges and crevices. Behind the reefs, this is a reasonably sheltered dive on the bottom of the flood when most of the Knavestone is visible above the surface, but it is best avoided on the ebb and especially on spring tides because you can quite easily end up on the wrong side of the island. On the ebb tide, the current splits into two, going around the island in two different directions, and if you get too close to the eastern end of the Knavestone and try to surface, you are whipped around the corner before ever reaching the surface. You wouldn't be the first or the last diver who has been picked up by another boat or, worse still, gone adrift from this site. When the island is showing it is difficult to see anything on the north side and a diver on the surface would very quickly disappear into the distance in these strong currents.

(4) ★ ★ ★ ★

On the eastern edge of the plateau, 75 metres from the seaward corner of Knavestone, there is a nice gully and reef wall which runs away in an arc to the southwest. It has lots of interesting overhangs, boulders and large rocks where you can usually pick up a nice

Squat lobster or 'little men'
(Courtesy Bob Jolley)

crab or two. Cod, ling, conger, ballan wrasse, squat lobsters, whelks and a host of other critters can be found for those with a torch and an eagle eye, but more interesting still are the swarms of lovely juicy prawns, measuring up to about 7.62 cm (3 in.), that live along the base of the reef. However to catch and contain them takes a bit of pre-planning because you need to go armed with a child's fishing net in which to catch them.

Depths start at about 8 metres on the plateau top, with the gully bottom at 15 metres, but it shelves away deeper the further south you go until the reef wall peters out at 20 metres. The seabed at 20 metres is covered in small jagged rocks and is ablaze with small marine life, but it is worth remembering that above you is a very strong current going south on the flood or, heading into Seal Gut, on the ebb. A surface marker buoy is seriously worth thinking about on this dive site. Visibility is usually good all around Knavestone, except maybe during spring tides or after rough weather.

(5) ★ ★ ★ ★

This is another exciting site with depths ranging from 5 to 25 metres and the sheer, eerie walls of the reef are covered in marine life, but this is definitely a slack water dive. On the flood tide, the current of water surges around the corner of the island at 20 metres plus, then drives up the gully and over the reef plateau, making it impossible for you to get down the wall. On the ebb, there is also a vicious downward flowing current going north around the Knavestone, which can be rather frightening on a big tide. At the base of the reef wall is a gloomy canyon with lots of wreckage strewn around and well worth a closer inspection, because a couple of ship's bells were discovered there in recent years. All that was visible of them at the time was the brass loops protruding out of the stony bottom at the base of the reef. There must be dozens of such goodies just waiting to be found by someone willing to take a little more time to look a bit closer at the bottom. Because of the currents, this site is probably the least dived area around the Knavestone. Lots of seals play around this area and there is a profusion of marine life covering the reef walls. Visibility is generally pretty good.

A lucky escape

This site reminds me of the time my buddy Trevor and I came out with one of his so-called 'friends', a guy called Clayton. My little Flatacraft Force Four had enough room in it for two divers and four bottles but Clayton was stuck for a lift, so we reluctantly decided to make do with one bottle each. The sea had been running big for a couple of weeks and there was a 2–3 metre swell rolling in from the nor'east. We decided, nonetheless, to take a run out to the Outer Farnes to weigh up the prospect of a dive somewhere sheltered. We choose the inside of the Longstone which seemed fairly quiet. Then, while Trevor and his 'friend' were preparing to kit up, the inshore lifeboat came alongside. The crew informed us that an unforeseen storm was imminent and asked if we would help in telling the other dive boats in the area to head for Seahouses harbour immediately. We agreed and set off for the Knavestone where we knew there were two small inflatable boats moored up with divers. As we approached we saw one of the boats was moored up about 20 metres off and south of the reef but that the other one, which had been milling around, had broken down and was drifting. They could not start the 15-hp outboard and the boat was perilously close to the Knavestone. The sea was horrendous and the huge rollers which built up over Whirl Rocks were crashing down onto and over the Knavestone. Their colleagues in the other boat had no quick release system and were having difficulty in retrieving the anchor. We moved in close to assist the boat with the engine problem, but suddenly the suction from the deep surging groundswell caught the little boat and pulled it onto the jagged rocks of the islet. One minute the Knavestone was high and dry and the next it was covered in two or three metres of foaming white water. There was nothing we could do in those conditions without seriously jeopardizing our own safety but then, without any warning, Clayton grabbed a rope and leapt across the bow dodger of my little RHIB towards the inflatable. Trevor and I both instinctively grabbed his feet and pulled him back on board. We asked what he thought he was trying to do and he mumbled that he was going to swim to the inflatable with the rope, which by this time was being pounded and clattered up and down on top of the Knavestone amidst a mass of foaming water. Their bewildered colleagues, still struggling with the anchor, could only look on in horror and Clayton then realised both how stupid and how lucky he had been. What would have happened to him had he tried to swim in those conditions, and especially without any fins on, did not bear thinking about. All we could do was to motor over to the other side of the Knavestone and wait and hope. They took a real bad pounding as the boat and its occupants were clattered up and down and spun round and round at the mercy of the huge rollers, but fortunately they made it over to the other side in one piece. The outboard engine's bottom leg was badly damaged, as was the floor of the inflatable, but they were alive and that was the main thing. We threw them a rope and towed the boat over to their mates, then helped them free the anchor. We had not realised it at the time but, amazingly, they both had divers down. After some ten minutes or so, their divers surfaced well out into Seal Gut and we had to assist in picking them up, which was a tricky operation with three of us in my small Flatacraft and in such turbulent conditions. We transferred the divers over and left the two inflatable boats to make their way back to Seahouses – without, needless to say, as much as a 'thank you'.

(6) ★ ★ ★ ★

The north side of Knavestone is a very popular site for many visiting divers because it provides an interesting mixture of scenery and lots of life on the seabed mixed with wreckage from a number of ships which have collided with the island. The best time to dive this site is at low slack water and the bottom half of the ebb tide. It is not recommended diving on the flood because you can quite easily be swept around to the other side and out of sight of the boat cover. The tidal streams are exceptionally strong on spring tides and depths range between 15 and 23 metres, with the seabed mostly stony. The area is so popular with divers in the summer that it can be like Piccadilly Circus, with up to 20 dive boats struggling for somewhere to anchor.

(7) ★ ★ ★

A shallow plateau covered in a dense jungle of kelp with depths between 2 and 5 metres. There are a few small gullies and holes where you have the chance of picking up the odd lobster, but it is also an excellent rummage dive where anything could turn up, as it has in the past. For those intrepid divers interested in swimming with a couple of dozen young seal pups, it is the perfect location, as at certain times of the year this area is like a seal kindergarten. At the edge of the plateau, it drops away down a steep wall and levels out onto a stony bottom at 15 metres, where rusting steel plates and framework litter the bottom. Here the current is very noticeable and more care should be taken, especially on the flood tide. There is no movement of water whatsoever in this position on the bottom half of the ebb tide. It is also possible to dive on the bottom part of the flood tide, while the four rocks of the Frying Pan Shank of the Knavestone are still above water. These are a string the rocks that dry on a low tide and are situated on the northwestern side, linking up to form the reef resembling a pan handle.

SS *Horley*

(8) ★ ★ ★ ★

An excellent dive in a gradually-sloping gully to 10 metres, which is full of wreckage from the steamer *Horley*, including steel prop shafts, winches, huge pipes, plating, framework and anchors. At the eastern entrance to the gully is a rusting ship's boiler, now split open and exposing lots of pipes, including some copper ones, and the boiler often has one or two large resident 'beetles' in it. Last season, one diver from a London club discovered what he thought was a wooden box full of large brass shell casings: they turned out to be anti-personnel mines and were still filled with cordite. That was a very dodgy find. Every year the northerly gales rip up the debris that litter the gully floor to expose new artefacts. The force of water is so strong that even the heaviest items like the huge prop shafts get thrown about like toys, so it is little wonder that ships coming ashore on the Knavestone seldom stay in one piece very long.

Young seal pups are everywhere and can often give you a shock when they suddenly pop up in front of your mask or tug at your fins. Visibility is usually pretty good and, with no currents to worry about, it makes an excellent novice dive on the low ebb tide.

SS *Gastav Vigeland*

(9) ✫ ✫ ✫ ✫

Some 30 metres north of the gully on the last dive site are the remains of what is probably the SS *Gastav Vigeland* A large ship's boiler lies on its side next to an iron propeller, surrounded by masses of wreckage spread all over the place. Depths are in the 15–18 metre region and, because the wreck lies a bit offshore from the island and rather exposed, the current can be very noticeable. This is a good rummage dive and there are often a few crustaceans and large cod hiding under the steel plates and framework. The visibility sometimes appears a bit dismal compared to what it is closer in to the island. Depths just north of this position drop away to 25 metres plus where the seabed is very stony and currents are very strong.

SS *Abessinia*

(10) ✫ ✫ ✫ ✫

55 39'.962 N 001 36'.254 W

The northwestern corner of Knavestone is a steep sloping face which bottoms out onto hard stony ground strewn with rusting jagged steel plates and framework, possibly from the SS *Abessinia* at 10 metres. Lots of marine life can be observed, with soft corals, anemones and crustaceans. From here the seabed slopes away down into Seal Gut channel to around 15metres before rising up again at the base of the massive submerged reef that stands like a barrier all the way over to Longstone. The tide is exceptionally strong due to the funnelling affect in the channel. This is obviously best dived at slack tide when the Frying Pan Shank is showing above the surface.

SEAL GUT REEF

Seal Gut is in fact the local name for the long, narrow lagoon formed by the islets on the northeastern side of Longstone at low tide. My colleagues and I, though, have always referred to the section of water between the Longstone and Knavestone as Seal Gut as an easy reference when discussing dive sites.

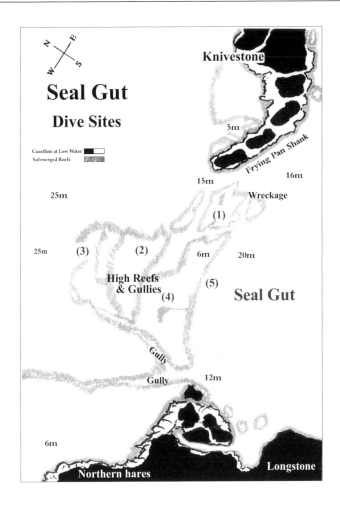

Seal Gut dive sites

(1) ✶ ✶ ✶ ✶

This site is located about 50 metres in a WNW direction off the western corner of Knavestone. This is an excellent dive site, the top of this huge reef in Seal Gut resembling a mini-mountain ridge with steep sloping sides. The vicious tidal currents rip up the life-covered slopes and whip the two-and-a-half metre tangleweed on the top of it into a frenzy. The surface during a spring tide boils with overfalls, causing massive surges and two-metre rollers. There are all kinds of marine life about and it is a very scenic dive, but one best made at slack water. It is possible to dive on neap tides where you can shelter behind the reef on the opposite side to the tidal flow, but a surface marker buoy is essential. Depths on the south side level out at 16–18 metres where bits of wreckage can be found. The seabed on the north side is a bit deeper, at 20 metres plus, and there are many deep channels containing large lumps of wreckage. There are also lots of coley and pollack to be found over the reef tops.

(2) ★ ★ ★ ★ ★

A superb dive site can be located in a northwesterly direction, over the 20-metre wide and 20-metre deep canyon at the end of dive site (1). There are high ridges, deep channels, crevices, wreckage and a fantastic amount of various marine flora and fauna with every inch of rock covered in some form or other. The only drawback is the current, which is very severe, so to enjoy it at its best, it should really only be dived at slack water. Depths range between 7 and 15 metres, but 25 metres can easily be reached over the northern edge.

(3) ★ ★ ★ ★ ★

55 39'.024 N 001 36'.625 W

With an echo sounder, this site is fairly easy to locate at slack water by driving halfway between Longstone and Knavestone then turning north until the reef drops away on the north side. A beautiful dive with overhangs, cliff walls, deep valleys and every square metre covered in an array of colourful anemones and soft corals, making for a very picturesque sight all the way up to the highest point of the reef at 7 metres. Individual pollack of four and five kilos sweep up to catch titbits being swept over the reef top. On neaps, it is fairly easy to dive at any state of the tide, providing there is little or no wind, but a surface marker buoy is essential. The visibility can be exceptional during neaps and light westerly winds during the summer months.

(4) ★ ★ ★

A wide kelp- and tangleweed-covered plateau, harbouring an interesting array of small marine life, with a few small crevices breaking the monotony of this wide area of flat reef. The reef top slopes up from 15 metre s at the north end to 10 metres before it terminates in some wide channels and a steep cliff face at the southern edge. Definitely a slack water dive because there is not too much cover from the strong tidal stream.

(5) ★ ★ ★

55 38'.868 N 001 36'.337 W

An almost cliff-like hill drops down to a flat sloping seabed at 18 metres. A number of huge boulders are lying around at the bottom, along with a few large anchors and strings of lobster creels. The best time to dive is at low slack water, due to the strong

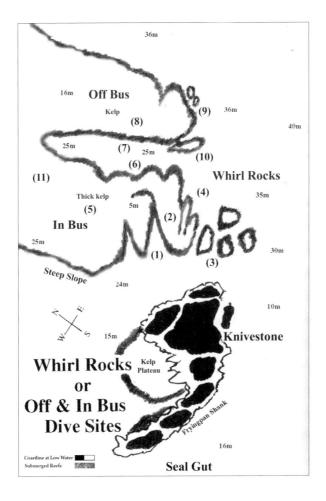

36m

16m **Off Bus**

Kelp

(8)

(9) 36m

40m

25m

(7) 25m

(6)

(10)

(11)

Whirl Rocks

Thick kelp

(5) 5m

(4) 35m

(2)

In Bus

25m

(1)

(3)

30m

Steep Slope 24m

10m

15m

Knivestone

Whirl Rocks Kelp
or Plateau
Off & In Bus
Dive Sites

Fryingpan Shank

16m

Coastline at Low Water
Submerged Reefs

Seal Gut

current. There is not the same quality or quantity of marine life about on the south side of the reef in comparison with the north.

WHIRL ROCKS OR OFF BUS AND IN BUS

Approximately 200 metres NNE of Knavestone is the beginning of the notorious reef known as Whirl Rocks, or the Off and In Buses. At the highest point of the In Bus, the reefs are only three metres below the surface on an ebb tide and are permanently submerged. They are the seaward end of the hard, black igneous dolerite seam of rocks which are mentioned in the section on the History of the Farne Islands. The dolerite reef, standing up to 25 metres high in places, is about 600 metres in length and lies in what appears to be two sections which are divided by a 100-metre wide funnel-shaped channel 25 metres deep. The two Buses, however, are in fact linked together a quarter of a mile to the north. They are a formidable barrier against which the sea is forced to change direction, causing

71

the treacherous rip tides and overfalls that have given the reefs the name of Whirl Rocks. This particular area is probably the worst and most dangerous site on the whole of the northeast coast of Britain. The site is even marked on the Admiralty Charts with whirlpool and eddy symbols to warn craft of the potential dangers they pose.

What we refer to as Seal Gut, between Longstone and Knavestone, is as bad as you would have thought the tide and currents could get, yet the tidal run on Whirl Rocks is about three knots faster and a lot more serious to navigate in a small craft. During spring tides the whole area is just a mass of foaming, seething, white rolling water in which it would be very easy to swamp even a RHIB of five metres. 'Whirls', as we prefer to call them, are a ship's graveyard, where 20 metre canyons and gullies are piled high with the wreckage of vessels, a real testimony to the ferocity of the treacherous tidal forces. During spring tides, the current runs up to ten knots and slack water is non-existent, because the current just stops and then immediately runs in the opposite direction. On a normal tide, slack water takes place approximately one-and-three-quarter hours after low water at Seahouses harbour, when you can expect about twenty minutes to half an hour of slack water. However the amount of slack varies with the size of tide, as mentioned earlier. It pays to get there early to save a wasted trip, but if you are unsure check the time first with Stan Hall or with one of the other charter boat skippers. Reliable engines are essential when diving Whirls and it is much safer to use two boats, with one as a back up. If the outboard gives trouble in starting and the tide is running, any divers in the water will very quickly disappear into the distance, travelling at a fair rate of knots. Any type of surface swell will be exaggerated three-fold over the top of Whirls and it should be avoided like the proverbial plague. The importance of making people aware of the danger cannot be too strongly emphasised.

On a calm day with light westerly winds and neap tides, Whirls is arguably one of the finest, if not the finest, dive sites in Britain. The top of the reef is a dense forest of two- and three-metre kelp stalks and tangleweed., their whip-like fronds covering deep canyons and gullies full of hundreds of pig iron ingots and lumps of wreckage. Lobsters, crabs, squat lobsters, spider crabs and even octopus can be found all over the two reefs of Whirl Rocks, while the 20-metre-plus vertical reef walls are covered in jewel anemones, Devonshire cup corals, soft corals and a whole host of other marine life. Shoals of coley and pollack hover over the reef edges and friendly ballan wrasse follow you around at the base of the walls. Large cod, ling and two-metre long congers hide amongst the broken hollow steel mast posts and caverns formed by the piles of twisted wreckage filling the V-shaped ravines and canyons, many of them so deep that you cannot see the bottom. Anchors lie everywhere and just a few metres away from the base of the first section of Whirls are the remains of the old steamer *Jan Van Ryswyck*, her boiler and engine frame still standing proud over the big jumble of engine parts. Regularly seen, but so far eluding capture, is an eight-pound lobster, which by now must be feeling quite secure after being attacked so often – and unsuccessfully – with poles and hooks by visiting divers.

On her final voyage and during thick fog on 21 May 1924, the *Jan Van Ryswyck* stranded on the treacherous In Bus reef; she was on passage from Antwerp for Grangemouth with a general cargo, cast pig iron and steel ingots. The crew took to the boats and were eventually rescued and landed at Berwick later that day. The steamer broke its back and then broke into two halves, spilling her cargo all over the reef. The bow section soon disintegrated, but the stern half, which included the superstructure, engine and boilers, slipped back over the submerged cliff wall at the southern edge of the reef, down into deep water, where much of the remains can be seen today at 55 39'.115N 001 35'.956W.

The *Jan Van Ryswyck* (Official No.125611) was a steel-hulled 2,152-ton Belgian steam cargo ship measuring 87.47 m in length, with a 13.41-m beam and a 6.09-m draught. Craig, Taylor and Co. Ltd at Stockton built and completed her as Yard No.125 in August 1907; she was launched as the *Baltic Sea* on 25 July 1907 for Finland-London Steam Ship Co. Ltd, London; W. R. Medhurst was the manager. The single steel screw was powered by a 210-hp, three-cylinder triple expansion steam engine that used two single-ended boilers and gave 9.5-knots. In 1911 she was sold to H. G. Harper and Co., London (Cardiff). Dampfschiff Ges. Joachim Zelck GmbH, Rostock, Germany, purchased and renamed her *Joachim Zelck* in 1912 and O. Zelck was the manager. The Belgian Government – Régie de la Marine, Antwerp, Belgium – owned her in 1919. From 1922, La Maritime Belge, Antwerp, was the registered owner and she was renamed *Jan Van Ryswyck*; the Belgian company of F. Alexander fils et Cie became the manager.

LCR 1924, p. 9 (g); *The Times*, Thursday, 22 May, 1924, p. 28.

The cargo of ingots lie all over the top of the In Bus reef and fill many of the deep V-shaped gullies from top to bottom, along with the remains of the bow section that is now shattered into a thousand pieces, although larger lumps of big hollow masts, steel plates, ribs and framework can be found at the base of a gully on the western side. The main stern section of the wreck lies in 28–30 metres and about 25 metres away from the base of the cliff face on the south side of high reef wall.

The profusion of marine life, combined with the marvellous underwater scenery, makes Whirl Rocks without doubt a stupendous dive site.

Dive sites of the In Bus

Top centre of the In Bus: 55 39′.118 N 001 35′.999 W

(1) ✴ ✴ ✴ ✴

This dive is on the inside and western edge of the Whirls, where the bottom half of the largest of the two main canyons is full of wreckage from some of the many ships which have met their doom over the last century or so. The wreckage includes broken hollow mast sections, anchors, steel plate and framework, with much of it concreted into surrounding rocks. Thousands of pig iron ingots are strewn everywhere and last year at least three brass portholes and three sets of zinc anodes, weighing 30 kilos, were recovered from beneath the algae-covered girders and concretion. A massive wolf fish, with large horse-like teeth, lives in the largest pipe, part of a hollow mast, and never fails to make threatening gestures to anyone getting too close to its home. Big clumps of juicy mussels cling to the bottom of some of the kelp stalks and the surrounding gully walls and rocks are a thick carpet of tiny baby mussels. The bottom of the gully on this site, which is in the 18 metre range, is exposed to some strong currents. When the tide is running, it is strongly recommended that you move higher up the gully into shallower water before surfacing, to avoid being swept hundreds of metres down tide before you ever reach the surface.

(2) ✴ ✴ ✴ ✴

55 39′.101 N 001 35′.994 W

The whole of the top of the Whirls is covered in a dense forest of thick stalked kelp. Channels, or small gullies one or two metres deep, run across the top of the reef in an east-west direction. Fair numbers of crustaceans can be located in the small slots and crevices formed by twisted wreckage, which are usually hidden by the dense coating of brown algae-type weed, but a sharp eye is required to spot the red ends of the lobster's tell-tale antennae. Depths range from four to ten metres, with the gullies and channels a bit deeper. There is no problem swimming in any of the gullies on the reef top, even when the tide is in full flow, but once you move above the kelp level the force of water is strong enough to send you tumbling head over heels and purge your demand valve. Near to the southern edge of the drop-off, long strands of tangleweed wave frantically in the current once the tide starts to run, and if you don't want to dive when the water is boiling on the surface, this is the time to leave the area. On the ebb tide, the current sweeps along the reef wall in a northerly direction and it is literally impossible to get over and down the wall when it is running hard.

Close-up of a species of Hydroids off Knavestone

(3) ✴ ✴ ✴ ✴ ✴ ✴

The reef top is at four metres, with vertical drop-offs and giant monolith-type pillars rising like skyscrapers from the seabed at 24 metres. These are covered in a wealth of beautiful anemones, including Devonshire cup corals, jewel anemones, soft corals and peculiar, colourful little Hydroids, for those who look closely enough. Swirling shoals of coley and pollack hover near to the reef tops and on a good day, when the visibility is at its best, the scenery is magnificent. This is a really superb dive and one not to be missed.

(4) ✴ ✴ ✴ ✴ ✴ ✴

55 39'.109 N 001 35'.925 W

After diving in a great many places around the coast of Britain, including fabulous sites around the Isle of Lewis and Benbecula in the Outer Hebrides, my colleagues and I believe that this is one of the best dive sites – if not the best – anywhere. There are canyons full of wreckage, including everything that comes off a ship. Even if most of it is covered by or buried in piles of concretion and steel girders, it is all still there, just waiting to be recovered: pipes, masts, anchors, anodes, chain, winches, portholes, bits of pressure clocks, bronze valves and, somewhere under it all, will be the ship's bells and telegraphs. There are submarine cliffs alive with colourful life, along with the usual crustaceans and fish. This dive is very similar to site (3), but it has the added bonus of having a wrecked steamship in its vicinity. As mentioned earlier, the wreck makes a wonderful photographer's frame, especially when you catch the sun's rays shining through the engine framework with the boiler in the background. On the flood tide, it is quite easy to swim where you want to over the cliff face and down around the bottom, although when you start to ascend and approach the reef top, the current whisks you away as if caught by a tornado. The best time to dive is about 20 minutes before low slack water on a neap tide. If the tide has started to run on the ebb, you will have difficulty in getting down the cliff faces because of the force of water pushing along and upwards. Once the tide begins to run, overfalls develop and the surface boils like a cauldron, with white water up to two metres high even on a calm day. It is also very unwise to anchor a small boat over the reef when the tide is in full flow. It is best to throw in a heavy shot (weight) attached to a large surface marker buoy (a medium-sized surface marker buoy will be pulled under the surface) with sufficient rope or cord, equal to about four times the depth of water, and then go and wait a little way downstream below the boil on the surface. It is also wise to have some form of quick release and a surface marker buoy on the end of the anchor line when the boat is at anchor, to save losing the divers because you cannot retrieve the anchor quickly enough. It sounds like common sense, but this happens on a regular basis.

(5) ★ ★ ★

Two hundred metres north of the cliff face, the reef top shelves gently down to between 15 and 18 metres where there is not much of interest apart from a few urchins and little spider crabs. The rocks lack the life that they have closer to the drop-off. The undulating seabed has very few gullies and the kelp is short and becomes much sparser the deeper you go. Further north, the reef shelves away and levels out onto a stony seabed at 35 metres with exceptionally strong currents. There may possibly be a few scallops and queenies in the deep water, because the scallop dredgers from Seahouses work in those depths, but a fair bit of pre-planning would be required to gather them.

(6) ★ ★ ★ ★

55 39'.171 N 001 35'.980 W

Depth to the reef is about 12–15 metres with the kelp thinning out but, at the reef edge, the sides slope down in large steps with a number of interesting crevices leading down to the bottom at 20 metres: this whole area is one big blanket of colourful anemones. It is a beautiful sight when the sun is shining, because the different colours reflect the light back, making the place like a garden of bright yellow flowers. The reef runs north-south in the same direction as the tide and this means that there is no shelter from the tremendous current. Definitely a slack water dive.

(7) ✶ ✶

Moving east from dive (6), the seabed at 25 metres is still a carpet of anemones but there is no cover from the rip tide, which is caused by the water being funnelled in between the two buses of Whirl Rocks. There are a few small boulders and rocks but unless you are interested in the small marine creatures, like shrimps and prawns, that live among the anemones, this site is not worth bothering about, even at slack water, which is the only time you could reach the seabed.

Off Bus

Centre and top of the Off Bus: 55 39'.227 N 001 35'.890 W

(8) ✶ ✶ ✶

A pleasant dive into a thick kelp bed with a number of nice little gullies and a few crevices that often hide crustaceans. In the latter months of summer, masses of huge lion's mane jellyfish are whipped over the reefs of the Outer Farne Islands. Their poisonous stinging cells, sometimes 10 metres long, are dragged through the kelp, leaving the broken thread-like ribbons trapped in the fronds. They very commonly get caught around the regulator's second stage and against the diver's mouth and lips, leaving a nasty burning sensation that lasts for three or four hours. The sides of the Off Bus rise up fairly steeply from the seabed at 20 metres, up to 12–15 metres, and then it tapers away north into deeper water. The reef top is around 100 metres wide, east to west. The current and its direction are the same as the last dive site but the little gullies which criss-cross over the Bus from east to west provide a little shelter from the ferocity of the overhead gale when the tide is running. This is definitely a slack water dive site.

(9) ✶ ✶ ✶ ✶ ✶ ✶

55 39'.264 N 001 35'.774 W

A superb dive around the edge of the cliff face, which has a number of monolithic boulders, covered in the same beautiful marine life as seen on dives (3) and (4). The seabed at the base of the wall is in 30 metres and drops away rapidly to 40 metres plus. The masses of tangleweed growing on the top edge of the reef waves like bunting in a gale when the tide is flooding, while the rest of the reef top has a dense covering of thick kelp. Numerous narrow crevices are spread across the undulating reef top and there is a good chance of collecting a couple of crustaceans. Pollack weighing an estimated five or six kilos are regularly seen, as are large shoals of coley, and it is always worth doing a spot of rod fishing after the dive. When visibility is good, looking over the cliff face is an awesome sight because it looks so mysterious and bottomless. Beautiful anemones absolutely cover the walls and giant boulders and it is a fantastic experience just to float slowly down with outstretched arms, like a glider into an abyss. This is also definitely a slack water dive.

(10) ✷ ✷ ✷ ✷

55 39'.187 N 001 35'.815 W

An excellent dive with some good channels and gullies on the inside (western) corner of the Off Bus. This site is 50 metres away and west of dive site (9) and is more exposed than all the other dive sites on the reef because it takes the full brunt of tide in the channel. The reef face is more of a steep slope and drops down in steps and stairs, but it also has a wealth of life on it. The top at 15 metres has some short kelp growing on it, possibly due to the ferocity of the tide at this point, but there is still a lot of life covering the rocks and boulders. This is a slack water dive, without any doubt.

(11) Drift dive ✷ ✷ ✷ ✷ ✷ ✷

55 39'.194 N 001 36'.103 W

The location of this site is about 250 metres NNW of the reef drop-off at dive site (4) and the position of it warrants only two stars because the seabed has little of interest. There is a rather featureless sloping bottom at 20 metres plus, consisting of flat rock and small stones with a few anemones here and there. This, though, is the starting point for a fabulous drift dive on the flood tide, which takes you right across the In Bus. Obviously, the bigger the tide, the faster you will travel and on a spring, it is not for the faint-hearted. A first sight of the rolling white water is enough to deter the most stout-hearted of divers, as the tidal run can reach ten knots on the springs. Once in the water, you have no time to dilly-dally and should head straight down for the bottom, facing the direction of the current, which will not only slow you down but will also prevent you from rolling over out of control. On reaching the seabed, turn with the current and just go for it! Getting faster and faster, you flash over the reef top at a hairy rate of knots until you reach the cliff face on the southern edge, at which point you can fin down and finish the dive in reasonably sheltered gullies. Needless to say, surface marker buoys are essential on the drift over the Whirls. It is also very important to have a boat waiting downstream for the divers. Although it may again sound like simple common sense, I've seen dive boats waiting over the reef top or just pottering around with the engine running and nearly losing their divers when the surface marker buoy got snagged up and pulled down. Keeping the engine running can also create problems for divers trying to surface: they can hear the engine but don't know where the boat is. This is a great and exciting dive but needs a bit of careful planning.

LONGSTONE

55 38'.637 N 001 36'.658 W

Longstone is located 4.10 miles from the nearest mainland, 4.46 miles from Seahouses and 759 metres southwest of Knavestone. At low water, Longstone is the largest island in the Outer Farnes group. The island is unmistakable because it features the distinctive red-and-white banded lighthouse made famous by Miss Grace Horsley Darling and her father in 1838. It was built in the 1820s and replaced the round tower lighthouse situated on Brownsman, which was pulled down in 1826. The light on Longstone was first lit when the Darling family moved from Brownsman to the Longstone on 15 February. Longstone, at low tide, is about half a mile long and joins up the rocks and islets from the Northern Hares at the northern end to the horseshoe- shaped lagoon called Brada at the southern end. There are dozens of gullies and creeks between the various rocks, which fill in as the tide rises, forming a number of separate little islands, depending on the size of the tide.

The main island of Longstone has also been a graveyard for shipping over the centuries and at least fifteen known vessels has come to grief on it since 1800. The

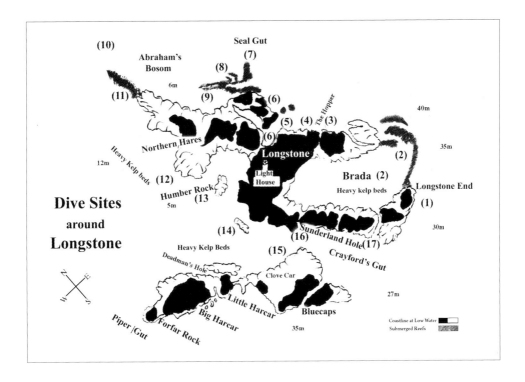

sea is horrendous during north and northeasterly storms and it must have been a virtual nightmare living in the lighthouse during such periods, as William Darling's records make clear:

> On 18th March 1852, at 0130 hours, the wind was blowing strong northwest, the sky dark and hazy, an Eider Duck struck the north by east tower square of the lantern carrying two thirds of the glass inside. As the bird weighed 4 pound and hit the middle of upper square sections the consequences might have been more serious.
>
> On the 5th July 1852, a severe storm was blowing with vivid lightning and the rain mixed with hail and was continuous from 1030 to 2000 hours. The barometer remained stationary at 2007 and the external thermometer read 62°.
>
> On the 4th January 1854 a severe storm blowing east-south-east with snow showers which continued for seven days, causing heavy loss of life and shipping, at Shields and South Sunderland. Later that month another seven day gale continued and the barometer was not observed being stationary, even for one hour.

All of the ships which were lost around Longstone are smashed beyond recognition, due to the ferocity and destructive elements of the wind and sea. Most have disappeared altogether, including the galliot *Maxamillion Frederick*, lost in 1800, and the schooner *Caladonian* of Montrose which foundered on the northern tip of Northern Hares in 1802.

In 1812 the *Humber Packet* foundered on Humber Rock, just west of the lighthouse (giving the rock its name). An unknown vessel was wrecked in 1852, as was the *Aid* of Newcastle in 1853, the schooner *William* in 1864 and the 55-ton ketch *Pallas* in 1901. The steam trawler *Patopiqa* was lost in 1913, the wooden-hulled 478-ton Norwegian steamer *Valhal*, built in 1890 and owned by A/S Valhal, Haugesund, was wrecked on 15 November 1914, while transporting coal from Blyth to Haugesund in Norway, and another vessel, among others that came to grief, was a steam trawler on naval duties in 1918.

Only the remnants of three ships remain as jumbled wreckage: the steamer *Chris Christensen* lies off the southern tip of Longstone in 32 metres and was identified by Selby Brown, who discovered the wreck by accident many years ago. Selby, originally from Newcastle, spent some time researching the ship and is responsible for sharing her location with many other grateful visiting divers.

The *Chris Christensen* was a steel-hulled 1,461-ton Danish steam cargo vessel measuring 76.25 m in length, with an 11.32-m beam and 5.48-m draught. Flensburger Schiffbau Gesellschaft, Flensburg built and completed her as Yard No.224 in June

1903 for Aktieselskab Dampskibsselskab Selsk. Vendila, Copenhagen; Svendsen and Christensen were the managers. The single steel screw was powered by a three-cylinder triple expansion steam engine that used two boilers and gave 10 knots. Flensburger Schiffbau Ges., Flensburg, also manufactured the engine and ancillary machinery. She had an amidships bridge, two holds forward and two holds aft.

The *Chris Christensen*'s final voyage was on 16 February 1915; she was in ballast and on passage from Aarhus via the Tyne for New York when she stranded in heavy seas on Longstone Point, Outer Farne Islands. The North Sunderland (Seahouses) self-righting and rowing lifeboat, the *Forster Fawsett*, was launched at 0440 hrs and rescued the nineteen crewmen, completing the mission and returning to North Sunderland harbour at 1830 hrs that evening. The stranding had torn a massive hole in the ship's bottom plates and she eventually slipped back and sank in deeper water.

Then there is the little steamer *Ilala* in Crayford's Gut, lying at the base of the reef in 18 metres. Its story and technical details are found at the end of this section.

The lumps of wreckage lying in about 7 metres off the Northern Hares is referred to as belonging to the steamer *Loch Leven*, which was wrecked in 1902, so maybe someone somewhere has found something to identify that vessel too. There could, though, be the remains of other ships intermingled in the pile of jumbled iron and steel. The *Loch Leven* was reported as wrecked on Knavestone Rock on 15 April 1902, while voyaging from Aberdeen to Sunderland, in ballast, according to the Starke/Schell registers. Some accounts suggest that she struck the Knavestone, slipped back to the north and sank in the area known as Abraham's Bosom.

The *Loch Leven* (Official No.78679) was an iron-hulled 852-ton steam cargo vessel, completed in 1878 as Yard No.88 by Gourlay Brothers at Dundee and launched in April 1878 for David Ireland of Dundee. She measured 64.10 m in length, with a 8.71-m beam. In 1881 the registered owner was Dundee Loch Line S.S. Co. Ltd and Ireland, Leitch and Co. was the manager.

In 1884 she had the same owner but was managed by A. Leitch and Co. In 1899 the registered owner was J. and A. Davidson, Aberdeen.

On 11 December 1977 the 23-ton MFV *Constance* ran aground on Longstone and later sank in 25 metres of water, 0.25 miles east of Longstone lighthouse, while en route from Peterhead to Bembridge; she was owned at the time by Mr Henley Bembridge.

Dive sites

SS *Chris Christensen*

(1) ✵ ✵ ✵ ✵ ✵

In approximately 32 metres, off the southwest tip of Longstone, are the remains of the SS *Chris Christensen*. The wreck lies up against a small reef and, although well

Steamer SS Chris Christensen

broken up, she is still worth a good rummage around. Until recently her huge iron steering wheel stood upright and proud from the bottom, making a lovely sight, but it may not even be there any more.

When Selby Brown found the wreck and saw the wheel standing upright, covered in soft corals and urchins, he was so impressed that he had a friend take some photographs of him standing holding the wheel, like a very determined Captain Ahab sailing after the great white whale Moby Dick. This was no mean feat by anybody's standards: to stand on the seabed in 32 metres, without his diving gear on and in this particular area.

There is quite a variety of marine life around the *Christensen*, with shoals of small coley and lots of seals. The current, though, is very strong and there is, at certain states of the tide, a pronounced downward flow near the bottom, much like an underwater waterfall, which can be very alarming if you are not expecting it. Visibility can be excellent during the summer months and may reach as much as 15 metres plus on a good day. The cliff face on Longstone end, at this point, is a mass of anemones and it is not uncommon to pick up a couple of lobsters.

One very important point to remember is that the trip boats visit this particular site in their droves during the summer, especially at weekends, and they don't always acknowledge a diver's 'A' flags and surface marker buoys, so extra vigilance should be maintained. Any problems from their skippers or dangerous encounters should be reported to the DTI and the Marine Police on the Tyne. Another important thing to remember is that, on spring tides, there are very large curling waves on the surface and strong currents caused by the concentration of water being forced around Longstone end.

Brada

(2) Inside Brada : ✷ ✷

55 38'.519 N 001 36'.405 W

Underwater at the southeast corner: ✷ ✷ ✷ ✷ ✷

55 38'.488 N 001 36'.158 W

At low tide, the south end of Longstone forms a nice quiet horseshoe-shaped lagoon called Brada and unless there is an easterly swell, it is an ideal site both for the beginner and the experienced diver. There is little or no current inside the bay and it is usually home to a colony of grey seals, which are quite happy to follow you around and allow you to get very close to them. Many divers spend their free time between dives just snorkelling with the seals. The further into the bay you go, the shallower and less interesting the flora and fauna becomes. The whole area is covered in a dense kelp forest, but there are some nice deep gullies and crevices to poke around in, near to the eastern and seaward end. The eastern and southern perimeters of Brada have lovely rocky cliff faces to 15 and 25 metres, where there is a profusion of marine life, but the tide flows fairly strongly on the surface out here.

The trip boats cut very close to the edge of the underwater cliff face to let their passengers see grey seals and you cannot always hear their engines underwater, so extra care should be taken when surfacing from the deeper water. I find it pays to swim back into the shallow part of the lagoon and out of harm's way; this also prevents a lot of unnecessary verbal abuse from the trip boat skippers. Always fly the 'A' flag too, or expect the verbal abuse.

(3) ✷ ✷ ✷ ✷

55 38'.612 N 001 36'.309 W

At the southeast corner of Brada, the seals often lounge around a large flat rock called The Hopper. Here, the walls of the submerged reef are nearly sheer, with wide cracks running all the way down to the bottom at 20 metres. Just to the south of this point there are some interesting deep canyons which meander all the way back into the Brada and they have plenty of interesting marine life in them. To the north, the steep rock face, over a distance of about 50 metres, is riddled with crevices and makes a very picturesque dive. Visibility is often excellent during the summer months, but the area is prone to a swell from the open sea. Depths away from the base of the reef drop away rapidly to 25 metres plus and there is a strong tidal run. On the flood tide, this stretch of water from the end of Brada and along the Longstone reef wall for about 200 metres is caught in a type of backwash, because the surface current runs north instead of south before turning out to sea. This site is also very popular with the trip boats because of the proximity of the large grey seal colony.

(4) ★ ★ ★ ★

This is a similar dive to dive site (3) but there are fewer seals around. Again the visibility is pretty good and there are some large boulders on the bottom at 20 metres, often sheltering those creepy-crawlies. It may be worthwhile taking a look away from the reef at this point too, because there are bits and pieces of wreckage scattered around which appear to have come from some kind of vessel. There is a possibility that the wreckage is from the 23-ton MFV *Constance* which ran aground on 27 September 1972, slipped back into deeper water and sank. It was en route from Peterhead to Bembridge and was owned by a Mr A. Henly of Bembridge. This area has now become a very popular dive site with many of the charter boats in recent years.

(5) ★ ★ ★ ★

This is a pretty dive site against the reef wall and a very similar site to (4), with lots of marine life in many forms, including shoals of small coley. Visibility is usually very good, often reaching ten metres. On the bottom there are some large boulders and a few nice crevices at the base of the reef wall, with plenty of anemones and the like. The current can be very strong.

(6) ★ ★ ★

55 38'.690 N 001 36'.543 W

At mid-tide there is a shallow channel close to this dive site, separating the islands of Longstone and Northern Hares, where the water races through on the flood and ebb tide. On a spring tide, the race is extremely strong, and although it is not exactly life threatening, it can be a nerve-racking experience to be swept through to the other bay on the inside of Longstone. This would be especially embarrassing if trip boats were dropping their passengers at the lighthouse landing stage in the same channel. The boat handler would also have to make a half-mile trip round to pick up his divers.

At low tide a number of small islets are created, forming a long narrow lagoon, locally called Seal Gut, between them and the Longstone. This is used as a kindergarten by a lot of young seal pups. The only entrance or exit at low water is at the southern end of the lagoon, through a narrow canyon, 13 metres deep and only 3 metres wide underwater, with a flat, sand-and-stone seabed. As you move through the narrow canyon, the bottom rises up in a couple of steps to 5 metres, where the lagoon then opens out to 10–15-metres wide and 150 metres long.

Visibility in the lagoon is usually excellent, with lots of life under the overhanging rocks and big boulders and there is no current at all. Although the dense kelp makes swimming on the bottom a bit of a struggle, this is the ideal location for a novice diver's first open water dive.

The islets themselves, on the seaward side, are huge, almost vertical pillars, rising up from the bottom at 15 metres and make an interesting dive site. On the seaward side the current can be very strong and it literally rages on a spring tide.

(7) ★ ★

55 38'.884 N 001 36'.501 W

Thirty metres out into Seal Gut, in a northeasterly direction from the centre of the islets at low water, is a shallow and rather flat, kelp-covered reef, which is the western end of the Seal Gut reef. The south-facing edge of this reef has a 3–5 metre wall down onto sand and stone with a few bits of wreckage strewn about but little else to recommend it. There are very few crevices on the reef at this end and the tide runs up to 5 knots on the springs. The top of the reef is in about 10–12 metres but gets deeper the further you go out, while depths on the south side drop away down to 20 metres. This is a rather uninteresting dive site.

(8) ★ ★ ★

Very shallow, rather flat ground, covered in dense tangleweed, 2–3 metres long at low water but with a couple of narrow, 10-metre deep gullies running south-north. The nearest one to the islets has a dark narrow cave at the southern end of it where the seals play about. Care should be taken not to trap any seals in the cave as there is very little room for them to pass by and it could be dangerous. This site is very shallow and the current is very strong, especially on springs, and it should be avoided if there is any swell. The long tangleweed on the surface at low tide makes picking up divers or mooring a boat rather difficult.

(9) ★

A shallow, rather flat and uninteresting rock seabed, with a few very narrow two-metre deep crevices covered in dense tangleweed. During the summer months the weed is so thick that it is impossible to push your way through.

(10) ★ ★ ★ ★

55 38.932 N 001 36'.968 W

About 200 metres northeast (seaward) off the end of Longstone – what is actually the Northern Hares – are some lovely drop-offs. The reef walls are covered in anemones, with lots of other life in the crevices, including crustaceans such as crabs, lobsters and squat lobsters. Visibility is usually very good, but currents are very strong, with depths ranging from 15 metres down to 25 metres. An echo sounder is required to locate the reef edge.

(11) ✳ ✳ ✳ ✳ ✳

This excellent site off the north end of the Northern Hares is one of the most popular dives around all of the Farne Islands. Sheer cliff walls and reefs are covered in an abundance of marine flora and fauna of all descriptions with numerous species of fish, including cod, conger, ling, pollack, coley, ballan wrasse and wolf fish. The whole area is carpeted in heavy kelp while the reefs are separated by channels 7–10 metres wide and gullies containing masses of scattered wreckage from those ill-fated ships which have struck the reefs, including that of the little steamer *Loch Leven*. There are still some massive lumps of plate and framework from this ship, which is home to a number of large ballan wrasse, and it is not uncommon to see cod of up to ten kilos sheltering underneath. On the flood tide, most of the water from the north side of the Outer Farnes is channelled around this area, so currents can be exceptionally strong off this point, especially during springs. The current runs out to sea for about 200 metres before turning south through Seal Gut. There is plenty of shelter from the current in the many deep gullies but it is best dived at low slack water or during the ebb on neap tides. This site is a bit exposed, so surface marker buoys are recommended if diving when the tide is running on the flood or if there is a strong wind blowing, as divers will quickly disappear into the distance. Visibility is usually good during the summer months after a spell of light westerly winds and neap tides. The submerged reef at the end of Northern Hares extends a long way out in a northerly direction and there are some lovely overhangs covered in anemones, even at 20 metres.

(12) ✳ ✳ ✳

Moving inshore for about 150 metres from the end of the rocks of the Northern Hares and lining up the end of the North Wamses and Bamburgh Castle tower brings you over two submerged hillocks, only three metres below the surface at low tide. Between these two hillocks is a 7-metre deep valley, with steep walls covered in soft corals and about 50 metres long in an east-west direction. At the western end of the hillocks, the reef and valley carry on for a further 150 metres before terminating at the huge reef called Keen'ys Bus out in the centre of the bay. Except for the two submerged hillocks, most of the ground around the dive site is undulating, smooth, flat rock, but there are some smaller interesting reefs just south of here, containing a few holes and crevices. There are plenty of urchins, a few edible crabs, lots of velvet swimming crabs but very few lobsters. On a flood spring tide, the current can be fairly strong and runs towards the Northern Hares or south towards Crayford's Gut, depending on where you happen to be on the dive site. It is, though, possible to dive at any state of the tide with care.

A word of caution, though: do not moor the diving boat anywhere near this position if there happens to be a northerly swell, because waves of 2–3 metres suddenly build up and curl over the two submerged hills, especially on the lower half of the tide.

(13) ✷✷

A number of small rocky mounds covered in kelp, with little walls around them. Shallow depths of only 3–5 metres and with moderate currents at low water, but on the flood, during springs, the tide sweeps strongly towards and around the Northern Hares. Diving here at high tide on the flood is not recommended, because the current runs strongly in three different directions. The western side of Northern Hares has a small reef wall with a few crevices in it. This is a decent novice dive on a low neap tide. The site is also subjected to a lot of white water when there is any northerly swell.

(14) ✷✷

All of this area, close in to the inside of the Longstone lighthouse, has a maximum depth of only about 4–5 metres. There are patches of sand, a few small reefs and occasionally, maybe, a few crustaceans, but generally speaking it is not very interesting, although you can collect a lot of winkles. The current is exceptionally strong on both ebb and flood spring tides.

(15)

Not a dive as such, because it is too shallow, but it is worth mentioning that the remains of an old steam trawler lie scattered among the thick kelp bed in very shallow water. The small rusting remnants of a ship's boiler can be seen just below the surface.

Sunderland Hole
(16) ✷✷✷

Submerged bank: 55 38'.442 N 001 36'.611 W

Close to the inside of Longstone and just south of the lighthouse, there is a gap in the rocks with a landing stage built into the side of it. This is called Sunderland Hole and is one of two landing stages used by trip boat skippers to land their passengers at certain states of the tide.

Just a little way out from here and 3–4 metres to the northwest, there is a 3-metre submerged bank which causes an underwater waterfall on the flood tide. On spring or big tides the current is severe enough to push you down to the bottom with quite some force, which can be an unnerving experience. For a distance of 20 metres north of this position, the water is so shallow that on a spring tide any attempt to cross it in a boat would probably result in a damaged outboard engine or broken propeller. The seabed south of the bank consists of kelp-covered rocks and sand, with little else of interest. Occasionally, though, at certain times of the year, thousands of large edible crabs congregate for some unknown reason on the sandy seabed just south of this position, all the way down Crayford's Gut to the 20-metre mark.

The tide is very strong in both directions as the water is funnelled into the narrows of the Gut.

As I have already mentioned, the trip boats use this site, so anchoring a diving boat at the landing stage or diving here, especially at weekends, will almost certainly result in some verbal abuse and friction from the boatmen.

(17) ★★★★

A good dive on a cliff wall to 18 metres and lots of life about on the steep reef. Plenty of crevices and holes and you can even go behind the reef into a deep canyon formed by the walls of rock. Visibility is often excellent with a moderate current close to the reef but during spring tides, especially on the ebb, the force of water is so tremendous it will easily drag a large surface marker buoy down to the bottom. It's a great place to lose the anchor!

Ilala, Steamer

Just away from the base of the reef in 18 metres are the scattered remains of the steamship *Ilala*. The *Ilala* was completed as Yard No.5 and was the very first ship to be built at the then new W. B. Thompson shipyard on the River Tay at Dundee in 1874. Mr Thompson, the owner of the yard, was born in 1837 and trained in Finland. When he came back to Britain, he built himself a foundry a mile from Dundee docks. His first four ships were actually hauled down to the River Tay on bogies driven by teams of horses, which was certainly not the most convenient way of launching ships, it wasn't until 1874, however, that he finally negotiated and acquired his very own riverside shipyard. The first ship he built at the new yard was the 178-ton SS *Ilala*. Unfortunately, he did not have any ready customers for it when it was completed so, being an enterprising chap, he decided to trade with it himself.

Then, just fifteen months after the launching ceremony, on 23 January 1876, she was wrecked on the Farne Islands and became a total loss.

The *Ilala* had left Gainsborough for Gateshead on Tyne, but strong nor'easterly gales forced her back to shelter in the mouth of the Humber off Hull. After she left Hull roads, a strong southwesterly gale sprang up, driving the *Ilala* before it past the mouth of the Tyne and right through the main mass of the Farne Islands until she struck hard on what was described as the hidden 'Swadman Reef'. The crew let go both anchors and lit the ship up to attract attention. Their signals were answered from the shore but no lifeboat came to rescue them. They decided to cut the anchors and drifted out and onto the Longstone. An account of the ship's loss was taken up by the Dundee Courier on 27 January 1876. The headlines read:

The Loss of the Ilala of Dundee...

Strange Conduct of the Lifeboat Crew

It went on:

> The crew then lowered their boat and four of them jumped into it, and made for the rocks. The boat was dashed forward towards the rock by the sea, and on nearing the rock one of the men sprang upon it from the boat. The boat was then carried away by the receding wave and upon again being thrown towards the rock by the sea, two other men jumped out of it to the rock. The fourth man, however, was unable to get out before the boat was carried away, and feared that he would drown. Fortunately however, a huge wave carried the boat above and close to the stern of the steamer, and at that moment the poor fellow sprang for his life. The steamer meanwhile was rapidly sinking and the four men still aboard were enabled with little difficulty to leap from the rail of the vessel to the rocks, and in this way saved their lives. About 20 minutes after all had safely landed on the rocks, the steamer swung round and tumbled to the side two or three times by the force of the tide and then went down in deep water, the crew remained on the rocks all night without food and exposed to the weather. At low water they made their way to the lighthouse.

The seamen went on to tell the reporter of their home town newspaper how a sinking smack had been ignored by the lighthouse keepers and they complained bitterly about Seahouses lifeboat not coming to their rescue.

The account of the *Ilala* makes mention of her grounding on the 'Swadman Reef' which I presume to mean the Swedman Rocks, some 500 metres west of the Megstone. The Swedman Rocks are about 2½ miles NNW of Seahouses so if the ship was lit up, it would have been clearly visible from the harbour there. If it was the

Swedman, then the ship must have drifted almost three miles east and out to sea after the crew cut the anchors away, missing the Megstone's surrounding reefs, Oxscar and North Wamses, before being swept through the very shallow water in Crayford's Gut and hitting the Longstone. This seems incredible with a strong southwesterly wind blowing. However, if the reef she struck was in fact the Callers and not the Swedman, then the crew, having cut the anchors away, would have been driven in a southwesterly direction directly onto the south corner of Longstone at the southern end of Crayford's Gut, where she now lies. This sounds much more feasible. They would still have been clearly visible from Seahouses harbour (North Sunderland).

Anemone gully at Swedman

There is only an engine block, parts of her keel ribs, steel plates and framework strewn around so there is not a lot left of the ship to get excited about. Recently, however, visiting divers on Stan Hall's charter boat found a very large porthole in 25 metres of water, about 50 metres west of the wrecksite towards the Bluecaps.

The wreck is fairly easy to locate on the inside of Longstone by positioning the tower on Staple over/in the channel between Bluecaps and Clove Car.

It is possible to make a pleasant drift dive from this position on the mid water spring ebb tide, taking you into Crayford's Gut, past dive (16) and beyond. During this time, the tide runs at about 5 knots and it is wise not to anchor the boat anywhere around here. It is also an area regularly visited by the trip boats as part of their route, so extra vigilance is required by both divers and boat cover. Make sure, too, that you are not too far along towards the southern end of Longstone, where the tide runs around the end of the island and straight out to sea into fairly deep water (40 metres).

BLUECAPS TO THE HARCARS

This group of five rocky little islets – the Bluecaps, Clove Car, Little Harcar and Big Harcar and Forfar Rock – are one big reef curving over half a mile at low tide. They are situated approximately a third of the way along the inside of Longstone and some 100 metres across Crayford's Gut, running in an east-west direction. The barrier that these islands represents means that over the centuries they have probably been responsible for more tragedies than all of the rest of the Farnes put together.

Bluecaps

55 38'.387 N 001 36'.707 W

At least five known vessels have collided with the Bluecaps since 1819.

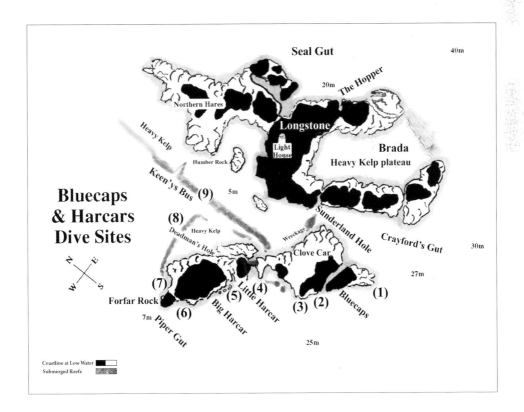

The first was the fishing smack *Hope* of Leith, which sank on 28 August 1819.

Four years later, on 17 October 1823, the British brig *Monkwearmouth* foundered on east Bluecaps, beside Longstone Rocks, and was lost with all hands.

On 23 November 1832 the British schooner *Sister* of Newcastle was transporting coal when she foundered just south of the Bluecaps.

On 27 January 1916 the steam trawler *Yagen* was wrecked and became a total loss.

Then, on 22 October 1955, the motor fishing boat *Grade* ran aground, but the crew were fortunate enough to be able to refloat her later without too much damage.

Little Harcar

55 38'.410 N 001 37'.037 W

The aptly-named Little Harcar is one of the smaller islets in the middle of the group, but its size is in no way proportionate to the number of fatalities for which it is responsible. At least 81 people have been drowned or killed and at least five known recorded ships wrecked on the jagged rocks surrounding the south side of this barren little islet. All of those 81 deaths came from just three sailing vessels which came to grief within hours of each other during the Great Storm of November 1774. The storm was so ferocious that it smashed off one of the huge black Whin Sill dolorite pinnacles at the southern end of Staple Island and partially destroyed the old tower lighthouse there.

Forfarshire

Peggy

Forfarshire *and the brig* Peggy

The brig *Liddle* was blown onto the rocks of Little Harcar and sixteen lives were lost. The sailing vessel *Industry,* owned by Drummond of London, was also destroyed while on a voyage from London to Leith, with an unknown number of people on board. Then the brig *Success* smashed into it, driven by the mighty winds and mountainous seas, with the loss of a further fifteen lives. Within hours of that catastrophe, the brig *Peggy* of Leith was dashed to pieces in the same place and a further 50 passengers and crew perished in the raging waters on the south side of the Little Harcar.

The *Peggy* was a large wooden sailing brig, owned by Charles Spalding of London. On 3 December 1774, she was on passage from London for Leith, under the command of Captain Thomas Boswell, when she encountered the Great Storm. On that fateful day, the *Peggy* was carrying fifty passengers and crew as well as a valuable cargo which included silver bullion belonging to the vessel's owner. Mr Spalding decided to salvage his treasures by using three enterprising local men who developed a kind of upturned, open, weighted barrel to use as a diving bell. The air was replenished from small barrels sent down, with the air from these released into the larger diving barrel. They were fairly successful in salvaging much of the silver for a company and became very rich from the proceeds. After their success, the men were in great demand and moved down to the south coast to work on other wrecks, but they were all dead from diving-related problems within a year of salvaging the *Peggy*. It is not known how much silver was recovered at the time, or even where the wreck of the *Peggy* actually lies, but the area is not very big and very few divers actually move very far out away from the reef into the relatively deep water. It is more than likely that the ship, which would have been smashed to little pieces in that one storm, just slipped down the slope into the deeper water. The seabed at 25 metres is just sand and stone, with – up till now – little of interest to tempt divers down to explore the bottom. Interestingly, though, a crushed bronze bell was recovered only a few years ago, lying in 15 metres on the steep sloping bank in this area.

On 19 July 1893, the 165-ton wooden-hulled steam yacht *Mermaid* also became a total wreck in the same area as the others.

Big Harcar

55 38'.348 N 001 37'.242 W

This island, which is the highest and largest in the group, has had eight recorded ships wrecked on it in the past 200 years.

On 31 January 1823, an unknown brig was lost with all hands. Then, on 26 September 1853, the sloop *Success* was wrecked and one person drowned. However the most famous shipwreck of them all was the steamer *Forfarshire*, a 400-ton wooden paddle steamer on which 43 people lost their lives.

She was a modern paddle steamer, being only four years old at the time of her loss. Built in Dundee in 1834 at a cost of £20,000, the vessel was designed to carry both cargo and passengers mainly between the ports of Dundee and Hull. She had twin 90-hp simple steam engines, supported by brigantine-rigged sails, and two masts with one funnel in between them. Her normal complement was 25 and she was carrying approximately 40 passengers. The true number of passengers would only have been known by the master, whose perk it was to go round collecting fares during the journey. The *Forfarshire* could make about 9 knots under her own power without the use of the sails. She left Hull for the journey to Dundee on the midnight tide on 6 September 1838 with a cargo of superfine cloths, hardware, soap, spinning gear and boiler plate. She'd had some problems with leaking boilers, which were repaired before she sailed from Hull, but by the time she reached the coast off Berwick, they had began to leak again. This time the trouble was much more serious and her engines were rendered useless. At 0100 hrs on the 7th, she started to lose ground and the chief engineer told the Master, John Humble, that neither of the engines could be used. The leaks soon got so bad that steaming hot water was filling the bilges. The only way the firemen could put the fire out was by dousing the boilers. They realised the ship was in trouble so the Master ordered it be turned round to head for South Shields: at the same time he had the sails set fore and aft to keep the ship well off shore. At this point she was not in any immediate danger, because she was still a sailing ship in her own right, equipped with auxiliary steam engines.

The weather was bad: a northerly gale was blowing and patches of thick fog made visibility extremely poor, but very soon the weather worsened. The gale increased to storm force and the combination of wind, heavy rain and fog was seriously affecting the ship's headway. The master soon realised that, with the strong tidal streams, she was actually being driven backwards in the darkness of night. Captain Humble decided to run before the storm in an attempt to find shelter behind the Farne Islands. He caught sight of a light which he presumed to be that of Farne Island on the Inner Farnes, although it was in all probability the Longstone light in the Outer Farnes. At 0400 hrs on 7 September, the *Forfarshire* smashed into the western corner of Big Harcar, now known as Forfar Rock. Within 15 minutes one of her paddle axles broke off, causing a massive hole in the hull through which the sea rushed, drowning most of the people on board. James Keeley, a ship's weaver of Dundee and witness at the inquiry, said:

> They had the hatches off nearly the whole way to admit air and let the steam out. A little before 4 o'clock on the Friday morning the ship struck, it was quite dark; all Thursday and during the night the weather was very thick and foggy. When the vessel struck, I was in the cabin and two or three minutes after I got on the deck the vessel parted in two. The fore-part of the ship struck upon the rock and the after part from the engine was washed away. I was told that there was two boats, but did not see either of them. I did not see any of the after-cabin passengers on deck after the vessel struck; they were washed away with the wreck. There was nine saved who were on the forecastle, amongst whom were the carpenter, cook, two coal-trimmers and a fireman. During the night about 10 o'clock, the captain and steward were in the fore-cabin

collecting fares from the passengers. The sails were up during the whole night and were up when the vessel struck; the main sail was down for a short while but was hoisted again. After the vessel struck, I never saw anything more of the captain or mate, or cabin passengers.

Later, Jordan Evans of Bamburgh, a Customs House officer, said:

I had been on the rock where the wreck of the *Forfarshire* lies; the fore-part of the vessel and paddle-wheels are lying there; the engine likewise is all there. All the materials before the paddle-box consisting of mast, rigging, anchors and cables are saved and may be worth £200, which belongs to the Hull and Dundee Steam Packet Company.

Fortunately, nine people had already left the ship in one of the lifeboats and had been rescued by a vessel from Montrose. They were eventually taken to South Shields but a further nine were left stranded on the Big Harcar, waiting for daylight and rescue. At 0700 hrs, Grace Darling and her father, the lighthouse keepers on Longstone, saw three or four men on the rocks and decided to launch their rowing boat to try to rescue them. By this time the tide had dropped, which made access to the Harcar slightly easier. On arriving at the rock they found eight men and one woman clinging to life, but because of the size of their boat, they could only take the woman and four men back to the lighthouse. Two of the men bravely agreed to return with William Darling and between them they rescued the others.

Meanwhile, North Sunderland lifeboat coxswain William Robson had been informed about the wreck of the steamer and decided to launch a local coble instead of the lifeboat, because he considered it would be better suited to getting close in amongst the rocks. He was, however, oblivious of the courageous rescue by William Darling and his daughter. Six local men – Thomas Cuthbertson, William Swan, James Robson, Michael Robson, Robert Knox and the lighthouse keeper's son, William Darling – bravely set out into the storm from North Sunderland harbour for the Longstone. In those days, of course, the boat had to be rowed. On reaching the Harcar Rock, they found that all had been rescued, but they picked up three dead bodies, a man and two children, which they placed higher up on the island and then made their way to the Longstone Lighthouse as the sea state made it impossible to return to North Sunderland. On reaching the lighthouse, however, the accommodation was found to be full and the crew had to take shelter in a derelict building for the next two days.

At about the same time as the lifeboat arrived, a fishing smack also reached the wreck and its crew began salvaging some of the cargo, including two boxes of soap. They carried it to the water's edge, but when they tried to load it onto the fishing smack, it almost capsized and all they ended up with was two light, hair-filled mattresses. The *Forfarshire* was so smashed up that wood from her was actually washed up at Beadnell, seven miles to the south. On 12 September, the moveable and loose objects from the wreck were taken to North Sunderland by a Mr Sinclair on behalf of Lloyd's of London and then the wreck itself was sold for £70 to a Dundee shipwright, a Mr Adamson.

Grace Darling and her father were both awarded medals by the Royal Humane Society and public donations of £800 were raised for Grace, but only £270 was raised for her father. Grace became a national heroine as word got out about the rescue, but very soon the truth became distorted. The public wanted a woman as a hero

Above: Memorial grave of Grace Darling

Left: North Sunderland, circa 1910

during this period and very soon the story was being told of how Grace performed the entire rescue on her own. Another tale was that after she woke her father up, she had to more or less force him to help her. A Board of Inquiry was ordered by Trinity House to get at the truth and William Darling wrote this letter to the Secretary of Trinity House in reply:

Dear Sir,

In answer to your request of the 29th, I have to state that on the morning of the 7th September, it was blowing a gale, with rain from the north, my daughter and me, being both on the alert before high water, securing things out of doors, one quarter before five, my daughter observed a vessel on the Harcars Rock, but owing to the darkness and the spray going over her, could not observe any person on the wreck, although the glass being incessantly applied until near seven o'clock, when, the tide being fallen, we observed 3 or 4 men upon the rock: we agreed that if we could get to them, some of them would be able to assist us back, without which we could not return: and having no idea of the possibility of a boat coming from North Sunderland, we immediately launched our boat and was enabled to gain the rock, where we found 8 men and one woman, which I judged rather too many for to take at once in the state of weather, therefore took the woman and four men to the Longstone. Two of them returned with me, and succeeded in bringing the remainder, in all 9 persons, to safety to the Longstone about nine o'clock. Afterwards a boat from North Sunderland arrived and found three lifeless bodies, viz, one man and two children, which they carried to the rock, and came to Longstone with great difficulty; and had to lodge in the barracks two days and nights, with scant provisions, no beds, nor clothes to change them with.

Your Obedient Servant

William Darling

The Inquest at Morpeth, Northumberland on 13 September, was reported in *The Times*:

The following individuals were saved from the wreck by Mr Darling and his daughter:

John Kidd, fireman of Dundee; Jonathan Ticket, cook of Hull; John Macqueen, coal-trimmer of Dundee; John Tulloch, carpenter of Dundee; John Nicholson, fireman from Dundee of the crew; D. Donovan, fireman and free passenger of Dundee; James Kelly, weaver of Dundee; Thomas Buchanan baker of Dundee; Mrs

Dawson who was bound for Dundee, passengers ...The entire number saved is 18, of whom 13 belonged to the vessel and five were passengers. The remainder of those on board, amounting to between 35 and 40 individuals, have all perished.

Even though officialdom knew the whole truth about the famous rescue and there is no doubt that Grace Darling performed a dangerous and heroic feat alongside her father, the rumours and twisted tales prevailed. People just believed what they wanted to hear. The fan mail to Grace poured in, with invitations to her to sit for portraits and thousands of requests for locks of her hair; in fact, she sent so many locks of hair that she was in danger of going bald. Busts of her were on sale everywhere, poems were written and offers of marriage galore came in. Each visit to the mainland was like a royal occasion. Grace did not want any of it, really; she just wanted to be left in peace with her family on Longstone. She had been born at Bamburgh on 24 November 1815 and was one of nine children brought to maturity by William and Thomasin Darling. The lighthouse was her home, her father's business and her principal interest. Books from the Castle Library were her greatest delight, seabirds and their eggs (for the larder) and seashells her pet diversions. Tragically, poor Grace only lived another four years after the famous rescue: she died of consumption (tuberculosis) on 20 October 1842 and was buried in Bamburgh churchyard.

Bamburgh church – resting place of the Darling family

Darling family grave at Bamburgh

Dive sites

(1) ✮ ✮ ✮ ✮

55 38′.388 N 001 36′.678 W

A very pleasant dive at the eastern end of the Bluecaps, with an overhanging cliff dropping away to 23 metres and large boulders at the bottom against the wall. Lots of small fish swimming around, mostly coley and the odd codling and ballan wrasse. Low water is the best time to dive because you can see where the Bluecaps drop away, although it is quite easy to pick it up with an echo sounder. The submerged part of the cliff runs well out into Crayford's Gut and slopes down until it bottoms out onto sand and stone at around 28 metres. It is an excellent scenic dive and a good first 'deepy' for the novice diver, as there is not too much current, except on springs, and you are close to the islet. A few crustaceans can sometimes be found in the crevices and under the large boulders at the bottom.

(2) ✮ ✮ ✮

Behind the end of Bluecaps in Crayford's Gut there is a narrow channel or cut that runs right through the Bluecaps and is a popular haunt of young seals. The channel is fairly interesting with a few ledges and crevices at the eastern end at Crayford's Gut, where the bottom drops away down in steps to 18 metres. The depth inside the channel is only 5–8 metres. This dive can be combined with site (1) unless you wish to explore the kelp-covered rocky reefs further north into Crayford's Gut. After a spell of heavy weather, though, lots of dead kelp gets washed into the gullies to the north where it quickly goes stagnant.

(3) ✶ ✶ ✶

A sheltered dive site, or at least one protected from the main tidal streams and a good place to introduce a novice diver. There are a number of submerged 'hillocks' only a couple of metres or so below the surface, forming deep channels and cul-de-sacs, with the surrounding depths between 8 and 15 metres. Some of those close to the main reef often contain stagnant seaweed at certain times of the year but many others are teeming with marine life. On the outside of the hillocks there are lots of rocks and small boulders, which go down a steep slope to a seabed of dirty sand at 20 metres plus. The area seems to attract fair numbers of small fish too, including little ballan wrasse. Visibility is usually only moderate, due to the lack of tidal movement, but can be good after a spring tide.

(4) ✶ ✶ ✶

55 38'.438 N 001 36'.954 W

An interesting dive with some very large boulders on a patchy sand and stone bottom, with a 4–5 metre submerged cliff face just out from the main reef. A strong current runs on the top half of the tide in the channel between the Bluecaps and Little Harcar, but on a spring tide it develops into a raging torrent. It is still possible to dive on the flood, as the current is mostly near to the top half of the water and you can find plenty of shelter, but on the ebb you may end up in the bay on the northern side of the reef. It was in this location a couple of years ago that an 18th century ship's bell was found: it was badly crushed and had no name on it but it could nonetheless have been from one of the ships wrecked in the Great Storm.

(5) ✶ ✶

A number of boulders and rocks on a steep sloping bottom from 6 metres down to 20 metres plus and a rather boring dive, lacking in marine life.

(6) ✶ ✶

An old ship's anchor has lain jammed in a gully on the top of Big Harcar for many years. How it got there was a complete mystery to me until a few years ago. A good friend of mine told me that he and some of his colleagues had raised it with lifting bags, because they believed it to be the actual anchor from the wreck of the *Forfarshire*. They had intended to present it to the Grace Darling Museum at Bamburgh, but their transport did not arrive to take it ashore and it weighed so much that they had no other way of removing it from the rock. It has now gone and I was told that a helicopter had picked it up and dropped it off at the museum.

Underwater, this is another rather boring dive site with very little of interest. There is very little current near to the island, which has a small cliff face running along it but very few holes or crevices. Depth to the stony seabed, close to the base of the island, is around 6–7 metres. Away from the island towards Piper Gut, the bottom consists of sand and weed-covered rocks, but the current is considerably stronger. When there is a big northerly swell running, this is one of the very few sheltered places where you can actually dive, and it is a favourite with some of the charter boats (although if they took me there to dive, I would not bother to get wet). The depth is about the same all the way along to the Little Harcar, with the same boring scenery.

(7) ✯ ✯ ✯

55 38'.325 N 001 37'.421 W

The western end of Big Harcar is now called Forfar Rock and is where the *Forfarshire* struck on the northern side during her ill-fated voyage. The submerged walls of the reef at this point are covered in anemones and soft corals, caused by so much water being funnelled through Piper Gut, and the seabed at six metres has lots of pieces of wreckage 'melting' into the rocks and stones. By staying close to the reef wall on the north side, you can quite comfortably fin around as long as you don't venture too far out into Piper Gut. What is very surprising is that only 20 metres or so round on the north side of Big Harcar, there is little, if any, current close to the reef. There are some huge square rock ledges dropping down to the bottom, resembling very large steps. Travelling a further ten metres brings you to a shallow undulating kelp-covered plateau, 2–5 metres deep, that stretches out from the Big Harcar in a NNW direction for over 70 metres. There are a few small gullies and channels, often filled with lots of dead kelp and seaweed and with not much of interest. At the edge of the plateau there is a steep wall down to the bottom at 12–15 metres, made up of small boulders often covered in sediment and rather dismal. From here the seabed gradually slopes away down in a northerly direction into 20 metres plus, with a lifeless-looking bottom.

(8) ✯ ✯

55 38'.535 N 001 37'.160 W

More or less out in the middle of the bay on the north side, in between the two Harcar islets, there are lots of undulating 'hills and valleys' covered in kelp. Unfortunately, everything always seems coated in a layer of sediment, making the scenery dark and drab, and even the marine life is sparse except for urchins and an occasional crab. The reason may be because the area is in a type of tidal void, where there is not too much current but where what there is runs in two or three different directions on the flood; on the ebb tide at low water, there is no movement at all and maximum depth is around 12 metres.

Keeny's Bus

(9) ★ ★ ★ ★

55 38'.612 N 001 37'.119 W

Keeny's Bus s a long high reef facing west, commencing on the north side between Clove Car and Little Harcar and running parallel to Longstone for almost its full length. There is lots of everything amongst its boulders and crevices, including lobsters and crabs, cod and some fair- sized conger. Opposite the lighthouse, the reef almost touches the surface and in fact is only half a metre below the surface on a low spring tide. There are some very high reef walls covered in soft corals and it is also one of the few places around the Farnes where you can see the photogenic plumose anemone. Visibility is often good in the summer months and tidal streams are light to moderate, except at top half of the flood, and especially on spring tides. During the big tides it runs in two directions, through Crayford's Gut and between the Bluecaps and Harcars. A lot of divers have ended up shooting through the channel between the islets before the boat could reach them, often causing some panic. The easiest way to locate the reef is to run west from the lighthouse, until the centre/top of the Little Harcar lines up directly due south. That puts you roughly midway along the reef and right over the cliff edge. An echo sounder will pick the reef up easily because it is up to 9 metres high in places. The top is covered in heavy kelp while the bottom leads onto a 10-metre wide patch of sand.

NORTH WAMSES TO STAPLE ISLAND

Crossing over the tidal race of Piper Gut from the Big Harcar at low tide is a chain of islets and islands stretching in a southerly direction for over three quarters of a mile: North Wamses, Roddam and Green, South Wamses, Nameless Rock, Brownsman, Staple Island, The Pinnacles and the Gun Rocks in Staple Sound.

North Wamses

55 38'.348 N 001 37'.805 W

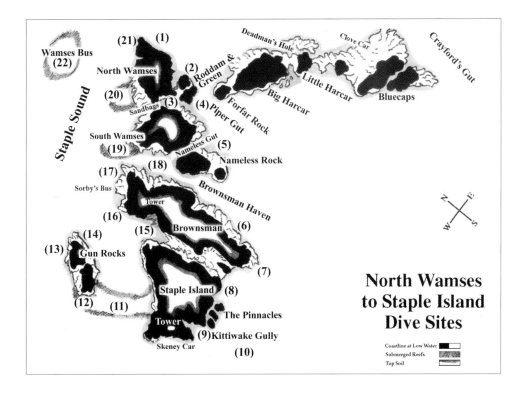

(21) (1)

Deadman's Hole

Clove Car

Crayford's Gut

Wamses Bus
(22)

North Wamses

Staple Sound

(2) Roddam & Green

Little Harcar

Big Harcar

Bluecaps

(20)

(3)

Sandbags

(4) Piper Gut

Forfar Rock

South Wamses

Nameless Gut

(19)

(18)

(5)

Nameless Rock

(17)

Sorby's Bus

Brownsman Haven

Tower

(16)

(15)

Brownsman

(6)

(14)

(13) Gun Rocks

(7)

N
E
W
S

(12) (11)

Staple Island (8)

The Pinnacles

**North Wamses
to Staple Island
Dive Sites**

Tower

(9) Kittiwake Gully

Skeney Car

(10)

Coastline at Low Water
Submerged Reefs
Top Soil

South Wamses

55 38'.240 N 001 37'.695 W

The North Wamses, as its name implies, is the most northerly in this group and lies on the seaward side of the mile-wide, relatively shallow channel of water known as Staple Sound. The two islands of North and South Wamses are connected at mid low water by a low shingle/stone bridge called Sandbags and a large seal colony is always present around the western side of the North Wamses. The grey seals have their breeding nursery on the shingle-covered south-facing side of South Wamses and with more than 500 pups born every year, it has become the main nursery of the Farne Islands. When approaching the islands downwind you are greeted by the horrible stench emitted by the thick carpet of white guano and accompanying bulky, smelly nests of the main colony of breeding cormorants on the Farnes. The top of the two Wamses have a light covering of peaty soil which encourages small numbers of puffins to breed and, to add to the putrid smell, nesting alongside their burrows are some 800 pairs of guillemots, fulmars, shags, eider ducks, kittiwakes, lesser black-backed and herring gulls.

At least three recorded sailing vessels have been wrecked on the North Wamses: in September 1842, a lighter (a sailing vessel carrying fly ash) was wrecked there, then in June 1894, the brig *Formica* came to grief and on 2 January 1916, the schooner *Spica* of Riga ran aground.

In 1987, I discovered the identity of another vessel which was wrecked on the North Wamses but was never recorded.

The Pearle 1717

In February 1987, my wife Rose and I were strolling around the old harbour at Seahouses, which was almost deserted except for the odd trawler coming or going and a few boatmen preparing their trip boats for the expected tourist invasion at Easter. We met up with an old friend from Wakefield, Peter Zemlik. Peter and his pals from Wakefield BSAC invited me out for a dive with them at the Farnes, even though the islands were shrouded in a wintry, icy mist and looked really desolate.

Aware that I knew the islands like the back of my hand, Pete asked me to choose a site that was rather sheltered and suitable for his two novice divers. I suggested we try the western side of the North Wamses, with ample shelter in the lea of the protruding reefs and a depth of only 7 metres. Two of the guys agreed to handle the boat and I went in with Pete and his two novices, although Pete told me just to 'do my own thing' and not to worry, as he would look after them. I hung around for a while watching his young novices enjoying the marine life and the scenery of the overhanging reefs before going off to search for something for tea. This was my first dive of the year and the icy water temperature quickly numbed my face. It took me a while to settle down and relax, especially as two seal pups decided to pester the life out of me for the first half of the dive. I soon found a nice three-pound lobster, in an area where I didn't normally dive and well away from the main reef. I tried to persuade it to come out of the deep awkward crevice in which it was hiding, but no amount of coaxing would bring it closer, so I decided on another tactic. I gave the hole a good rattle with my pole, moved back out of sight and waited for a minute or so, which usually arouses their curiosity. I happened to glance to one side and could not believe my eyes. There, only two metres away, in a small sandy clearing amongst the kelp, in all its majesty, was a huge bronze bell. My heart missed a beat and I tried to control my breathing as clouds of bubbles surrounded me in the excitement. I checked my contents gauge but had plenty of air left. I easily pulled the bell clear of the seabed because only about three inches around the base was under sand. There was no clapper but the top inside was flush and it appeared that there never had been one. On the top of the bell was a kind of crown on which it hung, while close to the shoulder, in a band around the side, were the words *The Pearle 1717*.

The problem was that I had no lifting bag with me and I would have trouble recovering it. I removed my fins and tried to carry it to a more recognisable area closer to the reef, but after a few attempts which ended in my falling in a heap on my face, I had a rethink. The bell must have weighed in the region of 30 kilos. On went my fins and 1 rechecked my contents gauge: my air was OK. There was only one thing left to do. I half-carried and half-rolled it along on the bottom of its rim to a familiar place at the base of the main reef. By this time I was absolutely shattered and was about to head for the surface when I caught sight of Peter and Sean. After ushering them over to view my prize, Pete signalled to use our drysuits together to lift it to the surface. All that happened, though, thanks to its awkward shape and weight, was that we lifted up and the bell stayed put on the bottom. By now, the other two lads had used up their air so we decided to surface and return with a lifting bag. The boat quickly picked us up and there was a hum of excitement when we told them what I had found. A lifting bag was produced and I decided to recover the bell with my remaining air, accompanied by Sean Hunt. In less than two minutes I had relocated it, slipped a nylon rope through the crown loop, filled the bag and looked on, ecstatic, as it headed the few metres to the surface. The lads in the boat – Peter and Bob Raby –wasted no time pulling it on board but nearly forgot that we were still in the water. The guys returned to Wakefield that evening full of excitement, especially Sean, who'd been involved with a ship's bell on his first sea dive.

Needless to say, the first thing I did on the Monday morning was to report my find to the Receiver of Wrecks office in Sunderland because I knew that when news got out of what I had discovered, HM Customs would confiscate it. The Sunderland office reported the matter to their Blyth branch, which then passed the information over to the Berwick office, and by the time I arrived home they were on the telephone demanding that I hand the bell over to them as I had not reported it to them as soon as I had found it. I pointed out that their office was not open on a Sunday and that I had reported my find first thing on Monday morning, but that did not satisfy the person I spoke to. He still insisted that it was to be confiscated. A number of heated arguments followed before I threatened to put the bell back where I had found it at the Farne Islands and let them look for it themselves. More arguments followed, with numerous phone calls from the Customs Office, and then finally somebody in authority informed me that I had taken the right course of action. I was told that the bell could stay with me and that they would make inquiries to try and locate the owners. After that, HM Customs were extremely helpful and informed me that the vessel's owners were unknown and the ship was not of any historical interest.

Unfortunately, the bell had started to develop the dreaded 'bronze disease', which was beginning to eat into its surface and also meant that it would crumble into a powder when it dried out. I had to keep it in a drum of fresh water for several weeks until I found out how to preserve it. Eventually, after lots of letters and numerous phone calls around the country, I received advice from Bob Williams at Aquascan, a company which makes magnetometers and related equipment. I first had to have a fibreglass bell-shaped housing made, which was done by Reiver Boats of Stanley, County Durham, and I then had to apply to HM Customs and Excise for a permit to acquire some special chemicals, which were very costly and difficult to get hold of.

The bell was placed in the housing, covered by the chemicals and left sealed in for nearly five months. When it was taken out, the disease had been cured but, sadly, the bell had kept its dark green hue and would not polish or shine like bronze.

I tried for many months to trace the history of the ship without any luck, chiefly because she was built in 1717 and there are few, if any, records dating to before 1760, when most records were destroyed in a fire. I later discovered that the vessel was a large wooden British sailing ship, probably a schooner, brig, snow or barquentine of around 200–250 tons. She was built in the period when the infamous pirate and hellraiser Blackbeard roamed the seven seas. On 19 February 1740, *The Pearle* was in ballast on a voyage from London to Newcastle upon Tyne with a crew of six and under the command of a Captain Emmett. She ran into southwesterly storm-force winds while approaching the Tyne and was driven before the wind and way past her destination until she encountered the barrier of islands in the Outer Farnes. With little or no control, the ship struck the shallow reefs on the western side of North Wamses and was lost with all hands. The official report from Lloyd's quotes: 'From London to Newcastle, is lost to the northward of Newcastle, and six men drowned.' The bell now takes pride of place in the Wakefield BSAC clubhouse.

Very little else remains at the site where the bell was discovered, apart from a big old anchor that could have come from anything. We did, though, find two huge brass rudder hinges and a lot of copper pins close in to the island in three metres of water. There are also a few bits of metal concreted into the rocky seabed close in to the reef face, towards the northern end of North Wamses, but nothing very significant.

Roddam and Green

55 38'.333 N 001 37'.586 W

These two small bare islets, which still show at high tide, lie on the eastern side of North Warnses and across the swirling waters of Piper Gut opposite Forfar Rock. During northerly storms they take the full brunt of the huge waves that pound into this barrier of islands. It is said that when the *Forfarshire* ploughed into the rocks at the western corner of Big Harcar (now known as Forfar Rock), she swung round and hit the two rocks of Roddam and Green before breaking her back. It sounds very feasible, because there would have been an enormous amount of pressure on the ship both from the mountainous seas and the tidal rip through Piper Gut, especially on the flood tide.

On 26 November 1825, an unknown vessel was wrecked on the two islets and another, the schooner *Est* of Montrose, was destroyed on 26 July 1871.

Nameless Rock

55 38'.178 N 001 37'.503 W

Nameless Rock is just a bare rocky islet off the southeast corner of South Wamses and, as far as I know, there have been no major shipwrecks around it, although there are supposedly some cannons close to it in Piper Gut. Between the small islet of Nameless and South Wamses, on the top half of the tide, there is a navigable channel called Nameless Gut that is used by the trip boats to save time, but the shallow channel has also been the cause of a few bent and broken propellers in its day.

Brownsman

55 38'.015 N 001 37'.489 W

Brownsman is what you would call a proper island, as it is one of the largest in the Outer Farnes and has a covering of peaty soil in which plants are able to grow. There are also the remains of the old square beacon lighthouse and a cottage which was built in 1810. The cottage was the one used by the Darling family who moved there when the Staple tower lighthouse closed down. It is now used as a home by the National Trust wardens who protect the Farne Island wildlife. Brownsman has huge numbers of kittiwakes, shags, guillemots and a sprinkling of fulmars that nest on the southern cliffs. The peaty soil on the top of the island is honeycombed with the burrows of puffins, which often line the cliffs along with hundreds of sandwich terns. It makes an impressive sight when the whole colony takes to the air at once.

Although Brownsman is not as open to the sea as many of the other islands, it has still had six recorded ships wrecked on it since 1795, three of them involving the loss of life. On 3 December 1795 the sloop *Friendship* of Bo'ness was lost and four of her crew were drowned.

On 2 February 1823 the wooden brig *George and Mary* was lost with all hands, while on passage for London with a cargo of coal; she sank after striking the eastern point of Brownsman during a severe easterly gale. On 14 October 1881 the barque *Snowdonia* smashed into the western corner of Brownsman, reputedly hitting it so hard that she left a groove in the rock face, and all her eleven crew members died in the incident. She was a sailing ship of 419 tons, measuring 42.8 m in length with a 8.95-m beam and a 5.3-m draught and was bound from the Coosaw River in South Carolina to Berwick with a cargo of phosphate rock. The *Snowdonia* was a wooden vessel with the hull protected by a sheath of copper.

The Times, Tuesday, 18 October 1881, p. 10.

The most dubious story of a ship wrecked on the Farne Islands has to be that of the old Norwegian sailing vessel *Spika*. I personally have never seen any records of a ship called *Spika* coming ashore on Brownsman, but there may have been some confusion with the Russian wooden schooner *Spica* of Riga (now in Latvia) which was wrecked on the North Wamses in January 1916. She had been on passage from Kristiania, Norway for West Hartlepool with a cargo of pit props; the crew was taken off by lifeboat. Even today, some parts of this ship still lie on top of the island, but most of her valuable oak timbers were gradually salvaged many years ago by people from Seahouses.

The strange story of the *Spika* on the Brownsman was that in 1915 she was bound for Hartlepool with pit props but was supposedly abandoned during a storm and left to the elements. She was never seen again until 6 February 1953 when she was reported as having been seen by local fishermen off the mouth of the River Tyne. They said they had seen 'a tall sailing ship with rotting timbers and bare ribs, slipping in and out of the fog banks.' Then, on 16 February, only ten days later, she was found aground on Brownsman Island in the channel known as Brownsman Haven, situated between Brownsman and South Wamses, It sounds like a regular *Marie Celeste* story and the tale sounds as tall as the ship itself! It is difficult to believe that any type of vessel could just float around aimlessly for 38 years, especially in the North Sea, surviving two world wars, hundreds of storms and even hurricanes without either being driven ashore or sinking, which would be more likely. That, though, is the story, if you want to believe it.

Staple Island

55 37'.852 N 001 37'.448 W

Staple Island is an ornithologist's delight and a photographer's paradise between May and July when it is possible to get very close-up views of the hundreds upon hundreds of nesting kittiwakes, shags, guillemots, razorbills, gulls, puffins and fulmars, as well as the occasional oystercatcher and ringed plover. Being similar to Brownsman, it is one of the few islands that have a covering of soil suitable for puffins to dig burrows for nesting. Both of the islands are reputed still to have a few rabbits on them and the puffins use their burrows.

The old tower lighthouse was partially destroyed by the Great Storm of 1774 and all that remains of it today is part of the walls, which stand up to 3 metres high. The old tower was used as a beacon light during the time of William Darling's father.

Saint André

55 37'.8798 N 001 37'.2702 W

Just off the south side of Staple Island are the scattered remains of the steamer *Saint André*.

On 28 October 1908, on her final voyage, the ship stranded on Crumstone in dense fog; she was carrying a crew of sixteen and a cargo of iron ore from Caen to Grangemouth. The vessel stood there for several days before being washed off and drifting across to Staple Island, where she sank against the cliff face. None of the crew was lost.

The *Saint André* (Official No.1502) was a steel-hulled 1,121-ton French steam cargo ship measuring 70.10 m in length, with a 9.06-m beam and a 4.19-m draught. Craig, Taylor and Co., Stockton built and completed her as Yard No.98 in November 1903; she was launched on 21 October 1903 for L. Larue of Caen in northwest France. The single steel screw was powered by a 900-ihp, three-cylinder triple expansion steam engine that used two Scotch-type boilers working at a pressure of 180 psi. North Eastern Marine Engineering Co. Ltd manufactured the engine and ancillary machinery at Sunderland. From 1908, Fernand Bouet of Caen was the registered owner.

The Pinnacles

55 37'.782 N 001 37'.421 W

Just off the south end of Staple and inshore of the *Saint André* stand the three huge Whin Sill pillars of the Pinnacles which, along with the nearby cliffs, are home to hundreds more guillemots.

Gun Rocks

55 37'.875 N 001 37'.791 W

The name of Gun Rocks came from the pile of cannon guns discovered on the south side of the islets in the 1700s. One of the cannons was used in Bamburgh Castle to alert the villagers when a ship was wrecked. The Gun Rocks wreck was first thought to have been an Armada ship dating from when the Spanish fleet was driven up the

Above: The Pinnacles

Below left: Guillemots on Staple Island

Below right: Kittiwakes and chicks nesting on Staple Island

North Sea coast, but she was later found to be an armed Dutch merchant vessel that was wrecked between 1650 and 1715; the cannons and other artefacts were later dated. Gun Rocks, of which there are two, are situated about 150 metres west of Staple Island and are dry to 3.6 metres. They are connected to Staple at the southern end by a shallow underwater sand and stone bank which is visible on the bottom of a spring tide, and it is then too shallow to navigate even in a small RHIB.

On 17 August 1939, the steam trawler *Excel* ran aground on Gun Rocks, but was later successfully refloated.

Dive sites

(1) ✵ ✵

There are submerged cliff walls all the way to the end of the eastern side of North Wamses with a few crevices near to the bottom at 10–12 metres. The seabed slopes down from 10 to 16 metres out from the island and goes much deeper to the north with a monotonous bottom. Currents are reasonably strong, especially on the flood tide.

(2) ✵ ✵

The islets of Roddam and Green are well and truly washed by the exceptionally strong currents of Piper Gut. On the eastern side the rock walls below the surface are covered in anemones, while the other sides are just covered in kelp. There are a couple of narrow crevices between the islets and they are surrounded by fairly shallow water, with the deepest part, at 6–8-metres, being in Piper Gut. There is very little of interest because the sand and stone seabed is well scoured by the current. It is possible to dive on the west side of the islets during ebb tide, but not on the eastern unless you are prepared for a rapid drift dive.

(3) ✵ ✵ ✵

55 38'.310 N 001 37'.572 W

At low water and on the ebb tide, this little lagoon makes an excellent novice dive and usually produces a few buckies (whelks) for the sharp-eyed diver. The flat sand and stone bottom has a patchy covering of kelp and is only 4 metres deep at the entrance, but becomes more shallow as you move in to the western end. There are small rock walls on both sides at the Piper Gut end and one or two decent holes to look into. On the top half of the tide the water rushes in from the north and west producing strong swirling currents, making it impossible to stay in one place, and at high tide the lagoon disappears altogether.

(4) ✷ ✷

55 38'.279 N 001 37'.476 W

The centre of Piper Gut is strewn with the wreckage of the *Forfarshire* and many other wrecks. There are still bits of non-ferrous metal to be found including a number of zinc anodes amongst the weed-covered rocks and stones, especially at the southern end. The problem is that, with the current running at up to 8 knots, it is not exactly the best place to go scrapping with a lifting bag. A few years ago there used to be full lengths of brass handrails from the *Forfarshire* but they are more than likely to have gone by now. The depth between Forfar Rock and Roddam and Green is only about 6 metres, but it slopes away to 16 metres on the north side and 25 metres to the south. The seabed consists mostly of sand and stone and patches of kelp-covered small rocks and is definitely a slack water dive. The drift dive, though, is something else.

Drift dive ✷ ✷ ✷ ✷

The best way to see Piper Gut is to drift dive it on the flood tide, north to south with reliable boat cover and surface marker buoys. It is an exhilarating dive during a spring tide, but not for the faint-hearted. The coxswain needs to keep an eagle eye on the surface marker buoy, bearing in mind that there is a considerable amount of boat traffic passing through the Gut all day long from Easter to about the end of September.

(5) ✷ ✷ ✷ ✷

55 38'.224 N 001 37'.421 W

Along the southeast side of Nameless Rock, the depth varies between 4 and 13 metres, with steep rocky steps and underwater hills harbouring plenty of marine life. Close in behind the island in this area it is possible to dive on the ebb tide, because it is sheltered from the main flow. The extreme eastern corner of Nameless is a beautiful sight and ablaze with soft corals living off the benefits of the strong tidal flow, but you need slack water for this part of the dive site.

George And Mary, Brig
(6) ✷ ✷ ✷ ✷

55 38'.022 N 001 37'.242 W

The northeastern end of Brownsman, close in to the island in Brownsman Haven, is an area of kelp-covered flat rock which just slopes gradually away downwards. The tidal run is fairly strong and there is not much of interest except for a few sea urchins. However, quite close by in 25 metres and at coordinates 55 38'.0118 N 001 37'.0572 W, the remnants of the wooden brig *George and Mary* can still be found; she was on passage for London with a cargo of coal but struck the eastern point of Brownsman during a severe easterly gale and was lost with all hands

(7) ✯ ✯ ✯

55 37'952 N 001 37'.160 W

A kelp-covered rock shelf dropping down a cliff face to a shingle seabed at 20 metres plus and a strong tidal stream running south and away from Brownsman on the flood. It is best dived at slack water to get the full benefit of the dive site, as it is a rather exposed corner and subjected to a lot of passing boat traffic.

SS *Saint André*

(8) ✯ ✯ ✯ ✯

55 37'.813 N 001 37'.380 W

Halfway along the southern side of Staple Island and lying at the cliff base are the smashed-up remains of the French steamer *Saint André*. The wreck is orientated in an east to west direction and lies in depths between 17 metres and 23 metres. It is now totally collapsed, well broken up and rather decayed, with just ribs, steel plates, framework and the boilers and broken engine remaining. There is very little to find in the way of artefacts, but this is still a nice and very popular dive site during the summer months. The builder's nameplate, which was located in 1974, positively identified the wreck. It is sheltered from the main currents and it is possible to dive the site at most states of the tide, although the area is prone to a lot of backwash from the island during strong south and southeasterly winds. A bit more care should also be taken when diving close to the northeast corner on the flood near high tide, due to the strong current running between Brownsman and Staple Islands. Visibility is often in the region of 15 metres during the summer months after a spell of westerly winds.

Kittiwake Gully

(9) ✯ ✯ ✯

55 37'.774 N 001 37'.462 W

Kittiwake Gully is a dead end V-shaped canyon at the southern corner of Staple Island and very close to the Pinnacles. Depths vary from 2–7 metres and the visibility is usually excellent. The canyon will be of special interest to the avid underwater photographer who wants that one-off picture of diving seabirds, as they dart by in their dozens. It is sheltered from the currents but very prone to a southerly swell. The sheer cliff walls of the Pinnacles next door are also an interesting dive site and you can combine the two sites into one. The smell around this area, especially during the nesting season, can be quite overpowering on the surface and you get a lot of the bird droppings in the water, but as a photographer it can be worth putting up with.

(10) ✷ ✷

Swimming south for about 200 metres brings you into 25 metres plus and onto a sand and stone seabed. Here, if you are lucky, it is possible to collect a few queen scallops (*Chlamys opercularis*) and great scallops (*Pecten maximus*) for the pot. Swim for a further 100 metres and you will find a whole scallop dredge, complete with its steel wire ropes stretching out across the seabed in an east to west direction.

(11) ✷

This is not a recommended dive site, because there are very strong currents and really nothing to dive on. It appears to be a reef but is in fact just a sloping bank in both directions which almost dries on a spring tide. The bottom is covered in short seaweed on small rocks, stones and sand.

Gun Rocks

(12) ✷ ✷ ✷

55 37′.820 N 001 37′.737 W

This is the Gun Rock wrecksite where there used to be as many as 26 cannons lying scattered around. Unfortunately, people with their own peculiar motives have removed many of them over the years, spoiling the site for everyone else. The wreck has never been a protected site because it was not deemed to be historically important enough, yet lots of encrusted artefacts, such as sword hilts, cannon balls, bar shot, musket balls and at least two brass swivel guns have been found here. A couple of years ago, some university divers recovered a small tin box with an inscribed lid. There has been an enormous amount of digging into the concretion, leaving holes of more than a metre deep, and literally piles of cannon balls and bar shot have been taken in the last 25 years. The wrecksite is on the south side of Gun Rocks in 7-10 metres, but you really have to look hard to find the rusting concretion

Looking down into Kittiwake Gully

under the thick covering of kelp. Even the remaining cannons are not as obvious as you might expect because they lie half-buried, with some even concreted into the surrounding rocks. The first time I visited the site in the early 1970s, I swam right over them, and at the time the guns were all over the place. The site is fairly sheltered on the bottom half of the flood tide, but the current is exceptionally strong away from the rocks in the Sound.

(13) ★ ★ ★ ★

55 37′.859 N 001 37′.846 W

This is an excellent colourful dive, where lots of anemones and soft corals cover the steep boulder-strewn sides of the reef. Even the stony seabed out in the Sound at around 13 metres is brightly lit up, with lots of life about. Tidal streams are very strong on this side of Gun Rocks and it is really a slack water dive; the visibility is also usually excellent. The boulders on the reef edge often hide a few crustaceans too, adding a bonus to the site.

(14) ✷ ✷

55 37'.899 N 002 37'.750 W

This side of the reef is rather more sheltered from the strong currents but it always appears gloomier. You can still, though, find the odd crab in the undulating mounds of rock which are covered in long kelp strands. Moving out east away from Gun Rocks and towards Staple Island, depths are in the region of 10–12 metres with a sandy seabed.

(15) ✷ ✷ ✷

55 37'.899 N 001 37'.750 W

At the entrance to the channel between the two islands of Staple and Brownsman are a number of large boulders on the sloping bottom at 10 metres and it always worth looking under them. On the flood tide there is a considerable amount of water being funnelled between the islands and on the top half of the flood tide it is possible to make a drift dive, bringing you out between dives (7) and (8). If a drift dive is contemplated, then the boat cover should wait at the south end and not attempt to go through the channel because it is rather shallow in the middle.

Snowdonia, Wooden Barque

(16) ✷ ✷ ✷

55 38'.612 N 001 37'.791 W

This is the wrecksite of the barque *Snowdonia*, where a number of nice little artefacts have been recovered in recent years. One diver found a complete sextant while another picked up the compass. The ship was copper-sheathed and after storms it can sometimes be seen protruding from the sand. There are still a few remnants of the wreck left, including the anchor, chain, keel and a few spars and frames. It lies at the base of the cliff face in only 8 metres of water but is little difficult to locate, because most of the remains are buried close to the rock face. These last two dives can be combined if you do not wish to explore the channel, but make sure the tide is on the low ebb.

Sorby's Bus

(17) ✷ ✷

55 38'.092 N 001 37'.723 W

The northwest corner of Brownsman has a couple of shallow kelp-covered rock plateaux called Sorby's Bus, which dry to half a metre on a low spring tide. They have steep, sloping rocky walls down to a sandy seabed at 10 metres. There are a few crevices and holes while the visibility is often good and the sides of the plateau provide some shelter from the current.

Brownsman Haven

(18) ✷ ✷

55 38'.147 N 001 37'.613 W

Drift dive ✷ ✷ ✷

The channel between Brownsman and South Wamses and Nameless Rock, called Brownsman Haven, is very shallow, being only 2 to 7 metres deep at low water. The seabed is sand with patches of kelp-covered boulders and large rocks with little of interest, although you might find the occasional crab under the boulders and a few whelks out on the sand. However, it is possible to have a nice drift dive down the middle of the channel because the current is fairly brisk. A word of caution though: most of the trip boats pass along this route every day between Easter and the end of September.

(19) ✷ ✷

55 38'.185 N 001 37'.846 W

Just off the South Wamses, a 200-metre long reef curves out into Staple Sound. The reef has a four metre-high wall facing south with the top plateau covered in dense kelp. The seabed at the base of the reef is sand with kelp-covered boulders. There are not many crevices in the reef but you can often pick up a few whelks on the sandy bottom. To the northwest of the reef there are a lot of little reefs covered in really dense kelp but little variety of marine life about.

The Pearle

(20) ✷ ✷ ✷ ✷

55 38'.387 N 001 38'.011 W

At the southern end of North Wamses is the site where I discovered the old ship's bell from *The Pearle*. This whole area has a thick covering of kelp and tangleweed with a shallow plateau of rock running two thirds of the way along the North Wamses, commencing just past the large V-shaped cut towards the northern end. The shelf or plateau is only a few metres deep beneath the surface and extends up to 30 metres out and west from the Wamses. There are a number of gullies and three pot-holes a couple of metres deep on the top, surrounded by overhanging, dense tangleweed. Currents are fairly mild on the neap ebb tide but can be very strong on the flood and especially so on spring tides. On the flood, the sea rushes up over the shallow ground from deep water to the north and can turn you upside down when crossing over the reef. The depth immediately around the plateau is around 7–10 metres.

(21) ✯ ✯ ✯

55 38′.410 N 001 37′.929 W

The northwest tip of North Waees has an excellent underwater cliff face up to 5 metres high and starting at about 4 metres out from the island. It extends out about 200 metres to the north, taking you down to 25 metres and eventually onto sand. There are some nice overhangs covered in soft corals and a large old Admiralty type anchor in 20 metres. Tidal streams are very strong in the deeper water, especially on the flood tide.

At the top of the Wamses, a large V-shaped gorge cuts deep into the island and looks as if a ship has ploughed into it. The gorge is very narrow at the top, 4 metres deep, and you often find seals playing around in it. It was close to this area on the top of the submerged cliff and under the tangleweed in only 3 metres that we discovered, in the little gullies and crevices, two bronze rudder pintles and dozens of nine-inch copper pins.

Wamses Bus

(22) ✯ ✯

55 38′.401 N 001 38′.012 W

One hundred metres due west from the end of the North Wamses is a submerged, rather undulating rock plateau covered in a thick kelp forest and aptly called Wamses Bus. There is not much to see and the currents are very strong but on the spring ebb tide there is a downward flowing current off the northern edge of the plateau with depths dropping down to 25 metres, and the surface boils from the amount of water being pushed up Staple Sound. Further inshore towards the island there are some nice big canyons and sweeping gullies but not much marine life except for the seals.

STAPLE SOUND

Staple Sound is approximately one mile wide and divides the two main groups of islands of the Inner and Outer Farnes. With a maximum depth of around 16 metres in the centre it is quite navigable, but, because of the proximity of Gun Rocks, Wamses Bus and some of the submerged reefs or 'shads' extending out from the western side, most large vessels give the Sound a wide berth. The tidal run can be extremely vicious and especially so on the spring tides. Large volumes of water are funnelled into the Sound on the ebb and flood tides causing a considerable amount of confused surface boil and choppy water.

The last section of the book covered a number of dive sites which are actually in Staple Sound, but these next seven sites are located more or less in the centre of it.

Dive sites

✶ ✶ ✶

55 37'.417 N 001 37'.599 W

This is a permanently submerged reef which can be located by using an echo sounder and motoring due south down Staple Sound, passing Gun Rocks 100 metres on the port (left) side. The reef lies approximately 450 metres past the end of Staple Island. The seabed goes away down from 15 to 24 metres before coming up fairly sharply to 10 metres and then dropping back to 28 metres plus. A double echo often registers on the sounder giving the impression that it may be a wreck; this, though, is caused by the proximity of a large sand and stone bank close by. The reef runs in an east-west direction with a small cliff face on both sides creating sufficient shelter from the very strong tidal run, depending which side of the reef you are on, but it is best dived at low slack water. The reef has lots of soft corals on it, while the odd crustacean may be found sheltering in the overhangs and crevices. Very often large individual pollack and shoals of coley are to be found hovering around the reef top. The steep sloping bottom on the north and south sides, away from the reef, mostly consists of stones and shell.

(2) ✶ ✶

55 37'.556 N 001 37'.256 W

Anywhere within half a mile east and south of the last dive site is in fairly deep water, between 28 and 32 metres, so there is the possibility of collecting a small bag of great scallops and queen scallops, although the scallop dredgers from Seahouses occasionally work this area too. The currents are very strong so it is advisable to dive at slack water and use a surface marker buoy because there is a lot of boat traffic around at weekends, during the summer months.

(3) ✶ (?)

The sand and stone seabed in this area is close to 20 metres with strong tidal streams and very little to recommend it, but I have been informed that last year some visiting divers on a random drift dive passed over the large upturned steel hull of a wreck half-buried in the sand. Unfortunately they were near to the end of their dive and, with poor visibility and a strong current running, they had not realised what it was

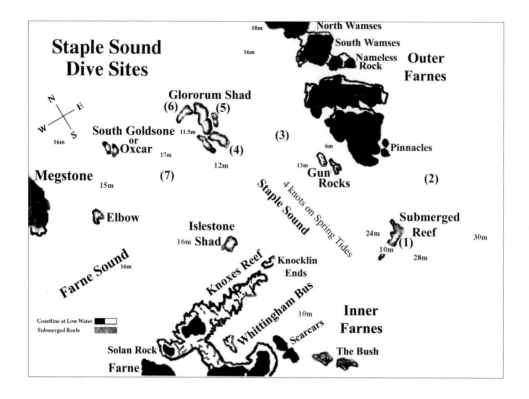

until they had shot over it. Who knows what it might be? Maybe one day the storms will turn it back over and it could make a worthwhile dive site. With the help of a magnetometer it should be fairly easy to relocate.

Glororum Shad

55 38'.165 N 001 39'.220 W

Glororum Shad, as its name implies, is the ancient medieval name for this permanently- submerged area of shallow seabed in the middle and towards the northern end of Staple Sound. It consists of a number of underwater hills which vary in length, at a depth of 5–8 metres. The surrounding seabed at 12–15 metres is mostly flat, stony and covered in a carpet of brittle stars. Tidal streams are very strong with overfalls developing in the proximity of the Shad during spring tides, so low slack water is the best time to dive the area and surface marker buoys are essential.

Unless you have a GPS, the easiest way to locate Glororum Shad is to motor away from Brownsman Island towards Megstone using the echo sounder: the Shad is approximately halfway over.

Dive sites

(4) ✯ ✯ ✯ ✯

55 38′.021 N 001 38′.767 W

The hill at the southern end of the Shad has a steep cliff-like drop-off from 5 metres to the stony sloping seabed at 12 metres, which is covered in brittle stars. This end is also probably the best and most interesting because it has plenty of crevices and overhangs, which shelter a few crustaceans and the rock sides are covered in soft corals. On spring tides, the thick two-metre long stalks of kelp which blanket the reef top are almost flattened, but it is still possible to dive and find some shelter in the many gullies which criss-cross over the 'hill'. Big individual pollack can often be seen weaving their way through the kelp fronds, while large resident shoals of coley are sometimes so dense they can blot out the light. Best time to dive is at low slack water or on neap flood tides.

After the dive it is worthwhile trying a spot of fly fishing because pollack and coley are very tasty, and when you hit the shoals you can catch them six at a time.

(5) ✯ ✯

55 38′.157 N 001 39′.040 W

The centre area of the Glororum 'hills', which run north-south in Staple Sound, is rather flat with only the occasional shallow channel on the top of it and, with the exception of a few little hairy spider crabs and multitudes of sea urchins, there is not much variety in the marine life. The eastern (seaward) side has a steep uninteresting wall to the flat seabed at 12 metres, while the west side is a gradual slope from the kelp-covered hill top to a boulder-strewn bottom.

(6) ✯ ✯ ✯

55 38′.203 N 001 39′.232 W

The northern end of the Shad slopes away steeply to 12 metres with a small wall running east-west and plenty of soft corals on it, obviously attracted by the strong tidal stream on the flood, although there are not many crevices to poke around in. This is best dived at low slack water or on the neap ebb tide.

(7) ✯

55 38′.000 N 001 39′.547 W

Midway between Glororum Shad and Oxscar (or South Goldstone) the bottom is very flat, stony and carpeted with brittle stars. Depths average about 17 metres at low water and there are strong tidal streams on both the flood and ebb. Not worth the effort, unless anyone wants to make a drift dive and take pot luck on finding something.

The Nature Reserve

This is an area of undulating hills, many with steep cliff-like walls, located approximately up to one mile northwest of the North Wamses, where interesting scenery and marine life can be found. However there is no record of any vessels having sunk in the area.

(8) ★ ★ ★

55 38'.644 N 001 38'.638 W

This site has very strong tidal streams, although it is possible to get some shelter behind the reefs, but it is generally a slack water dive. A 6-metre cliff wall at the southern end has lots of established soft corals on it and shoals of fish can usually be observed, especially during the summer months. The seabed is at just over 16 metres on a low spring tide, while the top of this mound is in 10 metres, with short fronds of kelp. It is over half a mile NNW of North Wamses but it is worth a visit.

(9) ★ ★ ★

55 38'.964 N 001 38'.903 W

This site is on the edge of steep slope dropping from 12 metres on the lowest spring tide down to 18 metres. Short seaweed covers the top but diminishes as you drop down the slope to a rocky seabed. There are a few crevices along the side of the hillock but tidal currents are quite brisk as the water surges up and over the top. This is an interesting area but there is no wreckage, just a variety of marine life to be seen. It is also best dived on a low slack tide.

(10) ★ ★ ★

55 38'.976 N 001 39'.057 W

This is the top of a very large submerged mound or hill at around 12 metres on the lowest spring tide, where very strong currents sweep up and over. Large pollack shelter behind it catching morsels of food, swept up with the current. A short distance to the north and south, depths drop rapidly to over 18 metres. A few crustaceans can be observed but divers should remember that this area is a nature reserve.

(11) ✲ ✲ ✲

55 38'.890 N 001 39'.310 W

Depths at the top of the mound are about 15 metres on a low spring tide, but it quickly drops away towards the west, north and east and tidal currents are quite fierce, with little or no shelter, especially on an ebb tide. Quite a variety of fish can be observed all around the hillock, but very few crustaceans can be found. These last three dives are best done using a surface marker buoy, because it would be quite easy to get swept away while surfacing.

INNER FARNE ISLANDS

The Inner Farnes consist of seven islands and islets situated 1.25 miles off the Northumbrian mainland and approximately midway between Seahouses and Bamburgh. They include the 16-acre, wedge-shaped Farne or House Island, which is the largest, then the smaller West and East Wideopens (or 'Wedums'), Big Scarcar and Little Scarcar, Knoxes Reef and the little Solan Rock off the western end of Knoxes Reef. The Bush is not an island but it covers a considerable area just to the south of the Inner Farnes and dries to 0.9 metres on a spring tide.

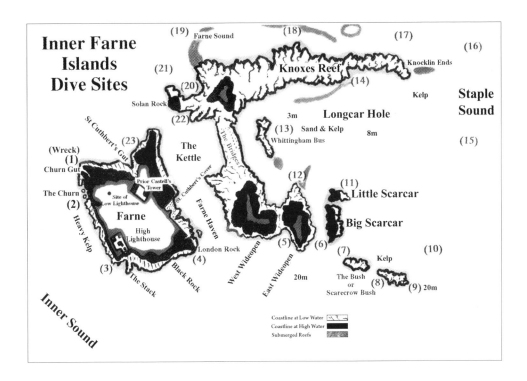

Farne or House Island

55 36'.992 N 001 39'.351 W

Farne Island, along with Staple and Longstone, are the only three islands open to visitors between April and September, but Farne and Staple have very restricted access during the breeding season. Like Staple, it has a magical attraction for the birdwatching community, who arrive at the sheltered landing site at St. Cuthbert's Cove in their hundreds during the spring and summer. The peaty soil covering almost two thirds of Farne Island is honeycombed with old rabbit warrens, attracting large numbers of breeding puffins that use the burrows to nest in and raise their chicks. Eider ducks and hundreds of Arctic, roseate, sandwich and common terns also nest on the grassy surface of Farne, while the rocky cliffs and ledges are occupied by hundreds of kittwakes, shags, fulmars, guillemots and razorbills. After so many years, the ever-clicking cameras of dozens of eager, chatting twitchers seldom disturb the nesting birds. The Pele tower on Farne Island is generally not open to visitors, because it is where the National Trust wardens live, although another three or four live on Brownsman.

Farne is the biggest island in all the Farnes, but surprisingly it has had only four ships wrecked on it in the last 160 years: two sloops, a brig and, most recently, the tug *William Follows* and a lighter on 12 March1934. It is not known whether anyone lost their lives on any of those vessels.

Knoxes Reef and Solan Rock

Knoxes Reef lies about 200 metres off the northeast corner of Farne Island and stretches over half a mile in an easterly direction on a low spring tide. The western end of Knoxes, the highest point, is the only part that is not submerged at high tide, along with the barren little Solan Rock, which is actually connected to the reef at low water. Knoxes Reef is also about 30 metres at its widest point at the western end, while below the surface at the eastern end, except for a couple of narrow channels breaking it, the reef curves a further 200 metres out into Staple Sound. This latter part of the reef, being so shallow, has caught out many an unsuspecting diving boat. The dry part of Knoxes Reef is comprised mostly of small stone and shingle and attracts a few nesting waders in the breeding season.

There have been a couple of recorded ships wrecked on the north side of Knoxes Reef: on 27 July 1852 the schooner *Breeze*, and on 29 October 1864 the brig *Myrtle*. Between Farne Island and Knoxes and just south of Solan Rock is the so-called safe anchorage of Farne Haven, a place regularly used by the trip boats when waiting for their passengers visiting Farne. On 27 December 1849, there was a terrible calamity in the Haven when the 327-ton paddle steamer *Britannia I* (1847 - Edinburgh and

Dundee S. P. Co.), which was sheltering from a storm along with a number of other vessels, dragged her anchors in the strong wind. Four of the boats – the *Arab*, *Nellie*, *Liberty* and the *John* – were sunk.

West and East Wideopens or 'Widems'

Opposite Farne and 75 metres to the south of Knoxes Reef, across a stony shingle ridge called The Bridges, which dries to 1.7 metres at low tide, are the two connecting islands of West and East Wideopens. West Wideopen, which has a covering of shingle and peaty soil, was where the monks in days gone by buried any drowned sailors they found, while East Wideopen, although it now has a fine covering of soil, is mostly solid Whin Sill rock. Oystercatchers and ringed plover nest and breed on the shingle areas of West Wideopen and the peaty soil provides a home to numbers of puffins. The craggy rock ledges on both of the islands during the springtime are full of nesting gulls, kittiwakes, shags, guillemots, fulmars, cormorants and razorbills.

Over the last 180 years five known ships have collided or been wrecked on the high barrier of rock on the south side of the two islands:

On 2 December 1818, the sloop *Kincardine* hit the wall between the islands.

On 31 October 1855 the schooner *Doore* of Drum smashed into the same area.

In March 1885, the schooner *St Fergus* foundered while rounding the southern tip of West Wideopen.

Since then two other vessels have ran aground on the lower boulders: the 320-ton steamer *Empire Ford* (1941 - Ministry of War Transport, Hull) on 11 January in 1943 and the 165-ton steam tug *Dunelm* (1883 – France Fenwick, Tyne and Wear Co. Ltd, Newcastle) on 18 June 1949, but both were later refloated.

Little Scarcar

55 37'.085 N 001 38'.404 W

Big Scarcar

55 37'.033 N 001 38'.387 W

The two little bare rocky islets of Little Scarcar and Big Scarcar lie 40 metres east of the East Wideopens across a stretch of water only a few metres deep. The islets take a real pounding in an east or southeasterly gale, remaining just above the surface at high tide by only 1–2 metres. Many of the trip boats use the narrow channel as part of their route around the Farne Islands to show the passengers the dozens of cormorants which usually line the top of the rocks during the summer months.

On 30 December 1852 the Newcastle brig *Manchant* was wrecked on the Little Scarcar and on 24 August 1899 the St Ives keelship *Rebecca* was lost in the same place. Since then, two more ships have run aground but were refloated.

The Bush (or Scarecrow Bush)

55 37'.062 N 001 37'.991 W

The Bush or Scarecrow Bush is the submerged shallow rocky kelp-covered ground lying approximately 100 metres east of Big Scarcar. The Bush dries to 0.9 of a metre on spring tides and the part that dries covers an area about 50 metres in diameter. The top is a dense kelp forest with lots of deep gullies criss-crossing it and at high water a colony of grey seals is always present around the top, so it is fairly easy to find without an echo sounder.

Eight known ships have run aground on The Bush over the years: three of them were refloated but two were wrecked with the loss of lives. On 3 March 1856, the 180-ton Banff-registered brig *Strive* was lost and seven of her crew were drowned, then the Gardenstown schooner *Lord Adolphus* was wrecked on 7 January and one man died.

Many diving boats pass over The Bush on their journey from Seahouses to the Outer Farnes without ever being aware of its presence, so every year the jagged rocks account for a number of damaged propellers and outboard legs.

Dive sites

(1) ✳ ✳ ✳

At co-ordinate 55 37'.033 N 001 39'.586 W, just a short distance from the northwest corner of Farne Island, lies the remnant of an unknown wreck; the site was surveyed in 2002, but little remains of it.

This is the northwestern corner of Farne Island, near to what is known as Churn Gut. The submerged, rather smooth, steep rock wall ends on the sand and stone seabed at about 7 metres and gradually slopes away to the north and west into slightly deeper water at around 12 to 14 metres. The area away from the wall has lots of medium-sized boulders with soft corals growing on them and clumps of kelp on the tops. There are fairly strong tidal streams in the Inner Sound running north-south with quite a lot of marine life about in the form of urchins, starfish and soft corals, and sometimes, if you're lucky, even the odd crustacean can be found hiding under the boulders. The steep smooth walls near to the corner of the island contain very few crevices but the north face at this point is very sheltered from the tide. Visibility can be very good out in the Sound.

(2) ✮ ✮

About one third of the way along the west side of Farne and just past The Churn is a rather boring dive site. Close to the island there is shallow water of only a couple of metres or so and the seabed, with a heavy covering of kelp to about 100 metres out, gradually slopes away and down to 15 metres before dropping more steeply to 18 metres onto sand and stone. There is the possibility of finding the occasional crab and a few whelks amongst the weed, but the tidal stream is strong and it is generally not even worth the effort of kitting up for a dive.

(3) ✮ ✮ ✮

55 36'.875 N 001 39'.358 W

A steep rock wall goes down to a few boulders and eventually onto sand at about 10 metres but there are some interesting creeks and gullies to explore near to the Stack around the southwest corner of Farne. Visibility in this particular area always seems to be rather tedious, however. Further out to the southwest the bottom slopes away rather steeply before levelling out onto sand and stone at 18 metres.

(4) ✮ ✮

A drift dive ✮ ✮ ✮ ✮

The southeast corner of Farne Island has a wall to the bottom at 7 metres and a very strong tidal stream runs between the islands in what is known as Wideopen Gut. Away from the wall to the south, the bottom slopes down steeply before levelling out at about 16 metres. On a spring ebb tide, an excellent drift dive can be made from Wideopen Gut over the very shallow seabed in the centre, past St. Cuthbert's Cove and down past the Kettle, ending up at Solan Rock. Anyone contemplating a drift dive should take into account the trip boats that use this channel all the time, so a lot of pre-planning is called for. Visibility is very often up to 10 metres in this stretch of water.

(5) ✮ ✮

55 36'.954 N 001 38'.718 W

The area on the south side between the two islets of East and West Wideopen is called Stamford Haven. There are a number of huge boulders lying close to the underwater cliff face at a depth of 15 metres. The seabed drops down in steps, a few metres at a time, with a few nooks and crannies between the boulders. Visibility is usually only moderate in this area and the rocks are often covered in sediment with very little marine life about.

(6) ✱ ✱

55 37′.131 N 001 38′.724 W

The centre of the channel between East Wideopen and the Scarcars is only 3 metres or so deep, with a strong tidal stream. There is little of interest and the seabed is rather bleak, but as you swim south, the seabed drops away in big steps to 18 metres and onto sand and stone where you can collect a few razor-fish and edible *Venerupis* clams under the sand; little hairy sea potato urchins can also be found here.

(7) ✱ ✱

55 37′.028 N 001 38′.137 W

Scarcar Gut is the channel between the Big Scarcar and The Bush. The area is strewn with boulders and shingle with strong currents and a depth of 10 metres all along the Gut to the east (seaward), however to the southwest (shore-facing side), a steep slope of small boulders drops away down to 18 metres onto a stony seabed. There are much better dives elsewhere around The Bush.

The Bush

(8) ✱ ✱ ✱ ✱

55 36′.983 N 001 38′.024 W

This site is a very steep slope down to 18 metres, strewn with small boulders and rocks, with a small reef wall at the top. The top is covered heavily in kelp, with lots of gullies and channels containing urchins, spider crabs, squat lobsters and other small marine life, as well as the occasional edible crab or lobster. The edge of The Bush drops away more steeply as you move southeast, towards the end, until it forms more of an underwater cliff. A nice dive, with moderate currents on neap flood tides, and visibility can be excellent during the summer.

(9) ✱ ✱ ✱ ✱ ✱

55 37′.058 N 001 37′.884 W

All along the southern-facing edge to the southwestern corner of The Bush is a first class dive, taking in some sheer cliff walls and brilliant overhangs. There are large crevices and gullies at the top half of the reef and lots of soft corals, etc. Depths drop to 18 metres onto stone and sand, with lots of big razor-fish buried in the sand, plus edible *Venerupis* clams can also be found about 5 cm under the sand. A dense bed of kelp covers the whole of the reef top, which has numerous channels and gullies criss-crossing over it. On the ebb tide, the water runs northeast into Staple Sound and there is a strong upsurge on the south side making diving difficult. Best time to dive is at low slack water and at the beginning of the flood. Visibility can often be excellent on this corner but young seal pups can sometimes be a nuisance on the top of The Bush.

(10) ✳ ✳

55 37′.118 N 001 37′.870 W

On the seaward side of The Bush, the reef tapers away to a flat pebbly seabed, although there are a couple of small, desolate-looking and sediment-covered reefs. Depths on this side vary between 12 and 15 metres and there is not much of interest, but one of the ships that was wrecked is supposed to be somewhere in this area, so it could be worth keeping your eyes open for any tell-tale-signs. The seabed on the northeastern side of Little Scarcar has a few kelp-covered boulders on it, at a depth of 11 metres, and then it gives way to sand and stone and slopes down to 20 metres away from the island. Currents are only moderate on this side and it is possible to dive around both of the Scarcars in one go, but beware of the frequent trip boats on the north and western sides.

(11) ✳ ✳ ✳

55 37′.123 N 001 38′.377 W

The seabed on the northeastern side of the Little Scarcar has a few kelp-covered boulders on it at a depth of 11 metres and then it gives way to sand and stone and slopes away to 20 metres, away from the islet. Currents are only moderate on this side and it is possible to dive around both the Scarcar islets in one go but, again, beware of the frequent trip boats on the north and western sides.

(12) ✳

This is a shallow kelp-covered plateau with a 2–3 metre steep rock slope at the edge that levels out onto sand. From this point it curves out in a northerly direction for 30 metres or so and then turns south and round East Wideopen. There is very little of interest and only 4 or 5 metres at the deepest point, but at low water makes an ideal sheltered first open water site.

Whittingham Bus or Newbiggin Bush

55 37′.131 N 001 38′.910 W

This is a small 'bus', 'bush' or reef that is covered in kelp and other species of seaweed. The top of the bus dries on a low spring tide, but underwater and nearer the seabed there are lots of overhanging ledges and crevices that shelter numerous forms of marine life. However, once the flooding tide runs over The Bridges (the shingle ridge that connects Knoxes and West Wideopen) it is almost impossible to remain in one place.

(13) ✷ ✷ ✷

55 37'.131 N 001 38'.724 W

The centre of the bay inside Knoxes Reef is mostly sandy bottom but at the western end and about 50 metres east of The Bridges is an area of undulating little reefs, covered in dense kelp and tangleweed, sometimes so thick it is difficult to push your way through. This is another ideal site for the novice as it is safe, shallow and with no current at all at low water, and there is always the possibility of catching a nice crustacean for lunch. Moving east and seaward, the kelp forest disappears and gives way to sandy seabed. Digging by hand into the sand can

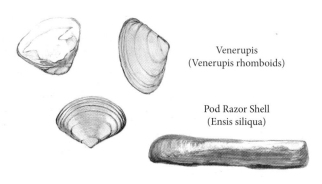

Venerupis
(Venerupis rhomboids)

Pod Razor Shell
(Ensis siliqua)

Clams off the Farnes

produce some nice juicy razor-fish and edible *Venerupis* clams that live just beneath the surface, although you have to be extremely quick to catch the razor-fish which burrow down into the sand like lightning. You can also come across little hairy sea potato urchins in the same area. The current is rather strong on the flood after mid tide and the surface can get a bit confused when the water races over The Bridges and comes south over Knoxes Reef from the north.

(14) ✷ ✷ ✷

55 37'.293' N 001 38'.538 W

This is another nice novice dive at low water, onto huge boulders inside Knoxes Reef. Carpeted in heavy kelp, the reef edge drops onto sand at 5 or 6 metres and is fairly well sheltered from any currents. When the water starts coming over Knoxes Reef on the flood, it causes a bit of disturbance on the surface, but is quiet on the bottom amongst the kelp and boulders. There is a reasonable amount of marine life under the boulders and a few whelks out on the sand.

(15) ✷✷

55 37′.341 N 001 37′.896 W

About 70 metres off the end of Knoxes Reef at low tide and a little south, there is a submerged kelp-covered reef. It is easy to locate with an echo sounder, because most of the bay is just sand. There is a steep sloping rock wall coming up about 3 metres to a rocky, undulating, kelp-covered plateau. Depth to the top of the plateau is about 10–12 metres and gradually deepens over the next 150 metres out into Staple Sound before sloping away steeply onto sand at 17 metres. The tidal streams running through the Sound are very severe, on both ebb and flood, at around 4 knots. It makes a good drift dive on the ebb tide, although there is not much to see other than kelp.

(16) ✷✷✷

At low tide and around 50 metres out from the end of Knoxes Reef, on the north side, is a four metre-deep channel, about 10 metres wide, which breaks the continuity of Knoxes. The channel runs north-south for around 150 metres and attracts a lot of rock-clinging life like soft corals, and there are a number of large boulders in the channel which sometimes harbour the occasional crustacean. Currents are very strong, and with so much kelp near to the surface on the flood, getting picked up by the boat can be quite a problem at low water. This is really a slack water dive.

(17) ✷✷

Close to the eastern end of Knoxes Reef, which is actually called Knocklin Ends, on the north side, is shallow water, with the flat rock seabed covered in thick kelp gradually sloping down to 7 metres, some way from the reef. There is not much tide to worry about on the ebb, but the flood runs fairly hard, especially near to the surface. The only marine life to be found consists of a few urchins and little weed-covered spider-crabs amongst the scattering of small rocks.

(18) ✷✷✷

Mid-way along Knoxes, off the north side, are a number of rock ledges and large boulder reefs which always have an interesting array of life on them, but the surrounding area is flat and you can waste a lot of time swimming about until you chance upon a reef. Not surprisingly, kelp is everywhere, so you need to look for the highest point in the kelp level. The reefs have lots of squat lobsters ('little men'), urchins, codling, the occasional crab or lobster and a few topknots, which are a small but rather thick-bodied type of flatfish. If you look closely enough, they can normally be seen slithering about on the roof of overhangs and ledges and make excellent eating. On the flood tide, the current can be rather strong and tends to run in two directions from this position, either east through Staple Sound or west around Solan Rock, depending exactly where you are in the dive sit. On the ebb, however, there is very little current at all.

(19) ✳ ✳

Two hundred metres north of the western end of Knoxes Reef is a large pile of flat rocks and some big boulders in 12–14 metres with only a thin covering of kelp. A few edible crabs can sometimes be picked up and large shoals of coley are often seen. Currents can be strong on the flood and very strong on the spring tide, but the ebb tide is only moderate.

(20) ✳ ✳ ✳

66 37′.250 N 001 39′.196 W

East of Solan Rock, the surrounding reefs form a quiet little horseshoe-shaped bay at low ebb tide and it is an ideal site for a novice diver. The centre of the bay is about 6 metres deep with very large boulders and dense kelp. Opposite Solan Rock and on the east (seaward) side of the bay, a big reef almost touches the surface and curves away from Knoxes in a northerly direction for around 200 metres. There are a couple of long crevices at the base of the reef and some huge boulders on the western side, near to the start of the highest section. Lots of squat lobsters and a few crabs can be found. When the tide starts flooding, the current runs quickly towards and around Solan Rock and past The Kettle, but on the ebb tide at low water there is little movement at all.

Solan Rock

55 37′.207 N 001 39′.277 W

(21) ✳ ✳

A drift dive ✳ ✳ ✳ ✳

Northwest of Solan Rock, a boulder reef stretches out about 50 metres and, even though it is in the main flow of water, has very little life on it. To the west, the reef slopes down to a stone and sand bottom at 14 metres with a rather strong current. The west side of Solan Rock itself has a bit of a wall with a couple of slots in it, while the surrounding seabed is sand and stone and of very little interest. From this position it is possible to make a drift dive on the flood, past The Kettle and St. Cuthbert's Cove, down to Wideopen Gut at the opposite end, but keep a watch for the trip boats.

(22) ✳

Behind Solan Rock and the extreme western end of Knoxes Reef, in The Kettle, this area is very sheltered from the main current, with long stringy whip-like stems of slimy weed and mosses growing from the shallow stony seabed. The type of marine life on the bottom makes it one of those areas where the water just seems to stagnate, as it must be by-passed by the main tidal flow.

(23) ✳ ✳

55 37'.068 N 001 39'.404 W

Roughly a third of the way along Farne Island, on the north side, is a deep V-shaped fissure, known locally as Assy Hole, although its proper name is St. Cuthbert's Gut. Names like that make me wonder if St. Cuthbert and all the other monks in medieval times would have used the Gut for their ablutions. (Have a nice dive!). I believe that the tower and accommodation were appropriately built next to the Gut for easy access, due to its shape and size, as well as because it is constantly washed out in a northerly swell. The shallow bottom is strewn with the rubbish from the nearby 'house' but there is nothing of any value.

Moving west from the Gut, depths are shallow and a small smooth wall to the seabed leads all the way along to the Churn Gut at the western end, but there is nothing of interest. Twenty metres north and out from the wall, the seabed slopes away down to 14 metres onto a stony uninteresting bottom.

At the eastern corner of Farne, facing north, the seabed slopes down gradually for the first few metres then drops down in steps to 12 metres, forming a small cliff face with a few slots in it. On the flood, the tide runs fast into the channel between Farne and Knoxes from this position.

MEGSTONE, SWEDMAN AND OXSCAR

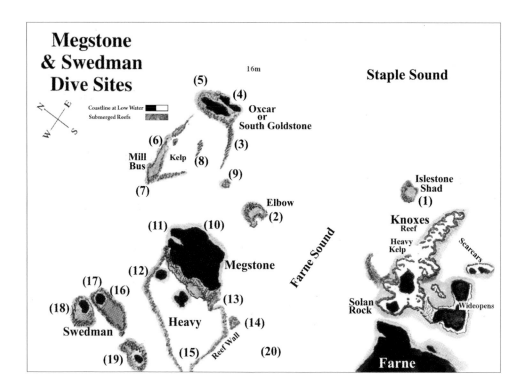

Megstone & Swedman Dive Sites

16m

Staple Sound

Coastline at Low Water
Submerged Reefs

N E W S

(5)
(4)

Oxcar or South Goldstone

(6)
(3)

Mill Bus
Kelp (8)

(7)
(9)

Islestone Shad
(1)

Elbow
(2)

Knoxes Reef

(11)
(10)

Heavy Kelp

Scarcars

(12)
Megstone

Farne Sound

(17)
(16)

(13)

(18)

Solan Rock

Wideopens

Heavy
(14)

Swedman

Reef Wall

(19)
(15)
(20)

Farne

Many of the rocky islets and submerged reefs around the Farne Islands are referred to as a 'shad', a 'bus' or a 'car', the medieval Northumbrian names still used on today's Admiralty charts. A shad or bus is the name for an area of shallow, permanently-submerged rocky ground, while a car is a submerged jagged reef that normally partially dries at low tide. The word 'car' is usually found as the last three letters in the name of a reef, as in Oxscar. This more isolated group of rocks, reefs and islets lie in a line, east to west, approximately one mile northwest of Farne

Island and Knoxes Reef. The best and easiest time to locate them is during low tide.

Megstone

55 37'.771 N 001 40'.515 W

The Megstone dries to 5 metres on the lowest astronomical tide and is the only island or reef in this group that is permanently visible at high tide; it can be seen clearly from Seahouses, nearly 3 miles away to the SSE. Being nothing more than a small, jagged, rocky island, holding no soil or vegetation, it is split halfway down in the centre at the northern end by a long, narrow V-shaped gully a few metres deep. Hundreds of squabbling cormorants and guillemots nest on Megstone and during the summer, when the young cormorants have left the nest, they muster together in large crèches, paddling around, moving and diving in unison and making a generally comical sight. At this time of year, the adult male birds have a beautiful, almost fluorescent green-purple sheen on their chest and a back of shiny bronze brown. Megstone has also been adopted by a large colony of grey seals, the majority of which are found at the southern end. This is probably due to the proximity of the low flat rocks at the southern corner, which are sheltered from a northerly swell and are convenient and accessible to them after high water. The island is governed by National Trust regulations and is a protected nature reserve, so landing on it is strictly prohibited. The National Trust wardens visit Megstone in their inflatable dinghy on a regular basis, checking on the birds and seals. The flat rock on the western (shore) side of the island dries out over an area of about 30 metres at low tide while beyond that, except for a few small ridges, the seabed, which is covered in dense kelp, just very gradually slopes downward for a further 250 metres to the west. It's not surprising that Megstone, given its location, has seen a few disasters over the years.

Ten known vessels have come to grief on the Megstone, three in which lives were lost:

The Dundee schooner *Eclipse* was wrecked on 5 March 1851 and all hands were lost.

On 16 December 1873 the schooner *Ocean Bridge* perished with all her crew.

In 1886 the schooner *Leda* was also wrecked, and lost with all her crew.

With the Megstone being so remote, ship's crews in the 1800s would have stood little chance of being rescued, especially during rough weather.

On 26 January 1949, the 616-ton Leith steamer *St Abbs Head* (1914 - A. F. Henry and MacGregor Ltd, Leith) ran aground but was able to re-float later without suffering too much damage.

Swedman Rocks

55 37'.654 N 001 41'.182 W

The Swedman Rocks are 648 metres to the west and inshore of Megstone and 1.57 miles southwest of Bamburgh Castle. On a low spring tide the rocks can easily be seen from Seahouses, which is 3.39 miles away to the southeast, and they dry to half a metre on the lowest astronomical tide; at other times, however, an echo sounder will come in handy. If you haven't an echo sounder, the next best way to find them is to approach the area from the direction of Megstone when the tide is in full ebb flow and look for where the current is swirling around the three highest points of the reefs, then throw a heavy shot weight with plenty of line on it, attached to a large surface marker buoy, onto the seaward side of the rock. The western (shore) side of Swedman is just a flat stony bottom in depths of around 10–12 metres, which gently slopes away to 17 metres over a distance of 100 metres or so. If you drop the shot on this side it will probably be dragged away in the tide, so make sure it goes into the kelp and gullies on the eastern side. Tidal streams are fierce and run at something like 5 knots on a spring tide, but if you can get down to the bottom, there is plenty of shelter behind the high reef walls. The Nunn Buoy, which marks the safe channel for shipping to the west, is 463 metres further inshore, to the west of Swedman, at position 55 37'.655 N 001 41'.622 W.

A considerable number of ships have come to an untimely end on the Swedman Rocks, which is only to be expected, as they are difficult to see at any time and are usually just submerged beneath the surface. Fourteen recorded vessels have been totally wrecked and another two grounded but later refloated. The three following vessels were wrecked with loss of life:

On 7 January 1830 the sloop *Waren Packet* was lost with all hands.

On 28 November 1842 the Sunderland ketch *Garent* was destroyed with the loss of all her crew.

The Dundee schooner *Jessie* was lost on 11 March 1847 and all her crew perished.

The last known ship alleged to have been wrecked on the Swedman Rocks was the steam trawler

Helios on 26 June 1940, but no records can be found of that vessel.

To date, all that has been found underwater of those 14 vessels are a few anchors and bits of a steel mast.

Oxscar, or South Goldstone

55 38'.049 N 001 39'.900 W

The Oxscar, or aptly-named South Goldstone, because it is roughly the same size and shape as the Goldstone five miles to the north, off Holy Island, is a craggy little 'car' roughly half a mile east of Megstone. It dries to 1.7 metres on a low spring tide and appears as two tiny islets, but just beneath the surface it covers a considerably larger area. At low water, during slack and neap tides, with a little wind blowing, it is notoriously difficult to see and seems to appear from nowhere, but most of the time the rock is submerged by just a few metres. During the days of sail, it must have been a terrifying experience, driven on by a storm, suddenly to run aground this far from land.

Tidal streams around Oxscar are very strong in both directions, but vicious during spring tides and there is an obvious 'boil' on the water surface over the top of the rocks. A large colony of grey seals have adopted the Oxscar as a resting place at low water and stay around and close to the top of it when it is submerged; they serve as a warning that you could be in danger of running aground.

Three known vessels have been wrecked on the Oxscar: the lugger *Paciline Defecamp* on 4 September 1850, Three of her crew were drowned.

On 9 January 1851, the Berwick schooner *Byron* was wrecked.

The schooner *Lilly Miles* from Douglas was also a total wreck when she ran aground on 25 August 1899.

Although I can find no records to show that any steamships were wrecked on Oxscar, there are some scattered remnants of a steamer, possibly a stern trawler, lying in the reef-top gully and around the west side of Oxscar. A boiler can be also found in about 15 metres over the north side, just away from the steep sides of the Oxscar; the seabed here is also quite colourful.

Dive sites

Islestone Shad

55 37'.682 N 001 38'.775 W

(1) ✷ ✷

Islestone Shad is one of those shallow rocky areas I mentioned at the beginning of this chapter. It is a permanently submerged, undulating rock plateau 5 metres deep, covering an area some 200 metres in diameter and carpeted with dense kelp, while the surrounding seabed, at 12–15 metres, consists of sand and small weed-covered rocks. The top of the plateau is rather monotonous, with very few gullies or crevices, and the steep slope all around the perimeter is of a similar nature. Occasionally there are shoals of coley and pollack swimming around, with a few ballan wrasse, small spider crabs and urchins, but overall it is a very boring dive site. Visibility is usually good but the site is well out into Staple Sound and is subjected to very strong tidal streams. The plateau is also difficult to locate without the use of an echo sounder, except at low slack water on spring tides when the kelp fronds are clearly visible on the surface, but the effort of finding it is hardly worth the bother. Probably the best way is to go to the north side and eastern end of Knoxes Reef at low tide, then motor in a northerly direction for about 300 metres. During a northerly swell, big rollers curl and break over the Islestone Shad and it is marked as such on the Admiralty charts.

The Elbow or Horseshoe Bus

55 37′.849 N 001 39′.988 W

(2) ★ ★ ★

The Elbow is another 'shad' or 'bus', a permanently-submerged area of shallow hilly ground and, as such, difficult to locate without a sounder. It covers an area of around 200 metres and is situated about 300 metres east of the south end of Megstone. The tidal.flow is strong so you could use the same technique as that for the Swedman. Look for it when the tide is running hard and this will reveal where the ground is, as the water boils over the top of the bus. Then throw in a heavy shot line with a large marker buoy and come back later; it is, though, possible to dive when the tide is in full flow on the flood, except during springs. When the visibility is good, the kelp fronds can easily be seen at low water. Depths are very similar to that of the Islestone. There is a lot of heavy kelp and a fair number of rock ledges and gullies but very few crevices or holes and the scenery is rather boring in general due to the flattish nature of the rock. A number of different species of fish can be seen, however.

At the southern end of the Elbow is a large, deep, horseshoe-shaped bay, with 4-metre cliff-like walls surrounding it, which is what gives the reef its name. Seventy metres to the west, the seabed is strewn with large rocks and boulders at 13 metres. There is a reasonable amount of marine life about, with soft corals on the southwest corner. Fifty metres south of here is a medium-sized reef covered in soft corals and a colourful array of anemones, but it is very exposed to the strong tidal stream.

Oxscar or South Goldstone

55 38′.049 N 001 39′.900 W

(3) ★ ★ ★ ★

This dive site is 50 metres off the southwest corner of the Oxscar, where a submerged reef wall some 3–5 metres in height runs away out from the Oxscar in a westerly direction for about 300 metres. The seabed at the base of the reef in 15 metres consists of sand and sporadic rocks with plumes of short kelp on the tops. The reef top, which has lots of boulders, gullies and channels running over it, covers a large area to the north and west and has a thick covering of kelp. At the northern side of this rocky plateau, the boulders and rocks have soft corals growing on them, which is a sure sign of the strong currents that sweep around the Oxscar. This is a nice dive where a fair amount of shelter from the current can be found under the long thick kelp strands and a good selection of marine life can be seen.

(4) ★ ★ ★ ★

An interesting dive can be made on the top of the Oxscar, with lots of life on and around it. Tidal streams rip over and around the east and west sides, so the best time to dive is definitely at low slack water or on neap tides. The sides of Oxscar at the east and southern ends have very steep, almost cliff-like rock-slopes down to 14 or 15 metres with the east side covered in a variety of marine growths, including soft corals and short weed. The top of the rock resembles a mini-volcano, as it is hollowed out with a canyon about 5 metres deep by 30 metres long, and lots of lumps of tangled wreckage have collected in the centre. It is well worth a rake about among the lumps of debris: very often you stand to pick up a few decent-sized edible crabs. To the west and northwest of Oxscar there are a number of large boulders with lots of soft corals on them and a kelp forest at 6 metres.

(5) ★ ★ ★

Twenty metres out from the Oxscar on the NNE end is a ship's boiler at 15 metres, with the seabed thick with anemones and soft corals clinging to the small rocks, making it a bright and pretty dive, but with very strong currents in both directions. Lots of prawns and shrimps can be found amongst the rocks. This is definitely a slack, low water dive site.

Mill Bus

55 38'.015 N 001 40'.247 W

(6) ★ ★ ★ ★

Mill Bus covers a fairly large area but at the northern end there are two large reefs about 250 metres long that stand 5–8 metres high, running east to west. In fact, the furthest reef west curves out nearly as far as the Oxscar, except for a couple of wide channels breaking its continuation. There are some nice overhangs and small cliff walls on the north face, all covered in a multitude of soft corals and hundreds of urchins. Many of the crevices hold resident conger and ballan wrasse and large shoals of coley and pollack swim above the long kelp fronds on the back edges of the reefs. The seabed on the north side of the most northerly of the reefs levels out at 14 metres. Here, the kelp thins out on a few low reefs, but there is not as much marine life about. Tidal flow can be very strong in both directions but, with a little care, it is quite easy to dive at any state of the tide. This is a nice, picturesque and interesting dive, providing you drop into the right place. On low spring tides, the depth to the reef top is only 3 metres at its highest point, but during a big northerly swell, the surface water breaks into a curl and the whole area should definitely be avoided.

The Wave

In the mid 1980s, my buddy Trevor and I were diving Mill Bus on a nice, warm summer's day and we thought the big northerly swell which was running at the time was nothing to worry about. I was in the water on my dive in the vicinity of the reef, with Trevor boat handling; this is the way we have always dived, one in the water and one in the boat. Half an hour into my dive, there was a surge of water and everything went dark as if a cloud had passed over head. At the time I did not think anything of it and carried on to finish my dive. The current had subsided as I had hit slack water right at the end of my dive. I surfaced, knowing I must be close to the place where we had anchored. I looked towards the Flatacraft (my little RHIB) and was amazed to find Trevor standing on the upturned hull, with gear floating around everywhere. He shouted for me to hurry and I quickly swam the few metres over to the boat and clipped my gear onto the side handles. All I could save was Trevor's demand valve, which had lodged in the coil of ropes beneath the hull. I climbed onto the slippery hull, we secured some ropes to the handles at one side, and after a number of attempts of slipping and sliding on the glossy fibreglass, managed to right the upturned boat. The engine had been submerged upside down for half an hour and the carburettors and fuel tank had lots of sea water in them. We tried desperately to start the 50-hp Mercury outboard but without tools, which had been lost with everything else, it was useless. We managed to bale the water out by using our hoods before beginning the long paddle back towards shore. By this time, unfortunately the tide was running hard, causing a bigger swell, while the wind was blowing us towards the huge mass of white water crashing over the Megstone. With some strenuous paddling using our fins we managed to pass the danger and carried on for another hour until we were caught in the tide going north. Relief came an hour later when we managed to attract the attention of an angling boat passing by half a mile inshore of us and they were kind enough to tow us back to Seahouses. We had no sooner arrived at the harbour when the coastguard arrived to ask a lot of questions, as he had seen us being towed back while off Bamburgh.

On the way back, Trevor explained to me what had happened. Everything had been OK, he said, and he had settled down to rest, when after about 25 minutes he heard an almighty roar in front of the boat. He leapt up to see what it was, and was horrified to find a massive wall of foaming white water, 5 or 6 metres high and over half a mile long, approaching him rapidly. Having no time to start the engine, he just dropped below the windscreen while hanging tightly onto the side handles of the RHIB. The huge wave crashed over the top of him, smashing the windscreen, ripping the bow dodger and tearing the echo sounder and compass off their fittings in the process. With the boat anchored, the awesome power of the wave dragged the RHIB down to the bottom, where she turned turtle, before surfacing again upside down. The force of water knocked the wind out of him and the pressure of being pushed down so quickly almost burst his ear drums, while the spare rope, which had been washed out from the bow section, got tangled round his legs on the way up. He said the length of time underwater felt like an eternity and he thought he was going to drown. After the boat surfaced, he dragged himself out of the tangled mass and out from underneath the Flatacraft, gasping for air, only to find his legs still trapped by the ankles. He then had to take another breath of air and submerge to free his legs before clambering exhausted onto the hull.

Fortunately it was a freak wave, being the only one that curled and broke, or the situation could have been a lot more serious than it was for both of us. We could not fathom out where it had come from, unless it was caused by the long trailing wake of a ship out at sea, which sometimes does happen.

Anyone contemplating diving in this particular area should also bear in mind that one of the lobster boats from Seahouses shoots his crab/lobster creels around here on a regular basis. He does not take too kindly to diving boats and divers being anywhere in the vicinity of his surface marker 'dans' or creels. and the creels zig-zag all over the place on the seabed. In recent years there have been a number of incidents in which creels have been cut open and the contents stolen, so it's not surprising that some of the fishermen have taken a disliking to the diving fraternity. I don't believe that many divers steal from creels, and I base my argument on the fact that fishermen bait and empty their gear early in the morning, long before most divers have managed to extract themselves from their beds. Crabs and lobsters, what's more, usually walk about in the open only after dark. In well over 30 years of diving, I have accidentally stumbled upon many creels and I can count on one hand how many contained a crustacean.

(7) ✭ ✭ ✭

55 37'.989 N 001 40'.501 W approximately

At the western end of Mill Bus, the high kelp-covered reef ends in a steep slope down to the seabed at 10 metres before low jagged reefs take over, running south-

THE FARNES & HOLY ISLAND

north in the same direction as the tide. The bottom gradually slopes down to the north, to 15 metres plus, where the kelp is very small and the seabed is flat rock. There are a few decent crabs about, but the tidal stream is strong and there is very little, if any, shelter from it.

(8) ✴ ✴

Fifty metres south of dive (6) and (7) is just shallow plateau of undulating, rocky kelp-covered ground, with little of interest unless you collect urchins, because there are plenty of them. Carry on south for another 100 metres and you arrive at a 3 metre wall, dropping down to sand and small weed-covered rocks at 9 metres. This is a very boring area and hardly worth the effort of getting wet.

(9) ✴ ✴ ✴

55 37'.947 N 001 40'.014 W

This site is about level with the centre of Megstone and directly south of dive (6). I stumbled upon it during a drift dive from dive (6) when the tide was flooding. There is a large 4-metre pile of flat rocks, resembling extra large paving stones in a heap, but spread out and forming some nice deep cracks and overhangs where all sorts of marine life shelter. Unfortunately the surrounding seabed is mostly rather flat rock with lots of short kelp.

Megstone

55 37'.771 N 001 40'.521 W

(10) ✴ ✴ ✴

On the east side of Megstone, and approximately halfway along it, is an area of large boulders covered in kelp with depths in the 10 metre range. The rest of the bottom is flat stony ground but there is the odd chance of picking up some crustaceans under the overhang of the boulders. The current is very strong on both ebb and flood, with very little shelter as it sweeps round the Megstone.

(11) ✴ ✴

55 37'.786 N 001 40'.548 W

Megstone is actually split at the north end by a V-shaped narrow canyon, running almost half the length of the island. The depth at the entrance is about 4–5 metres with kelp, but becomes shallower towards the centre of the island. If there is any swell on the sea, the canyon should be avoided, because the water is rammed right up onto the rocks in the centre of Megstone. There is sufficient room to navigate into it slowly but not enough to turn around, which means having to reverse all the way out and, because of the protruding underwater rock shelf, that can be a dodgy operation. Lots of tiny colourful nudibranches can be found on the walls close to and around the entrance of the canyon, but probably only the eagle-eyed, close-up underwater photographer will notice them. It is a pity that many divers don't look closely enough to spot these beautiful little gems but you do not have to be eagle-eyed to spot the silver streaks of cormorants and other seabirds as they flash past under the boat moored near the entrance. Depths at the north corner of Megstone are only around 10 metres but with very strong currents and the rock sides of the island are rather smooth. Topside, the rocks are 'ripe' with the droppings from hundreds of birds.

(12) ✶

A shallow weedy 3-metre reef runs out from the island with lots of tangleweed fronds waving from it. It is reasonably sheltered at low water on an ebb tide, but the current increases the further you go west from Megstone. A few little crevices but hardly worth the effort of getting your gear wet.

(13) ✶ ✶ ✶

A high, steep, sloping reef wall leads away south from Megstone for about 150 metres before turning west and levelling out onto the seabed. It is the edge of a very shallow flat rock plateau on the west side, covered in a dense jungle of kelp. There are very few crevices or overhangs and marine life is generally thin on the ground; at the southern end of Megstone there are a few overhangs which do sometimes bear fruit, though, and one deep slot at the top where a large conger lives. If you are interested in seals, there are dozens of them around this particular spot and they come up very close, especially the young pups. Best dived at low slack water or on the bottom half of the flood tide; it is best avoided altogether during spring tides.

(14) ✶ ✶ ✶

About 100 metres SSE of Megstone, there are a number of nice low reefs with only a moderate covering of long kelp strands and quite a good variety of marine life. The bottom is a mixture of boulders, sand and overhanging little craggy reefs, some with soft corals attached to them. A few crabs and maybe a lobster or two, lots of 'little men' (squat lobsters) and urchins can be seen in the crevices and a few big whelks can be found on the sandy part of the seabed. The current is fairly reasonable on the flood, except on the springs, but it is best avoided altogether on the ebb tide.

A close shave

I remember one dive on this site very well, because it was just after I had purchased a new and expensive 'wings-style' buoyancy jacket, complete with integrated weights, something rather new to me as I usually only wear one of these on diving holidays. I first tried the B.C. wings in Brada at the Longstone to check my buoyancy and weights and everything seemed satisfactory. We arrived at this site late in the afternoon after spending some time searching an area of seabed with the magnetometer and we were in a bit of a hurry. It was a high spring tide and on the ebb, with a lot of churning water flowing around the Megstone. I thought no more about it, though, having dived it dozens of times in the past. I quickly changed bottles, donned my new gear and slipped over the side of my mate's big RHIB with the intention of dropping straight down to the bottom into the thick kelp and out of the tidal run. Things didn't go exactly as planned, because I misjudged the position and dropped onto an almost barren rocky seabed with very little weed and no cover. The current, which was running like an express train, almost purged my valve and I had to claw my way inch by inch along the bottom towards a reef. I had almost reached the reef top and was pulling myself forward to get out of the current when I felt something bump onto the back of my legs. My first thought was that it was a seal pup bumping me and I turned quickly, but at the same time half stood up, facing into the tidal flow. Then everything happened so fast: my bottle slipped out of the harness, ripping the valve out of my mouth and at that same moment the current bowled me over along the flat rocks. I rolled over and over and tried to grab my valve, but the bottle, which was only held by the direct feed, was hanging right behind me and out of reach. The depth was only 10 metres, but when the valve ripped out of my mouth I had just breathed out and I was desperate for air. I was still rolling and could only grab the direct feed to the bottle and with the other hand press my drysuit inflation valve. It seemed like an eternity before I reached the surface, but I then found myself in the choppy riptide running north and close to the Megstone. I was dipping up and down in the waves, struggling to get my snorkel in and hanging onto my gear. I caught sight of the RHIB about 100 metres away and shouted for help. The boat was alongside me in seconds, much to my relief, because I was well and truly out of breath and just hung onto the boat for a couple of minutes before climbing on board. When I examined the harness, it was decided that although I had tightened the strap, I had not used a ratchet method to tighten it up. One of my buddies commented that he knew someone who would have taken the gear off on the seabed, sorted it out and put it back on! I asked him if that would have been while he was rolling along the bottom or before he surfaced, because I would like to have seen it. You are never too old to learn and I learnt something that day that I won't forget in a long time – and my 'wings' did not last long, either.

(15) ✷

This is a shallow, kelp-covered plateau and there is not much tidal movement or marine life below the kelp line, which gives it a stagnant appearance. There are a few half-metre reef ledges but no holes or crevices. Occasionally a few seals from the colony at the south end of Megstone play around, but that's about it.

Swedman

(16) ✷ ✷ ✷

55 37'.680 N 001 40'.962 W

In 7 metres, 150 metres to the east of Swedman Rocks in the direction of Megstone, are some nice gullies, channels and caves. One of the small caves is home to a large conger and, as a strange bedfellow, a 5-lb lobster. The dive site is quite sheltered from the main tidal flow because of the high reefs of Swedman, but because of this, everything is covered in sediment, making the scenery look dreary. The kelp is also a bit sparse, but overall it is not a bad dive.

(17) ✷ ✷ ✷ ✷

55 37'.658 N 001 41'.202 W

This is the northern end of a 200-metre reef covered in dense kelp and tangleweed, so thick on the top that you have great difficulty in pulling your way through it. A very small portion of the top at this northern end dries to half a metre on a big tide and it slopes down steeply on both sides to 10 metres. The west side is the most interesting, because of the amount of soft corals and various colourful anemones. There is a profusion of other kinds of marine life too, including a few crustaceans, which makes the dive worthwhile. A deep narrow gully splits the reef at the top and there are lots of soft corals on the walls. Continuing along the gully on the east side will eventually bring you to dive site (16). Down the steep west slope of Swedman Rocks, the seabed is just stones and sand. Moving south along the reef wall on the west side brings you to a horseshoe-shaped bay, surrounded by a steep overhanging cliff wall, complete with a number of crevices in it. Plenty of buck whelks can be found on the sand-and-stone seabed. Tidal streams around Swedman Rocks, especially at the surface, are very severe in both directions of the flood and ebb, but there is plenty of shelter by staying close to the reef. Care should be taken by the boat handler when picking up divers at low water, because of the proximity of the shallow reef tops and the presence of 2–3 metres of tangleweed that can stop a small outboard engine or damage a propeller.

(18) ✷ ✷ ✷

55 37′.639 N 001 41′.199 W

This is a very large rocky mound that has a tiny part of its highest point just visible on a low spring tide, drying to 0.4 of a metre on the lowest astronomical tide. The northeast corner of the mound forms a deep canyon between this islet and the last dive site, where the water funnels through like an express train and is strong enough to purge your demand valve. The top is covered in heavy tangleweed, kelp and soft corals. The sides of the mound are steep walls down to 12 metres on the west and north side with a rounded edge at the top and all are carpeted in soft corals. There are very few crevices or gullies in it except where the rock slopes down at the south end. There is a very old Admiralty pattern anchor lying up against the base of the west wall, but no sign of anything else. The tidal flow is very strong in both directions. It is most definitely best dived at low slack water, although there is a little shelter at the southwest side on the neap flood tide. The surrounding seabed is all stone, broken shell and sand and shelves away gradually to 18 metres. A few empty scallop shells are often found washed up at the base of the reef on the western side, which suggests there may be scallops between Swedman Rocks and the mainland.

(19) ✷ ✷ ✷

55 37′.560 N 001 41′.036 W

A kelp-covered reef, with its highest point drying to 0.2 metres on the lowest astronomical tide and the steep reef sides go down to a sandy bottom at 10 metres. There are plenty of gullies, with a fair amount of marine life in and around them, such as brittle stars, urchins, anemones and crabs. Although the tidal streams are very strong, this a nice, pleasant dive.

Farne Sound

(20) ✷

55 37′.351 N 001 39′.763 W

Farne Sound is the name for the rather shallow stretch of water between the Megstone and Farne Island, running west to east, with the majority of it being only about 12–15 metres deep. The bottom consists mostly of sand, broken shell, stone and small, weed-covered rocks. Currents are strong in both directions and the best way is to drift dive it, using a surface marker buoy. This is not a very interesting area to dive, but you never know what there might be lying around on the seabed, as quite a number of old ships have disappeared without trace or run aground and drifted off into the Sound before sinking. A couple of years ago, I was reliably informed by a local Seahouses diver of a very interesting bit of information regarding the chance discovery of what is referred to as 'the Holy Island Wrecksite'. It is rumoured to be lying somewhere between the Swedman Rocks, Farne Island and the mainland, where the maximum depth is only 17 metres on the lowest astronomical tide. During the reign of Henry VIII, there was an open clash between the Crown and the Catholic Church resulting in the dissolution of the monasteries. The King was also at war with the Scots and he assumed control of Lindisfarne in 1543 to garrison his military. During this period, much of the priory was destroyed to provide stone for his new castle. The priory church was converted into a storehouse 'for the king's use'. Then, in 1613, Lord Walsen, the Earl of Dunbar, ransacked what remained of the priory, removing the lead from the roof, the bells and anything else he considered of value. The ship carrying the stolen treasures sank in a storm shortly after leaving Holy Island and most of those on board were drowned. At the time this was looked on as an 'act of God's displeasure at his further desecration of the Holy Island.' As far as I am aware, nothing has yet been removed from the wrecksite and its location has been kept a closely-guarded secret. In fact, the person who allegedly discovered it does not dive anymore. It will certainly be very interesting to see what is recovered from this very historic shipwreck, if it is indeed the same one and if the information I was given is true. Unfortunately, the whole area is swept by very strong tides and with the bottom consisting mainly of sand and stone, it is very doubtful if much has survived. The one-star rating for this area would certainly rise significantly if the 'Holy Island Wrecksite' discovery is true, because there are many other ships, both ancient and modern, which must lie on the seabed in this area.

Dive Sites between the Farne Islands, Seahouses and Holy Island

There are a number of nice reefs just to the north of Seahouses. However, with one or two exceptions, there are very few decent dive sites in the stretch of water between Bamburgh and Holy Island because most of the seabed is just sand with a few rocks thrown in.

Shorestone Outcars

55 35'.593 N 001 39'.722 W

Located about half a mile north of Seahouses Harbour and a couple of hundred metres off the shore, the Shorestone Outcar is an area of very shallow sand and kelp-covered rocks that dry on a low spring tide. The Outcars are more or less in a line with the harbour entrance at Seahouses and they are a particular hazard to ships hugging the shoreline and approaching the harbour from the north. There have been a least six recorded vessels wrecked on the Shorestone Outcars since 1821, two of them where lives were lost.

On 26 February 1853 the Hull schooner *Nisus* was wrecked and three of her crew drowned.

The Sunderland schooner *Emerald* was lost with all hands on 18 October 1865.

As late as 1947, the Queensferry tug *Alexander* ran aground, but was later refloated with a minimal amount of damage.

(1) ✶

Except for some small edible crabs and a few pieces of twisted wreckage, most of which is well buried in the sand, there is very little of interest on the Outcar itself. At high tide there is only about 4–5 metres at the most over the top of Outcar and the tide is fairly brisk. I suppose there is always the odd chance that some long-buried artefact will emerge from the sand after winter storms, as happened to a lucky novice diver some years ago when he discovered a ship's bell lying just north of Seahouses harbour but, generally speaking, a dive on the Outcars is best forgotten about.

(2) ✯ ✯ ✯

55 35'.559 N 001 39'.436 W

On the seaward side of the Shorestone Outcars, four nice little reefs run parallel to each other in an east-west direction for about 100 metres and on low water spring tide, the kelp fronds over the top of them are visible on the surface. The small reef walls facing south contain numerous crevices and hold a variety of marine life, while the surrounding seabed is clean sand. Depths are between 4 and 7 metres at low water, but the tidal stream is fairly strong and runs parallel to the shoreline. There is shelter behind the reefs on the flood tide, but it is best dived at slack water.

(3) ✯ ✯ ✯

55 36'.755 N 001 38'.936 W

A little further out from the four reefs of the Outcars and about 150 metres south are two nice big reefs about 150 to 200 metres long, running parallel with each other, one behind the other and separated from one another by about 100 metres. The reefs are up to 4 metres high in places and run in a west-east direction, with the cliff sides facing south. Kelp fronds cover the reef tops while the seabed, which is often carpeted with common starfish, consists mostly of sand. A few blue creepy-crawlies and squat lobsters often shelter in the deep crevices and rocky overhangs at the reefs' base. Currents are very strong, especially on the spring tides, but you can find shelter behind the reef wall on the flood tide. It is also wise to use a surface marker buoy and to fly the 'A' flag too, because the trip boats pass quite close to this site on their return journey to Seahouses. Depth to the seabed averages around 8–12 metres.

(4) ✯ ✯ ✯

About 250 metres inshore of the Shorestone Buoy and around 250 metres north of the last dive site are two more nice reefs, also running parallel with each other in a west-east direction. They slope up out of the sand at the western end to about 3–4 metres, then slope back down on to sand after about 100 metres, but they have some interesting holes and crevices halfway along. The centre stretch has long kelp and tangleweed growing over the overhangs on the south cliff faces, while the surrounding seabed consists of sand and lots of common starfish. There is a strong tidal run, especially on the springs, and surface marker buoys should be used at this site because of its exposed position and the passing boat traffic to and from the Farnes.

Greenhill Rocks and Monks House Rocks

Greenhill Rocks - 55 35'.934 N 001 40'.661 W

Monks House Rocks - 55 35'.730 N 001 40'.441 W

The coastline north of the Shorestone Outcars has a number of rocky outcrops which lead onto sand just after the very lowest spring tide level. First, are the Shorestone Rocks, then the Monks House Rocks, on the south side of what used to be the ancient North Sunderland harbour, which the monks would have used when visiting Farne Island. A quarter of a mile north of the old harbour, the Greenhill Rocks protrude a bit further out to sea from the beach. They are hardly worth diving around, because they too just lead onto sand, below the low tide mark.

Over the last 200 years no fewer than ten sailing vessels have come to grief on the rocky outcrop of Greenhill Rocks, most of which, I should imagine, would have been driven in by heavy weather.

On 17 October 1865, the Whitby brig *Medora* was lost, along with her crew of twelve.

In 1922, a quarter of a mile north of Greenhill Rocks, the steam trawler *Saint Evelyn Joyce* ran aground while on fire and became a total wreck. Her boiler and engine can still be seen, half- buried, on a low spring tide and it is rumoured that her prop shaft, complete with brass propeller, are still buried under the sand.

Islestone

55 36'.500 N 001 41'.179 W

Half a mile further north from Greenhill Rocks is the long, high and very prominent reef known as the Islestone. It reaches well out to sea, drying to 2.1 metres on the lowest astronomical tide, at the point where the Bamburgh sands sweep back towards the Castle. The Islestone is a formidable barrier against the tidal flow, causing the water to funnel out seawards and creating a lot of surface disturbance. The change of direction of the sea here has caused a shallow sand bank to develop on the north side of the Islestone.

A total of seven vessels have been wrecked on the reef over the years, much of which is submerged and extends some distance out to sea:

In December 1821 the brig *Paragon* was wrecked and was a total loss.

The schooner *Joan of Wymiss* ran aground, was written off and salvaged on 14 March 1845.

On 6 February 1853 the Dunbar sloop *Helen* was destroyed on the reef.

The Thurso schooner *Cairnduna* was a total loss when she ran aground in rough weather on 9 March 1875.

In 1894 the brig *Inatje Baaf* from Groningen was wrecked and crewmen drowned.

On 13 July 1895 the Inverness schooner *Paragon* was also totally wrecked.

In 1916 the 3,764-ton steamer *Tredegar Hall* (1906 - Tredegar Hall SS. Co. Ltd, Cardiff) ran aground but was later refloated. (She was torpedoed and sunk by *UB 57* on 23 October 1917, 4.5 miles ESE of Flamborough Head, while voyaging from Melilla in Spain to Middlesbrough with iron ore).

On 24 May 1941 a steam trawler grounded on the reef.

(5) ✭✭✭

55 36'.500 N 001 41'.179 W

The Islestone has very little kelp growing on it compared with most other reefs, just long stringy weed, probably being too shallow for anything more. The long flattish nature of the reef is not very interesting with little obvious marine life on or around it except for masses of tiny mussels. It makes a nice starting point for a drift dive on the flood tide, though. Because of the strong tidal stream, you can cover a considerable area of seabed, including a number of submerged reefs that are not seen from the shore. They are of a similar nature to the Islestone, being black dolorite with the edges and corners being squared off like bricks and covered in millions of tiny little mussels. The south-facing sides of the reefs are by far the deepest, as they appear to have been scoured out by the tide, and because the south side usually has a few nooks and crannies to poke about in, they are also the most interesting. Depths are in the 8–10 metres range and I've had much worse dives.

Bamburgh Sands

This stretch of shallow sandy seashore with its magnificent rolling sand dunes has seen more than its fair share of wallowing, sinking vessels over the centuries, most of which would have been driven in by strong winds. The shallow seabed was made more lethal by the fact that there are a number of small submerged 'buses' lying just offshore and out of sight from the surface. A total of 19 various craft have been lost and at least half a dozen people drowned with them on this beautiful, peaceful-looking stretch of coastline. That peaceful scene changes dramatically, however, during a northeasterly gale, when huge waves come rolling in from over half a mile out to sea. Any ship caught in the surf would have been smashed to tinderwood in a matter of minutes. During the 18th and 19th centuries, so many ships were being wrecked all along this part of the coast that it comes as no surprise to learn that the people of Bamburgh had to organise a rescue system for shipwrecked mariners.

On 2 February 1823, the sailing boat *Mermaid* was washed ashore in the surf and one of its crew drowned. On 14 December 1842, the Lynn-registered brig *Paragon* was also wrecked and lost with two crew members. On 21 October 1894, the *May* of Stavenger was lost with all hands. In 1915 and 1917 two steam trawlers, the *Lucerne* of Grimsby and *Lord Strathmore* ran ashore but were successfully refloated.

It is very interesting to note that over the past 200 years, a number of Spanish gold coins have been washed up on the beach at various locations on the Bamburgh Sands. Although I cannot find anything about a Spanish ship sinking, records show that on 2 November 1462, two French caravels were wrecked on the sands, which could be the answer: they may have been carrying Spanish gold from trading or booty.

Black Rocks Point or Harkess Rocks

The next group of rocks on the shore are just north of Bamburgh Castle, where the lighthouse and coastguard station are situated, and at Black Rock Point, close to the southeast corner of Budle Bay. Only five recorded ships and fishing boats have come to grief on these rather substantial rocks, but at least nine people are known to have drowned.

In 1875 a Holy Island yawl was lost with five people on board.

On 9 March 1895, a Holy Island fishing coble was wrecked and the four crewmen lost to the sea.

One fascinating note in the records shows a ship called *Bonaventure* was wrecked in 1559. As records usually date back only as far as the early 1800s, why would the *Bonaventure* and the two French caravelles in 1462 be worthy of mention? There may be more to it than meets the eye.

(6) ✱

55 37'.000 N 001 43'.124 W

The rocks at Black Rock Point or Harkess Rocks drop onto sand and almost end at the low water mark so cannot really be classed as a dive site. Anyone wishing to catch a good flatfish for lunch could give this area a whirl, though, because I have seen many good plaice and flounders out on the sand, just off the rock ends.

Budle Bay and Ross Back Sands

Budle Bay - 55 37'.366 N 001 45'.056 W

Ross Back Sands - 55 38'.072 N 001 46'.202 W

Just north of Black Rock Point lies the wide sand- and mud-covered tidal expanse of Budle Bay, famous for its wide variety of visiting wading birds. In the 19th century, Budle Bay used to have a busy little harbour, where sailing vessels loaded up with stone from the nearby quarries, but it is now silted up by the shifting sands and only navigable at high tide by small vessels with a shallow draft. Only having a few metres of water over it at high tide, the bay is now used by ski boats and windsurfers because of its sheltered position. The sand bar at the mouth of the bay has the wooden and steel spars and frames from five wrecks, which protrude from it at low tide. It is certainly not advisable to wander around on the sand bar because of the possible danger of quicksand. Budle Bay has some fantastic lugworms that could be used for sea fishing, but it is now illegal to dig for them: someone was successfully prosecuted for the offence of 'causing suffering to lugworms' a few years back. There is also a lovely mussel bed in the river bed but that is now a private fishery. The rolling dunes at Ross Sands are a very popular nudists' spot and, not surprisingly, you get some suspicious glares when approaching too close to the beach by boat.

The harbour in Budle Bay was probably one of the main reasons why there were so many ships wrecked on the two-mile stretch of Ross Sands between Budle Bay and Holy Island. Budle Bay's small sand bar has seen as many as nine ships wrecked on it since 1833 with no fewer than five in which lives were lost:

In 1833 the Newcastle steamer *Ardincaple* was wrecked and nine of her crew drowned. On 28 October 1852 the schooner *Manly* was lost with all hands. The following year, another two unknown schooners came ashore during storms and were lost with all hands. On 4 January 1857 the Liverpool barque *Harmony* was wrecked and one of her crew was drowned. On December 14 1913, the 282-ton South Shields steamer *Glencona* (built 1907) came ashore, but she must have been refloated as she was later wrecked in 1926.

The main two-mile stretch of Ross Sands has actually had 31 recorded vessels wrecked or run aground on it, which must be something of a record for the British mainland:

In 1824 an unknown sloop was lost with all hands.

On 27 August 1837 the Newcastle-registered *Thomas* was wrecked with one man drowned.

The Whitby schooner *Euphemia* was blown ashore on 29 November 1848 and one man was drowned.

In 1853 an unknown sloop was lost with two of her crew when she became a total wreck after running inshore.

The schooner *Enterprise* was wrecked with the loss of all hands on 13 November 1876.

On 7 November 1890, the schooner *Flower of Ross* was lost with all the crew when she was blown into the shallow water of Ross Sands.

Ships approaching and attempting to cross the bar at the shallow awkward entrance to Budle Bay must have been part of the problem, but the strong local currents, combined with the topography of the surrounding land and islands, must also have played their part. They cause a type of void and would have interfered with the handling of sailing vessels during the strong northeasterlies off the Ross Back Sands.

SS *Coryton*

(7) ★ ★ ★

55 38'.358 N 001 45'.155 W

Left: SS Coryton

Below: SS Coryton transit marks

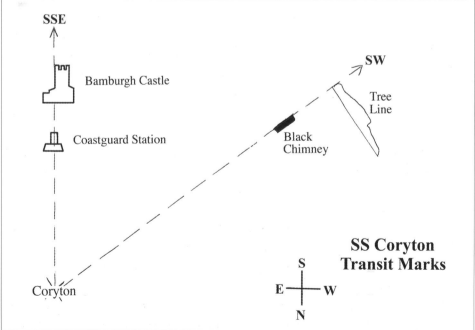

For divers, one of the most interesting wrecks along this part of the coast must be the SS *Coryton*. She was a cargo vessel loaded with grain which sank on 16 February 1941.

Unable to find out much about her history or sinking, I visited Holy Island and was able to track down the old coxswain of the last Holy Island lifeboat. He was at first very suspicious and the very mention of wrecks brought a torrent of verbal abuse about divers not being welcome on Holy Island, even though I had not said I was a diver. I spent about half an hour of gentle chat about the job of a lifeboat coxswain before winning enough of his confidence for him to relax a little – and then there was no stopping him. He was serving in the Royal Navy when the *Coryton* was wrecked, but he understood that she was bombed by a German aircraft a few miles northeast of the Farne Islands. With the ship being badly damaged, her captain decided to make a run for the shore at Ross Sands in an attempt to beach her. Unfortunately, the seabed off Ross Sands at low tide is shallow for some considerable way out from the shoreline, so when the *Coryton* came in she grounded about 300 metres out. The sea was absolutely mountainous at the time and the huge breakers which came crashing over the steamer were also pushing her beam-on to the sea. The crew soon realised they were in serious trouble, but their distress call had been intercepted by the coastguard and the Milburn lifeboat from Holy Island was already well on its way to their help. The lifeboat crew managed to rescue all 27 crew members of the *Coryton* but the ship's master stubbornly refused to abandon his ship. Throughout the night, the ferocity of the storm increased to such an extent that the ship's bridge and superstructure were washed off and smashed to pieces; the following morning the luckless captain's body was found washed ashore. The first mate was so depressed about the loss of the master and their ship that he would not leave Holy Island and, after many years, eventually married and settled down to live permanently on the island.

The ship is now broken into three separate parts and lies in 9 metres of water about 300 metres north of Budle Bay. Unfortunately the wreck is also at the whim of Ross's shifting sands and the rear half is sometimes prone to being covered, but the boilers and bow section, being the highest, usually stand well clear. The boiler tops are covered in kelp, are almost level with the surface on a low spring tide and are clearly visible. It is an ideal novice dive and shows exactly what can happen to a large steel ship when it is left to the wild elements of the sea. Care should be taken, as on all wrecks, because there are some very large jagged bits of metal all around. When uncovered by the sand, the three parts of the wreck are fairly substantial in comparison to most other shipwrecks so close in to the shore. It may stay covered or uncovered for a couple of years and usually there is a deep four metre scour in the sand all around each part. The boilers are split open and it is possible, with care, to swim through part of them, amongst the huge jumble of pipes and tubes. The wreck lies in a north-south direction, nearly parallel with the beach, while the stern and largest section is about 75 metres to the north of the boilers. The bows of the *Coryton* stand around 4 metres high and can be located about 250 metres southeast of the boilers, but they are rather more difficult to find and not really worth bothering about. Fair numbers of cod are to be seen, along with lots of nice mussels, and a few creepy-crawlies can sometimes be found under the steel plates, but they are not so easy to extract. This is a nice shallow second dive with very little current.

A friend of mine who, to save his embarrassment, will remain nameless, was diving on the *Coryton* when he put air into his drysuit and had the inlet button jam open. He tried to release the hose connector but that, too, acted up and wouldn't disconnect. He quickly filled up like the Michelin man and shot to the surface, where his fins were pushed out from his feet and he was unable to bend his arms or legs. It all happened so fast that his buddy had not seen the incident. Luckily he was outside the wreck in a depth of only 7 metres and with the boat anchored very close by. He used his wrist and caught the ropes on the RHIB with his crab hook where he was promptly helped out of the predicament. It was a laughable situation but could have resulted in a tragedy on a deeper wrecksite.

The *Coryton* (Official No.148303) was a steel-hulled 4,553-ton British steam cargo ship measuring 121.13 m in length, with a 16.15-m beam and a 7.49-m draught. William Gray and Co. Ltd, West Hartlepool built and completed her as Yard No.1009 in September 1928; she was launched on 2 August 1928 for Sir James Herbert Cory, Bart., at Cardiff. The single bronze screw was powered by a 423-nhp, three-cylinder triple expansion steam engine that used three single-ended boilers working at a pressure of 180 psi, with nine furnaces and giving 10 knots. The cylinders measured 66.04 cm, 106.68 cm and 177.8 cm with a 121.92-cm stroke (26 in., 42 in. and 70 in. with a 48-in. stroke). Central Marine Engineering Works at West Hartlepool manufactured the engine and ancillary machinery. She had one steel deck and a steel shelter deck with freeboard, six bulkheads cemented and bulkheads to the shelter-deck and a 9.7-m forecastle. Lloyd's classed her as 100A1 and her designated code recognition signal letters were: GSPV.

From 1932, British Steam Shipping Co. Ltd, Cardiff was the registered owner and J. Cory and Sons Ltd was the manager.

The History of the Seahouses Lifeboats by J. Morris; LR 1940–1941 No.72741 (C); LCR 1941, p.9 (g); LR 1930–1940; Starke/Schell Registers.

Tree o' the Houses

(8) ★★★

55 39'.263 N 001 43'.072 W

Tree o' the Houses is a shallow 'bus' covering an area of about a quarter of a mile in diameter and about two miles northeast from the position of the *Coryton*. It is fairly easy to locate when the tide is running by heading north from the Megstone towards the white pyramid-shaped landmark on Holy Island until you are approximately halfway between the two islands. You will then notice the area where water surges up over the bus, causing a lot of swirls and eddies. Depths over the bus are 7–10 metres with the highest part covered in a thick kelp bed. The middle of the bus is rather boring undulating rock with very few crevices and not much of interest, but plenty of urchins and small crabs. Around the edge on the western and northern sides there are small reef walls and lots of soft corals and anemones. Occasionally, the odd lobster or crab can be found under the overhangs at the reef' base, but it is a slack water dive because the tidal streams are very strong. It is worth bearing in mind too, that the Tree o' the Houses is a very exposed site and that there is very little passing boat traffic if you require help. Surface marker buoys are essential here.

Goldstone Rock

55 40'.240 N 001 43'.451 W

The Goldstone is about one mile further and almost directly north from Tree o' the Houses. It is also about 2.5 miles east of Holy Island and marked by a green conical buoy, approximately 150 metres inside (west of) Goldstone Rock, with the word 'Goldstone' painted on it. The rock dries to 1.7 metres on a spring low tide and is the western end of a submerged reef called the Stiel Reef, which slopes gradually down in a southeasterly direction over a distance of about 200 metres. The Goldstone Rock has been a serious hazard to shipping over the years; it was not buoyed in the old days and is so small and so far from land that most ships' crews would have been unaware of it until it was too late.

Among some of the ships known to have met their fate on this obstacle since 1823 are:

The brig *Augusta* when she ran onto it on 2 February 1823 and was lost with all hands.

The sailing vessel *Martha*, which was wrecked and lost on 5 July 1827.

The steamer *Northern Yacht* was alleged to have struck the Goldstone Rock and sunk with the loss of 23 passengers and crew on 11 October 1838, but newspapers of the day gave a different account.

The *Northern Yacht* sailed from Newcastle down to North Shields where three passengers embarked. She then left the Tyne for Leith at 0900 hrs on Thursday morning; however – and incidentally – the master's dog refused to go on board just before she sailed. The dog was beaten and put on board the ship, but it jumped ashore and ran away, adopting another vessel to sail on.

After leaving the Tyne, the *Northern Yacht* called into North Sunderland (now Seahouses) to put a passenger ashore, even though the master was not very happy to do so because of the prevailing storm force winds. The steamer had on board somewhere in the region of ten passengers and 13 crew, including a stewardess, the only woman, and 10–15 tons of iron which was being transported on the deck.

The lighthouse keeper of the Inner Farne had observed the vessel passing through the Farne Islands at 1700 hrs on the Thursday afternoon, the wind being at northwest; however, he also stated that, a 'perfect hurricane' blew that same evening. Following a statement by Captain Pattinson at Spittal Custom House, who through his glass witnessed a steamer apparently in distress some distance away, about one hour after the steamer was seen to pass Holy Island, it was presumed from a further report in the *Newcastle Journal* that the *Northern Yacht* probably sank somewhere in Berwick Bay. It was stated by various newspapers of the time, including *The Times*, that the vessel was not in a very seaworthy condition and that the iron on her deck would have caused her to be even more unstable. Fishermen from Eyemouth reported that a fair quantity of wreckage had been driven ashore on that coast, amongst which were some long, green-painted seats, such as used on the quarter-decks of steam vessels.

The *Dundee Courier* stated:

> The Northern Yacht was a slightly-built river steamer, very long in her shape and by no means fitted for contending with heavy seas. For some time she has plied between Dundee and Leith but was never reckoned a secure boat. We have several times made the voyage on board her, but with some alarm, arising from strange methods adopted in managing her boilers. It is not many weeks since an article appeared in the *Morning Gazette* condemning the *Northern Yacht* as a means of transportation, because machinery went wrong and she was obliged to trust in her sails.

The *Northern Yacht* passenger paddle steamer was completed at Glasgow in 1835 by Messrs R. Barclay for Mr Robert Barclay who was the registered owner. She was put to Lloyd's for classification but Lloyd's refused to grade the ship, reporting that she was more a river boat and not suitable for open sea voyages. The steamer was subsequently used over the next couple of years for making return trips from Glasgow down the Clyde to Ayr; in April 1838 the hull was eventually surveyed at Newcastle.

The Times, Tuesday, 23 October and Tuesday, 30 October 1838, p.6.

Pegasus, Paddle Steamer

55 40'.327 N 001 43'.591 W approximately

The most famous ship to be wrecked on the Goldstone and definitely the wreck with the biggest loss of life was the paddle steamer *Pegasus* on Wednesday, 19 July 1843. She left Leith with 50 passengers aboard on her regular trip to Hull and, at approximately 0029 hrs on a calm, clear night, struck the rock. Many of the passengers were still in their beds and at first totally unaware of what had happened, then panic broke out. Some of the crew and passengers scrambled into a lifeboat without clearing both ropes just as the captain ordered the great paddle wheels be put into reverse in an attempt to pull the ship back off the rock. The lifeboat overturned and was swamped by the paddles. The engines were stopped, but too late to save most of the people in the boat. As the vessel began to fill up with water, several people knelt in prayer on the quarter deck with a Rev. Mackenzie. In half an hour she went down, sucking many of the people down with her. Only 8 feet of mast were left showing and the sea was filled with bodies and screaming, dying people. Before she went down the mate managed to burn two rockets and a blue light, but to no avail.

One seaman, who was a passenger at the time, was in attendance with an invalid gentleman and by almost superhuman exertions managed to save himself. He gave the following account:

> I have been a seaman for about 18 years but was recently in attendance upon Mr Torry, who was one of the passengers on the *Pegasus* when she went down. I think it was about 20 minutes past twelve when the vessel struck. I was down in the cabin lying on a sofa and when I found that the vessel had struck, I ran on deck and having seen the state of matters there I went down to the cabin for Mr Torry. I told the passengers below that I believed the ship had struck, but they did not seem to comprehend what I meant. Some of the passengers, chiefly the ladies, were in bed. When I reached the deck with Mr Torry, I saw the crew in the act of lowering the lifeboats. I put Mr Torry in the starboard quarter-boat, when it was in the act of being lowered; and when it reached the water I jumped in myself. There were about nine of us in the boat. A lady, I remember, was sitting in

the bow. When we were in the boat there was a cry from the quarter-deck to 'stick to the ship'. At that moment the engines were set in motion and the boat, being hooked to the ship's stern, but unhooked at the bow, the back-water raised by the paddles filled the boat and upset her, throwing the passengers into the sea. I got hold of the ship's rudder chain and the chief-mate having thrown a rope to me, I got into the ship again. Seeing the danger increasing, I undressed myself to prepare for my life and laid my clothes upon the companion. By this time the engine had stopped and the ship was fast settling by the head. Looking around me, I saw the Rev. Mr Mackenzie on the quarter-deck praying, with several of the passengers on their knees around him. Mr Mackenzie seemed calm and collected. All the passengers around him were praying also, but Mr Mackenzie's voice was distinctly heard above them all. I heard the Captain say that we must do our best we could for ourselves. I saw a lady with two children, close beside me on the companion, calmly resign herself to the Almighty: the children seemed unconscious of the danger, for they were talking about some trifling matter. When I found the vessel fast filling, I leaped overboard: and the Engineer and I were the first drawn into the sea by the suction occasioned by the vessel sinking. I soon got up again, however, and got hold of a plank and the steps which led to the quarter-deck. The Stewardess attempted to get hold of me, but I extricated myself from her to save my own life. By this time the scene was a most dismal one; the surface of the water was covered in the dead and the dying, the screeching was fearful. One of the Firemen also tried to get hold of the plank which I had, but I swam away from him. I remained floating about till half past six, when I was picked up by a boat from the *Martello*, I was then about a mile from the wreck and people in the *Martello* for some time did not observe me, till I attracted their attention by waving a stick. One little boy kept himself afloat for about three hours on part of the skylight covering and made great exertions to save himself, but he sank at last. His body was still warm when he was picked up. I was once wrecked before about twenty years ago, off the coast of St Domingo, when I was three days and nights on a reef. It was the experience I learnt then which gave me the idea of taking off my clothes before leaping into the sea.

The Rev. Mr Mackenzie mentioned above was a devoted Christian, being the former pastor of the Independent Church in Nile Street, Glasgow and later Tutor of the city's Theological Seminary. At dawn the *Pegasus'* sister ship *Martello*, en route from the opposite direction, arrived at the scene to find only six people still alive; the mate, the engineer, the ship's carpenter, one seaman and two passengers. In an account of what happened, it appears that the passengers and crew were responsible for their own misfortune when they panicked, upsetting and swamping the lifeboats which were their only means of escape. Herring fishermen, returning to Holy Island after a night's fishing, assisted in the rescue and, after picking up everybody they could find, both dead and alive, the *Martello* continued on her journey to Leith.

The disaster brought national interest and it was reported in the *Illustrated London News* on 19 August 1843:

> As proof of the morbid feelings of the British public, it may be mentioned that the Holy Island, scene of the disastrous wreck of the *Pegasus*, is daily visited by throngs of fashionably dressed persons, who were attracted thither by the most idle and most unveiling curiosity. One day last week, two open carriages, filled with ladies and gentlemen, and drivers in bright red livery forming most dashing and distinguishing equipages, visited the Island. They were said to be a party of bathers from Spittal. They had a large bugle or French horn with them, by means of which they awoke to the echoes of the dreary sands in their progress and astonished the inhabitants on the shore. It is said that the party formed a deputation from the Royal Humane Society, but the rumour has not been authenticated.

A type of person we still see today, rushing out to gaze at disasters. The *Illustrated London News* goes on:

> Divers employed on the Pegasus steamer at Holy Island have succeeded in picking up an additional number of dead bodies.

On 11 November 1843 another quote from the same paper read:

A relic of the *Pegasus*.

> The *Journal des Débats* states: 'A few days since, a bottle was found on the coast of Holland, containing a slip of paper, on which was written *Pegasus* steamer, to Fern Islands, night of Wednesday, July 1843. In great distress: struck upon the rocks. On board 55 persons, vessel must go down, and no Grace Darling.'

Although how anyone on a sinking ship and in panic would have the presence of mind to sit down, calmly write a letter and place it in a bottle makes me suspect the work of another twisted personality.

The wreck of the paddle steamer *Pegasus* lies midway between the Goldstone Rock and St Nicholas Rock, in a general depth of 15 metres on the lowest astronomical tide. The wooden hull has long since gone, but the boiler and steam engine can still be seen. The seabed is quite flat, with numerous little mussels attached to everything and lots of various types of flatfish.

Other vessels to perish after striking Goldstone were:

The schooner *Euphemia* on 9 January 1848; she was lost with all hands.

On 9 January 1851, the schooner *Lady Panmure* was wrecked and four of her crew were drowned.

The schooner *Fifeshire* came to grief when she struck the Goldstone Rock on 14 October 1852 and was lost with all hands.

The schooner *Cheviot* was wrecked and crewmen lost on 2 October 1853.

In December 1856, the wooden schooner *Jean and Jesse* came to grief when she was lost with all hands.

On 5 June 1860 the schooner *Peace and Plenty* was wrecked and lost with all of her crew.

On 20 December 1863 the schooner *Maid of Aln* was also lost in the same position, again with all hands.

At 2230 hrs on the night of Wednesday, 3 May 1876, the screw steamer *Calcium*, belonging to the Kirkcaldy and London Shipping Co., was voyaging from Middlesbrough to Leith with a cargo of pig iron when she struck the Goldstone Rock. The crew launched one boat and the steamer then floated off the rock and sank in 8 fathoms (14.63 m). Six of the crew were left struggling in the sea. Four men who were in the boat managed to pick up one of their comrades and then made for Holy Island, where they reached at 1300 hrs. The master and one sailor clung to the steamer's mast, where they remained until 0400 hrs the following morning when local fishermen rescued them. Three of the crew, the mate and two sailors were drowned.

Both steamer and cargo were covered by insurance. Her master, Captain Hogg was reprimanded at a subsequent enquiry but did not loose his ticket.

The *Calcium* (Official No.58421) was an iron-hulled 226-ton coastal steam cargo vessel, completed as Yard No.44 by Bewley Webb at Dublin and launched on 13 April 1870 for Kirkcaldy and London Shipping Co. She measured 42.79 m in length, with a 5.19-m beam and a 3.12-m draught. The single screw was powered by a 45-hp, two-cylinder compound steam engine that used one boiler. Rankin and Blackmore manufactured the machinery. Port of registration was Kirkcaldy.

The Times, Friday, 5 May 1876, p. 5.

On 30 October 1876, the Folkestone brigantine *Attwood*, which was on passage from Granton for Boulogne with a cargo of coal, struck the Rock at 0900 hrs and sank; the crew was saved, but the vessel was a total loss.

The steamer *Arbutus* sailed from Aberdeen in ballast on 13 January 1890 for passage to Seaham, but on 17 January 1890 she stranded on the Goldstone Rock; she was carrying a crew of twelve and four passengers. The sea was calm and the people all landed safely, but soon after they left the ship it broke in two, slid off the rock and sank.

The *Arbutus* (Official No.18205) was an iron-hulled 356-ton passenger steamer, completed by T. Toward at Newcastle and launched on 1 November 1854. She measured 54.86 metres in length, had a 7.1-m beam and a 3.65-m draught. The single iron screw was powered by a 75-hp, two-cylinder simple steam engine that used one square boiler. The cylinders measured 87.63 cm and 76.2 cm (34.5 in. and 30 in.). In 1884 she was renamed *Por* and registered to J. Tulloch and Co. of Aberdeen. Between 1884 and 1890 she was renamed *Arbutus*.

The Times, Saturday, 18 January 1890, p.7.

Interestingly, the bell from this little vessel was auctioned by Jim Railton near Durham in 2005, so divers obviously recovered it.

It has also been suggested that the 454-ton steamer *Gothenburg*, built in April 1854 by Scott Russell, struck the Goldstone Rock and sank in 1890. In May 1913 the 113-ton steam trawler *Scottish Prince,* built in 1899 by Eltringham at Stone Quay, was also wrecked on the Goldstone. And there were many more. .

(9) ★ ★ ★ ★ ★

55 40'.240 N 001 43'.451 W

The top of the Goldstone is mostly bare rock with a few strands of seaweed clinging to it, while the seaward, eastern part is a high, gradually-sloping reef covered in kelp and tangleweed. The western side, however, is a sheer face to 10 metres and absolutely covered in bunches of beautiful large plumose anemones. The seabed slopes steeply down to the west and south, levelling out at about 15–18 metres, and the bottom here is one big scrapyard of wreckage, where ships over the last two centuries seemed to have simply piled on top of each other. The tidal stream is very strong on the western end and over the reef top, but there is adequate shelter on the north and south sides of the Goldstone, depending on which way the tide is running. The site is best dived at low slack water on neap tides when the rock is showing above the surface. On springs there is very little slack water time and it is best avoided due to the ferocity of the tidal run. The site is very exposed, with very little passing traffic, and it is a long haul from either Beadnell or Seahouses so extra care should be taken. This is a lovely dive, where anything could turn up.

Stiel Reef

55 40'.229 N 001 43'.384 W

The Guzzard

(10) ★ ★ ★ ★

55 39'.776 N 001 43'.024 W

The Guzzard is almost half a mile SSE of the Goldstone and has the same very strong tidal streams. The Guzzard is actually two mini mountain ridges with a long deep valley running between them and both have steep sloping sides. There are not many holes or crevices but some excellent crabs can be found around the reef sides and large shoals of pollack and coley are attracted to the reefs. During big seas, surf breaks over the top of the ridges which are only 4 or 5 metres beneath the surface, while the surrounding stony seabed is between 12 and 15 metres. This is definitely a slack water dive, and an interesting one that is in need of more exploration.

St Nicholas Rock

(11) ???

55 40'.440 N 001 43'.744 W

To date we have not dived on this rock, which looks as if it could be a good dive site. It is only 5 metres below the surface and has a drop to the seabed of 7 metres. Surf also breaks over the top of this reef during heavy seas and it has the same strong tidal run as that around the last two dive sites. Its position is about 400 metres NNW of the Goldstone and it should be quite easy to find, especially at mid-tidal flow.

Burrows Hole

(12) ★ ★ ★ ★

55 39'.770 N 001 47'.322 W

Just to the south of *Lindisfarne* castle and 50 metres or so out from the stony reef called Long Ridge or Burrows Ridge, according to the Admiralty chart, there is a wrecksite, marked down on the Admiralty chart as a navigational hazard, which is possibly that of the *Caroline*. At low water, the depth is only around 2–3 metres and the visibility can often be excellent. For anyone who enjoys mussels, the Burrows Hole trench is a great dive, as the sides and seabed are covered in big juicy ones. On the flood tide from low water, however, the current runs inside (east side) of the island like a mountain river. The bar at low tide is also very shallow and only about 2 metres or so deep, but as you come to the southern end of the trench, it drops steeply away to 15 metres and there is a whirlpool affect on the surface. We found that, as the sea ebbs and floods around the island, the tide is drawn from both ends and meets at the lowest point, causing the whirlpool which must have scoured the hole out over hundreds of years. The 10–12 metre trench is narrow and V-shaped and stretches for over half a mile with almost sheer sides and little variation in depth. The steep trench walls and seabed are one dense concentration of mussels but the current runs so hard along the bottom that it is difficult to stop long enough to pick any up.

LINDISFARNE OR HOLY ISLAND

Remains of Lindisfarne priory

Lindisfarne, often now referred to as Holy Island, is 6 miles northwest of the Farne Islands and is linked to the mainland by a one-mile long tidal causeway. The name derives from the medieval name of 'farne', meaning 'retreat', while 'lindis' is an ancient word for 'a small tidal river adjacent to the island'. The nearest village on the mainland is Beal, two miles from the causeway.

The Great Whin Sill, the volcanic seam of rock that forms the Farne Islands, is also present on Lindisfarne. At the southern end, the dolorite dyke forms some spectacular sights, particularly at the island's castle. Very similar to Bamburgh, it is a natural fortress where the dolerite intrusion is about 65 metres wide and is what the castle is built on. The dyke disappears into the Ouse, perhaps as a

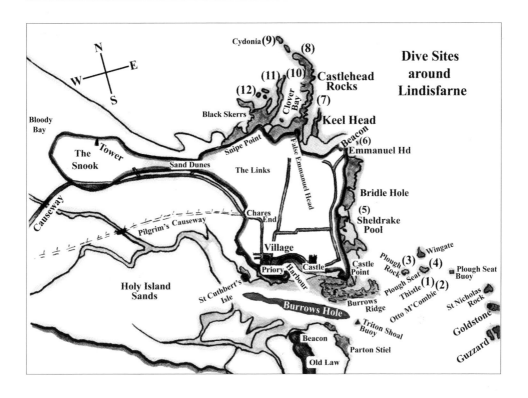

Looking northeast at Lindisfarne Castle

result of faulting, but reappears in the dolerite ridge south of the island's village. St Cuthbert's Isle, where the saint built his chapel cell, is also formed from the dolerite. The east coast of the island is mainly a platform of sandstone, with the lower coastal cliffs having a covering of boulder clay. The north shore is a fossil hunter's delight, because the extensive acres of limestone outcrop regularly produce unusual prehistoric fossils. Before the last Ice Age, Lindisfarne was just part of the mainland, but after the ice melted it became completely separated by a two-mile wide stretch of flat sand.

Lindisfarne is almost three miles in length but is only 1,050 acres in extent. It contains, though, a real variety of geological and historical features. The island, like the Farne Islands, is steeped in history dating back to the dark ages. St Aidan selected Lindisfarne as the site for his church and monastery because of its reasonably secure island position and its close proximity to the royal residence at Bamburgh; it was from here that Aidan taught Christianity to the barbarian people of north Northumbria. After listening to the saint's preaching, the feuding families laid down their weapons and gradually began to live in peace with each other. Aidan and Cuthbert, who followed in Aidan's footsteps, both became Bishops of Lindisfarne and their religious teachings of peace brought a tranquil calm and understanding to the people of the area.

Lindisfarne, like all the coastal villages, was still not exempt from the constant attacks by Norsemen who regularly came over the North Sea in their longships to pillage and plunder. Unfortunately, on 7 June 793, the priory and settlement on Lindisfarne was burnt to the ground and many of the monks killed. It was recorded at the time that:

> They came like stinging hornets, like ravening wolves; they made raids on all sides, slaying not only the cattle but priests and monks. They came to Lindisfarne and laid waste, trampled the holy places under foot, dug down the altars and bore away the treasures of the church. Some of the brethren they slew and some they carried away captive and some they drowned in the sea.

The priory never really recovered from the terrible slaughter and the few stalwart monks who were left finally deserted Lindisfarne in 875. In all probability the island remained uninhabited for the next 200 years.

In 1082 a group of Benedictine monks arrived and were granted the See of Lindisfarne; they then renamed the island Holy Island, to commemorate the holy blood shed during the Viking raids. Since then there has always been a permanent settlement on the island. The ruined priory was rebuilt by the monks and when it was completed in 1120, they dedicated it to St Cuthbert. The priory was built mostly of sand and stone and it was not significantly altered until the 1400s, when the apse at the east end of the chancel was made longer and reshaped into an oblong. The Benedictine monks remained at peace on Lindisfarne for 450 years and, unlike the mainland parishes, they even escaped attack by the marauding Scots. All that remains now of the once proud Norman priory is a roofless ruin. Above the entrance is an open gallery of five arches with pillars on either side that used to be a Norman archade. The patterns and ornamental details in the church are very similar to those in Durham Cathedral, which suggests that it was probably built by the same monks. The monks lived around the cloister on the southern side where there are the remains of a small stone spiral staircase. St Mary's parish church was built between 1120 and 1145 and still has its three original Norman arches on the eastern side of the north aisle.

There is a medieval tombstone decorated with a cross and sword on the north wall. In the 1700s, a small belfry was added to the church and this was totally restored in 1860.

By 1550, after the dissolution of the Catholic church, Henry VIII was having a lot of trouble with the warring Scots so he built the small castle, based on a Tudor fort, to garrison his army on Lindisfarne; most of the stone from the by-now defunct priory was used for the castle. He then had 'ten line of battleships' anchored in the harbour and the island became his front line of defence against the border enemy. The prior of Lindisfarne became Bishop of Berwick and it was shortly after a dispute with him that the king took control of the island. The Earl of Dunbar ransacked the remaining riches of the priory in 1613, along with the bells and lead from the roof, but his booty never reached its final destination: his ship sank without trace shortly after leaving Holy Island harbour (see dive site 20 in the Farne Sound).

In a border survey of 1550, there is mention of the 'forte' or castle as 'The Forte of Beblowe', which is the name for the hill on which the castle was constructed. At the start of the civil war, the fort was used as a Royalist stronghold, but it soon fell to the Roundheads. Then, in 1715, when the garrison was reduced to just seven men, the castle was captured by two Jacobites, although they surrendered without a fight as soon as reinforcements arrived from Berwick.

In 1820 the castle had its guns removed and it was partially dismantled; then, in 1880, the building was converted to a coastguard station. In 1944 the owners of the castle, Sir Edward de Stein and his sister, presented it to the National Trust. As well as the castle, the garden and nearby limekilns are also in the care of the National Trust while the priory, which is now just a ruin, is in the care of English Heritage.

Henry VIII's forte on Lindisfarne

LINDISFARNE'S WILDLIFE

The whole of the 8,000 acres around Holy Island, stretching from Budle Bay to the south and Goswick Sands to the north, is an important nature reserve. The sand habitats, mudflats, sea marshes and sand dunes give refuge to an extremely rich variety of animal and bird life and twitchers come from far and wide to view the hordes of different birds. So, unfortunately, do the wildfowlers, although they are now strictly controlled by licence. Holy Island and the adjacent mainland is world famous for its waders and overwintering wildfowl and in 1981–1982, it was recognised as the eighth most important site in the whole of the British Isles and Irish estuaries. The most common species of duck is the wigeon, which had over 2,600, at a peak count in the 1980s. Whooper swans, brent geese, greylag geese, mute swans, mallard and teal and even the occasional pintail visit the areas surrounding Holy Island. Very common off the coast are eider duck, common or velvet scoter, four species of grebe, great Northern divers, gannets, puffins and guillemots. Also arriving during the summer months are large numbers of curlew, oystercatcher, redshank, ringed plover, turnstone, purple sandpipers, little terns and sandwich terns – the list just goes on and on. A great many of these birds breed on Holy Island and the general public are requested not to disturb them. Another particularly interesting group of birds to be seen on a regular basis are the birds of prey such as short-eared owls, kestrels and sparrowhawks which are often to be seen chasing the small wading birds. Hares, foxes and vast hordes of rabbits are also very common all over Holy Island.

LIFE ON THE ISLAND

Access to Holy Island is now along a proper tarmac road built across the tidal causeway. About a quarter of a mile over the causeway from the mainland there is an emergency refuge tower on the small bridge which spans the little river, South Low. The sea acts like a river as it races in across the sand flats on the incoming flood tide and because of its speed, every year many unfortunate but careless people are trapped or drowned and their cars end up submerged by the rush of incoming water.

The route of the Pilgrim's Causeway across Holy Island Sands to Chare End on the island is the same as that used by the saints, Aidan and Cuthbert, and it remained virtually unchanged until 1860, when the authorities marked the route with a line of long posts to guide people across. Each year many hundreds of modern pilgrims still follow the traditional route used by the monks at low tide.

At high tide, emergency medical aid to the island's population has to come by helicopter because the ambulance service cannot reach them, but fires are another problem. They did have their own part-time fire service, but cutbacks in the service took it away from them. I believe they still retain a volunteer crew, however.

Today, Holy Island houses a thriving little community with its main revenue coming from farming, fishing and tourism; there is, though, local concern about many of the younger generation leaving for better jobs on the mainland. Over 100,000 people from all over the world flock to the island annually to visit the famous priory, castle and to sample the wonderful Lindisfarne mead. There are two public houses in the village, the Crown and Anchor and the Northumberland Arms, and both are very popular.

Mining used to be an established occupation when the people quarried limestone, sandstone, iron ore and even coal, which added to the island's economy. Sadly, however, this died out long ago. Now all that is left is the old coal mine tower at the Snook, but its six-inch seams were worked out by 1840. The limestone kilns can also still be seen on the pebble shoreline, just to the east of the castle, and act as a convenient nesting site for the gulls.

People living on Holy Island have always been involved in the fishing industry and by the 19th century it was a very lucrative business with huge catches of crab, lobster, cod and especially herring. Two thirds of the island's population were involved in cleaning and salting fish and in 1860 there were 36 fishing boats operating full time, By 1875, because of the better facilities and bigger harbours available at North Sunderland (Seahouses) and Eyemouth, the fishing industry declined to just a shadow of its former self. Now all that remains of what was the centre of the thriving herring industry are the old smoking sheds and the upturned hulls of some of the dozens of herring drifters, now made into convenient lock-up sheds. The lobster and crab fishermen still make a good living from the sea, but the mainstay of the population is tourism and the Lindisfarne Mead Company which was founded in 1962.

In the 17th century, there was a darker side to the Holy Island fishing industry which is not discussed locally today: like the Cornish fishermen they were accused of deliberately luring ships onto the rocks and then using their boats to loot the cargo.

LINDISFARNE'S LIFEBOATS

Old records on the history of Lindisfarne make mention of there being a lifeboat on the island as far back as 1786 and there was definitely one there in 1802, which probably qualifies it as the oldest station in the United Kingdom. The first official launching of a lifeboat on the island, however, was not recorded until 1829. It was at that time that a second boat was stationed at the Snook Point, making Holy Island unique: it was probably the only place in Great Britain to have two lifeboats at the same time. During the late 1800s and early 1900s, the Royal National Lifeboat Institute lifeboats were all of similar design to the *Lizzie Porter*, which now has pride of place in the Grace Darling museum at Bamburgh. This famous lifeboat, the original Holy Island boat and donated to the RNLI by a Miss Elizabeth Porter of Halifax, was rescued from a farmer's field in a dilapidated state and donated to the museum by a Mr Rowbotham of Nottingham. The one in question is the *Lizzie Porter* (Official No.597) self-righting boat. She was built at Thames Iron Works in 1909 at a cost of £823, weighed 4 tons and was 35 feet (10.66 metres) in length, with a beam of 8.6 feet (2.59 metres). The boat was built of diagonal planking on rock elm frames and had ten oars, two masts, a setting lugger sail and a jib.

Late in 1904 the Admiralty awarded £1,000 to the lifeboat crew who rescued the men of an 1800-ton steamer *Harcalo* in mountainous seas off Holy Island.

The *Harcalo* (Official No.118498) was actually a fairly new ship of 2,822 tons, completed as Yard No.274 in October 1904 by Furness, Withy and Co. Ltd, West Hartlepool, for J. and C. Harrison Ltd of London In 1907 she was renamed *Silver Wings* by the new owners Silver Wings S.S. Co. Ltd, London, and the manager was N. Hallett and Co.

In 1913 the registered owner was Wings S.S. Co. Ltd but she had the same manager.

On 18 August 1915, the ship was transporting a cargo of steel rails and general cargo from New York to Archangelsk in Russia when she was wrecked on Sable Island, a small Canadian island situated 111.8 miles southeast of mainland Nova Scotia in the Atlantic Ocean.

In 1907 Holy Island had one inshore lifeboat and a heavier vessel, which was used around the Farne Islands. The *Lizzie Porter* was used regularly until 1925 when she was replaced by a motorised boat and the *Lizzie Porter* was sent to North Sunderland (Seahouses) where she worked until her retirement in 1936. The boat was launched 35 times and rescued 77 people.

On 15 January 1922, the *Lizzie Porter* went to the rescue of the Hartlepool steam trawler *James B. Graham* in horrendous seas and freezing weather off False Emmanuel Head at the north end of the island. The lifeboat crew managed to weave between the shoals and shallow reefs in extremely difficult conditions and successfully rescued the nine crewmen on board the steam trawler. For 'splendid seamanship and great courage', Coxswain George Cromarty was awarded the Royal National Lifeboat Institute's Silver Medal. The three second coxswains were awarded Bronze Medals, while the rest of the crew received extra monetary rewards for their bravery. Unfortunately the RNLI withdrew the last of its lifeboats from Lindisfarne in 1968, and all that remains there now are the rescue memorial plaques on the wall opposite the priory entrance and the old lifeboat house at Jenny Bell's Well.

VESSELS WRECKED AROUND THE ISLAND

A considerable number of ships have been wrecked on the island's coast over the past few centuries, hence the need for two lifeboats on such a small place. The shallow sea around Holy Island is riddled with treacherous, jagged reefs, reaching far out to sea on the east coast. During north and nor'easterly storms, huge surfing rollers are created by the shallow seabed and they come crashing in from miles out to sea. This has made it particularly dangerous to shipping and it would have been a virtually impossible task to attempt to navigate vessels around the submerged shoals under sail. Bearing witness to this fact are the bits and pieces of wreckage, including anchors, chains, large brass rudder pintles and heavy planking full of copper pins, which can be found everywhere under the kelp beds and reefs on the seabed.

Unfortunately, as would also be expected, the wrecks inshore are literally smashed to smithereens, so the chances are slim for modern day scuba divers who live in hope of finding a decent wrecksite.

During the age of sail there were many dozens of ships lost on the seaward side of the island. Here is just a sample of those unfortunate casualties:

The 131-ton brig *Falcon* was transporting a cargo of wheat when she foundered off Emmanuel Head in October 1851; she was caught out in a Force 10 nor'easterly storm and driven inshore, where her crew of eight perished in the pounding surf.

In October 1852, a vessel called *Elliott* was wrecked and her crew of six all perished.

In February 1853 the 46-ton sloop *Janet Johnson* was carrying a cargo of wheat when she stranded on the rocks in a Force 10 nor'easterly storm and her two-man crew were drowned

Just to the south of Holy Island harbour, in January 1854, the 82-ton British schooner *Lancaster* was driven onto the shoals, where she stranded during a Force 10 east-south-easterly storm. One of her crew of five was drowned but the vessel was partially salvaged along with the general cargo.

In 1860, a 415-ton wooden barque, loaded with coal, stranded and was totally wrecked during a Force 7 east-south-easterly gale. She was driven onto the treacherous reefs close to Emmanuel Head and one of her crew of 16 was drowned.

The 29-year-old, 100-ton wooden schooner *Lady of the Lake* with a crew of five was wrecked on Plough Rock on 3 November 1866.

On 17 September 1867, the British schooner *Jane and Margaret* was carrying coal from Sunderland to Aberdeen when she was totally wrecked, but her crew survived.

On 27 March 1869, the British schooner *Cresswell* was wrecked while transporting coal from Sunderland to Montrose, but the crew were saved along with part of her cargo.

The steam tug *Courier* was carrying coal when she was wrecked during a gale near Holy Island bar and sank shortly afterwards. She was sold for scrap where she lay on 18 October 1875.

The *Courier* (Official No.5305) was an iron-hulled 323-ton paddle cargo steamer completed in 1850 as Yard No.4 by T. Wingate and Co., Glasgow, for Hull and Leith Steam Packet Co. She measured 54.40 m in length, with an 8.33-m beam and 3.68-m draught. Propulsion was by a simple 135-nhp, two-cylinder compound steam engine that powered a single paddle wheel and used one boiler. W. Simons, Glasgow manufactured the machinery.

In 1851 the registered owner was Thomas Wilson Sons and Co, Hull.

In 1854 she was owned by North of Europe Steam Navigation Co, London. The registered owners in 1858 were John Scott Russell, Robert Ford and Thomas Jackson, London.

Thomas Jackson owned her in 1864. In 1867 she was converted to a steam tug. Simons and Brown, Glasgow became the registered owner in 1867. From 1871, T. Adam, Aberdeen was the owner until she was lost.

On 19 October 1875, the day after the *Courier* was wrecked, the Leith-registered passenger paddle steamer *Britannia III*, which was en route from Newcastle to Leith, was wrecked on the bar and became a total loss. The *Grace Darling* lifeboat stationed at Holy Island rescued 35 survivors when she ran aground at Burrows Ridge, on the south side of Holy Island.

It was reported from Berwick that:

> At about 8 o'clock on the morning of 19th October 1875, the steamer *Britannia III*, from Leith for Newcastle, with passengers and a general cargo, stranded at Holy Island. The wind was blowing a gale from the southeast, with a heavy sea running. The sea was so tempestuous that the master was resolved to running the steamer into Holy Island harbour for shelter. However when that was attempted, the steamer stranded on the ridge at the entrance to the harbour, where it remained hard and fast, a short distance from the sunken steamer *Courier* of Aberdeen. The Holy Island lifeboat proceeded to render assistance, and all of the passengers, about seventy in number, were safely landed. The master and crew remained by the vessel, in the hope of being able to get her off when the tide rose, but it was feared that she would become a total wreck. The passengers were all then forwarded to their various destinations. The storm was continuing from the southeast, and the sea remained very high. The following day, reports stated that the steamer *Britannia III* was a complete wreck at Holy Island and the master and crew had no choice but to abandon her on the Tuesday, when it was found she could not be saved, the storm continuing and the waves breaking heavily over the steamer. Unfortunately she broke up when the tide rose. The cargo, consisting of 900 barrels of ale, besides whisky, wine and general goods, was strewn all along the coast. The steamer which was worth £12,000 was not insured and the cargo was worth a further £5,000. The barometer was still falling, and the storm was violent.

The hull of the passenger steamer was later sold for scrap. The *Britannia III* (Official No.52880) was an iron-hulled 420-ton paddle passenger/cargo steamer completed as Yard No.147 by Barclay Curle and Co. at the Stobcross Yard, Glasgow and launched on 3 June 1866 for Donald Currie, John Buchanan and Alexander Blackwood, Leith with Leith and Newcastle Steamship Co. the managers. She measured 59.18 m in length, with a 7.36-m beam and 3.50-m draught. The single paddle wheel was powered by a 150-nhp, two-cylinder compound steam engine that used one boiler.

On 31 January 1876, the iron steamship *Hibernia* stranded on the Holy Island harbour bar. The vessel was broken in half by the sea on the Saturday, just before the engine room and part of her cargo washed out. The steamer was a total wreck and was salvaged on 5 February 1876.

The *Hibernia* was an iron-hulled 658-ton steam passenger/cargo vessel that was completed by Gourlay Brothers at Dundee as Yard No.22 and launched in January 1865. The single iron screw was powered by a vertical direct-acting two-cylinder steam engine that used one boiler.

The Times, Tuesday, 8 February 1876, p.12.

In 1883 the 150-ton British brig *Sea Belle* was on passage from Nairn for Sunderland when she ran aground on the Goswick Sands during a storm; both of the two crewmen on board were saved. Though she was totally wrecked, some of her ribs and keel are still to be seen at low tide, firmly bedded in the sand

On 22 November 1883, the British steamer *Thistle* was transporting a cargo of coal from Sunderland to Montrose when she stranded on Plough Seat reef. She encountered storm-force 9 westerly winds off the north Northumberland coast and to ease the terrible sea conditions, her master, Captain J. Potter, brought the vessel closer inshore, but it stranded on the long Plough Seat reef off the east side of Holy Island. Of her crew of 11 and one passenger, only one crewman was drowned and the others were saved by Holy Island fishermen in their cobles. However, the *Thistle* was so badly damaged that she filled up with water and soon became a total wreck.

The *Thistle* (Official No.86371) was an iron-hulled 401-ton steam cargo vessel completed as Yard No.6 by Pearce Bros., Dundee in February 1883 and launched on 7 February 1883 for Robert Taylor and Sons, Dundee, who was the owner at the time of loss. She measured 46.22 m in length, with a 7.03-m beam and 3.58-m draught. The single iron screw was powered by a 60-hp, two-cylinder compound steam engine that used one boiler. She had one deck, four watertight bulkheads and was classed by Lloyd's as 100 A1. See Dive (1).

The Times, Friday, 23 November 1883; p. 12.

The small 71-ton steamer *Resolute* loaded with pig iron became another victim when she sank on the Holy Island bar in 1886.

On the night of Saturday, 28 March 1892, the 404-ton steamer *Holmrook*, of Newcastle, stranded on Emmanuel Head rocks, Holy Island, during a gale; she was on a voyage from Arbroath to Rotterdam with potatoes. Eleven of the crew were drowned and one was saved in the ship's boat. It was reported at the time by newspapers that:

> The Holmrook is badly holed and much of her cargo was washing
> out. The decks are submerged; the vessel is in an exposed position
> and will soon break up. It is considered the ship will then be a
> total loss. The survivor, John Rudolph Devries, states that the
> crew got into a boat, which capsized. It righted again, but capsized
> a second time. Mr Devries, who is a Dutchman, clung to the boat,
> and when cast ashore, he remained under it all night, much
> more dead than alive. The next morning ho made his way to a
> neighbouring farmhouse, where his needs were attended to. Mr.
> C. Percy, the Coroner for North Northumberland, held an inquest
> at Holy Island on the bodies of fire of the crew of the Newcastle
> steamer, which was wrecked on Saturday night and eleven men
> were drowned, The survivor, John Devries, described the wreck,
> and said that one boat was smashed and another capsized several
> times, all except himself being gradually drowned. It was agreed to
> ask the Board of Trade to erect a lighthouse at Emmanuel Head,
> Holy Island.

The eleven crewmen are buried in the churchyard on Holy Island.

The *Holmrook* (Official No.70242) was an iron-hulled 404-ton steam cargo
vessel, completed as Yard No.20 by C.S. Swan and Co. at Wallsend, Newcastle on
Tyne in August 1875 for Hall, Dyke and Hall, at Newcastle. However, C.S. Swan
was the official registered owner and in 1879, H.F. Swan was the registered owner.
She measured 45.72 m in length and had a beam of 6.77 m. The single screw was
powered by a two-cylinder compound steam engine that used one boiler. In 1880
and at the time of loss, J. G. Charlton and Co., Newcastle was the registered owner.

The steamer *Otto M'Combie* stranded on the Plough Rock and was lost – see
Dive (2).

On 9 January 1895 the *Otto M'Combie* (Captain A. Johnson) was voyaging from
Amble to Dundee with coal and carrying a crew of ten when she stranded on the
Plough Rock; the vessel broke in two and slid back off to become a total wreck

The *Otto M'Combie* (Official No.75257) was a 339-ton steam cargo vessel,
completed as Yard No.27 by W. B. Thompson, Dundee in June 1879; she was
launched on 7 June 1879 for J. M'Combie and Co., Peterhead. She measured 45.72
m in length, with a 6.7-m beam and a 3.96-m draught. The iron screw was powered
by a two-cylinder compound steam engine that used one boiler.

In 1884 the registered owner was Peterhead S.S. Co. Ltd, Peterhead

In 1890 she was owned by J. Service, Glasgow and R.B. Ballantyne and Co.
became the manager

On 9 January 1913 the SS *Fædrelandet* was on passage from *Kvæfjord* in northern
Norway for Stockton-on-Tees with a cargo of iron when she was wrecked on Goswick
Sands. The Holy Island's No. 2 RNLI lifeboat, the *Edward and Eliza*, was launched
early on the morning of Friday, 10 January and rescued 14 members of her crew; the

remaining four crewmen were taken off by rocket apparatus. A heavy southeasterly gale with foggy weather was prevailing at the time. On the first attempt the lifeboat was unable to save the men due to the tide, and to effect a rescue the lifeboat had to be transported four miles over sand and through broken water.

The *Fædrelandet* was an iron-hulled 1,556-ton steam cargo ship, completed as Yard No.7 by Martens Olsen and Co. at Bergen and was launched on 25 July 1884 for P.G. Halvorsen and Others, Bergen. She measured 79.24 m in length had an 11.27-m beam and a draught of 6.70 m. Her two screws were powered by a 160-hp, two-cylinder compound steam engine that used one boiler. The cylinders measured 86.36 cm and 160.02 cm with a 99.06-cm stroke (34 in. and 63 in. with a 39-in. stroke). She had five bulkheads and water ballast. Her designated code recognition signal letters were: JVTF. In 1888 she was registered to Bergh and Helland, Bergen. In 1902 the registered owners were Dampskibet Fædrelandet's Rederi, and Bergh and Helland was the manager. In 1911 she was owned by Dampskibs A/S Fædrelandet, Bergen and Thv. Halvorsen became the manager.

During calm weather on Tuesday, 14 January 1913, the 2,690-ton SS *Werner Kunstmann* was en route from Stettin to Newcastle in ballast when she ran aground on Goswick sand ridge near Holy Island, but none of her crew was injured or lost. The ship mysteriously caught fire and by 22 January her back was broken; she was subsequently salvaged in situ. The steamer was suspected of having been sabotaged by her crew, following reports that she was en route to supply her cargo of iron ore to German factories, which had been building up in their preparations for the start of World War One.

The *Werner Kunstmann* was a 2,690-ton cargo steamer completed as Yard No.301 in May 1891 by Soc. Cockerill, Hoboken, Belgium; she was launched on 24 February 1891 as the *Prince Baudouin* for Soc. Cockerill at Antwerp. She measured 97.5 metres in length and 12.2 metres across the beam. The single screw was powered by a three-cylinder triple expansion steam engine that gave 9 knots. In 1900 she was renamed *Frascati* by her new owners Rob. M. Sloman, Junior, at Hamburg. In 1912 she was renamed *Werner Kunstmann* by Wilh. Kunstmann, Stettin, Prussia (now Poland).

The steamer *Cydonia* was wrecked on Castlehead Rocks – see dive site (9).

The ship was employed by the Admiralty as a collier and on 28 September 1916, under the command of Captain W. Gill, she was on passage from Methil for Brest with a crew of 29 and a cargo of coal when, in heavy weather and mountainous seas, she stranded on the north (seaward) side of Castlehead Rocks at Holy Island. The self-righting lifeboat, *Lizzie Porter*, was launched from Holy Island and rescued all her crew, returning to render further assistance the following day. However, the *Cydonia* soon started to break up and became a total loss.

The *Cydonia* (Official No.127107) was a steel-hulled 3,085-ton British steam cargo ship that was completed as Yard No.165 by W. Dobson and Co. Ltd, Newcastle in April 1910 and launched for Stag Line Ltd, North Shields on 24 February 1910, with J. Robinson and Sons the managers; Stag Line Ltd also owned her at the time of loss. She measured 101.01 m in length with a 14.63-m beam and had a draught of 6.75 m. Her single steel propeller was powered by a three-cylinder, triple-expansion steam engine that developed 249-hp using two boilers and her machinery was manufactured by North East Marine Engineering Co. Ltd at Newcastle upon Tyne. She had one deck and a superstructure consisting of an 8.8-m poop deck, a 28.3-m bridge deck and a 10-m forecastle.

The trawler *James B. Graham* was wrecked and destroyed by the sea in 1922.

The women of Holy Island were sent a special letter of thanks from the Committee of Management of the Royal National Lifeboat Institution for gallant service on 10 January 1922. The lifeboat was called out at 8 o'clock in the evening in a gale with blinding snowstorms. The tide was low and the wheels of the lifeboat carriage got stuck in the soft mud. The brave women waded out waist deep into the sea and by their gallant efforts the lifeboat was got afloat.

The committee of management awarded Coxswain George Cromarty a bar to the silver medal of the Institution which he already had, and awarded bronze medals to the second coxswain and bowman, as well as special monetary awards to all of the crew of the lifeboat, for the rescue of the *James B. Graham*. The wreck was lying in a dangerous position among the rocks and the remnants of an old wreck. The lifeboat made three attempts and spent more than three hours attempting to get through the rocks, eventually succeeding in rescuing the trawler's crew. The trawler broke up and became a total loss.

On 24 July 1925 the *Yewdale* was in ballast and en route from Lerwick to Blyth when she grounded on Goswick's notorious Sand Ridge. The number two RNLI lifeboat at Holy Island was launched and rescued the nine crew members. On 20 October 1925 the vessel was refloated and subsequently sold for demolition.

The *Yewdale* was an iron- and steel-hulled 477-ton steam cargo vessel, completed as Yard No.79 by Scott and Co., Bowling, near Glasgow in September 1890; she was launched as the *Olivine* for William Robertson, Glasgow on 15 August 1890. She measured 50.34 m in length, with a 7.94-m beam and a 3.27-m draught. The single screw was powered by a 60-hp, three-cylinder triple expansion steam engine that used one boiler. Muir and Houston, Glasgow manufactured the machinery. In 1900 she was renamed *Yewdale* by her new owner, J. S. Hardman of Liverpool. In 1904 the owner was William Poslethwaite of Liverpool. In 1911 she was owned by George Poslethwaite, and William Poslethwaite and Son was the manager at Liverpool. In 1918 the registered owner was Earl J. Leslie, Liverpool (Dundee). In 1920 Henry

W. Renny at Dundee was the owner and E. J. Leslie became the manager. From 1923 and until the time of loss, John Stewart and Co. at Glasgow was the registered owner.

The 267-ton steamer *Grosvenor* ran aground on Castlehead Rocks at Holy Island late on the night of Saturday 18 December 1935, while on a voyage from Port Knockie to Sunderland. Her crew burnt blankets as distress signals when the coaster struck the rocks and then the men took to the boat. The flames and smoke were seen by the Holy Island lifeboat crew who launched and brought the crew of eight safely ashore. The vessel was very badly holed after striking Castlehead Rocks on the north side of Holy Island. A propeller blade had been lost and the pumps were unable to cope with the water entering the hold. She was written off as a total loss. Some salvage may have taken place, but nothing remains of her these days except for the boiler, which now lies on top of the rocks.

The *Grosvenor* was a steel-hulled 267-ton steam coaster completed as Yard No.64 by Garston G.D. and S.B. Co. Ltd at Garston in January 1908; she was launched on 23 October 1907 for R. Garner. She measured 36.60 m in length, with a beam of 7.12 m and a 2.81-m draught. The single screw was powered by an aft-positioned 40-rhp two-cylinder compound steam engine that used one Scotch boiler working at a pressure of 180 psi and used two plain furnaces. The cylinders measured 43.18 cm and 88.9 cm with a 55.88-cm stroke (22 in. and 35 in. with a 22- in. stroke). Crabtree and Co. Ltd at Great Yarmouth manufactured the machinery. She had a well deck, one steel deck, three bulkheads cemented, a 14.63-m quarterdeck, a 2.74-m bridge deck and a 7.62-m forecastle. The designated code recognition signal letters were: JLYN.

In 1933, A. Massie and Co. of Aberdeen purchased the vessel and was the registered owner at the time of loss.

The graveyard on Holy Island bears witness to the number of seamen that have perished on the hazardous reefs and rocks over the past few centuries.

DIVE SITES AROUND LINDISFARNE

The seabed and flora and fauna off the coast of Holy Island gather, for some reason, a fair amount of sediment, but with the very shallow depths around the island, even the tiniest swell very quickly stirs up the sediment and destroys the underwater visibility. A small swell coming from a northerly or easterly direction at Beadnell or Seahouses will be multiplied five-fold off Holy Island. The round trip by RHIB from Beadnell is approximately 23 miles, and from Seahouses it is 15 miles, so it is always worthwhile checking the sea conditions before setting out on a journey that might be wasted. There are no launching facilities on Holy Island and divers are certainly not welcomed with open arms by the local fishing community.

With the exception of Burrow's Hole there is no worthwhile diving on the south (Ross Sands) side of the island, because the depths are too shallow – only a couple of metres or so – with the majority of the seabed consisting of sand and small patches of rock covered in weed. There is also a strong tidal stream as the water ebbs and floods over the shallow Holy Island sand flats.

SS *Thistle*

(1) ✱✱

55 40'.200 N 001 45'.499 W

The remnants of the steamer *Thistle* can be seen but there is little of interest apart from a boiler and a broken, decaying engine. Various species of flatfish can be found all around this area, where the seabed is covered in tiny mussels and weed-coated boulders and rocks.

SS *Otto M'combie*

(2) ✱✱

55 40'.180 N 001 45'.300 W

All that remains of the old steamer is a battered boiler and rusting engine lying on a seabed of tiny mussels and short seaweed. There is very little else to be seen, but good flatfish can often be observed, feeding off the mussels.

Plough Rock

(3) ✱✱

55 40'.234 N 001 45'.875 W

Plough Rock dries to 2.6 metres on a low spring tide and the surrounding seabed, at six metres, is a flat rock bottom covered in minute mussels. There are a few large rocks and boulders around, which sometimes harbour one or two crustacean and the occasional flatfish that feed on the beds of tiny mussels, but in general it is not a very interesting dive site.

Plough Seat Reef and Wingate

Plough Seat - 54 40'.265 N 001 45'.600 W

Wingate - 54 40'.381 N 001 45'.628 W

Outer Wingate and Minscore - 55 40'.537 N 001 45'.486 W

(4) ✶ ✶ ✶

Plough Seat Reef is a high reef covered in kelp and tiny mussels with a steep south-facing rocky wall. In fact the whole seabed, and even some of the kelp, has a thick coating of minute baby mussels. There are a couple of very old Admiralty pattern anchors lying up against the reef on the south side, with a rusting anchor chain running over the top of it towards Wingate.

Tidal flow is very strong and especially so on the springs, but you can get sufficient shelter from the force of it on the flood by staying close in to the reef on the south side. Visibility varies a lot, from exceptionally poor to brilliant, depending how much rain has fallen, the size of the tide and which way the wind has been blowing – westerly is best. There also seems to be an abundance of little hairy spider crabs and brown nudibranchs (sea slugs) in this particular area, all living on the fronds of kelp.

A number of sailing vessels have been wrecked on the Plough Seat Reef so it may be worth a drift dive in either direction, either to the north or south. Travelling north takes you to Wingate reef, very shallow ground, only 2–3 metres with a dense kelp forest and those tiny mussels covering the seabed and rocks.

Further north of Wingate is the Outer Wingate, which is an extension of the shallow, rather flat reef: the highest part, 1.5 metres, at the northern end, is called Minscore. A fair number of various types of flatfish can also be observed all around this whole area. Bits of wreckage can also often be found under the kelp or jammed under rocks.

(5) ✶ ✶ ✶

55 40'.664 N 001 46'.314 W

Halfway along the island, and a couple of hundred metres out, opposite the gap in the rocks on the shore at low water, there is a small drop from 7 to 10 metres called Brides Hole or Shelldrake Pool. It is a nice little reef, approximately 500 metres long, with a few overhangs and crevices. The whole area is a thick kelp bed and it can be difficult to pull your way through during the summer months, but the effort can bring the reward of a lobster or two. The area is rather sheltered from the strong currents that run a bit further out, offshore.

(6) ✶ ✶ ✶

55 41'.369 N 001 46'.420 W

Off Emmanuel Head the seabed is made up of kelp-covered rocks with small reefs running out to sea, but the current is exceptionally strong in both directions, running at 2–3 knots. A good drift dive can be made, best done on the flood tide, taking you south towards the Plough Seat Reef and Wingate shoal. Plenty of sea urchins and small crabs can be found.

Keel Head

(7) ✯ ✯

55 41'.320 N 001 47'.242 W

Just round the corner from Emmanuel Head is a nice, fairly sheltered reef called Keel Head. The north side is a sandy bay but the reef, which is about 150 metres long, has plenty of holes and crevices in it and a few creepy-crawlies can be found. An added bonus is that when the main reef runs out, there are some smaller but interesting reefs spreading out in different directions. Depths are only in the region of 4–6 metres and the visibility is often very good, but the current gets stronger the further seaward you travel.

Castlehead Rocks

(8) ✯ ✯ ✯

55 41'.648 N 001 47'.161 W

Castlehead Rocks is an extension of the protruding headland called False Emmanuel Head, where the elements have worn the cliffs away over many centuries, leaving this long reef. At low spring tide, Castlehead Rocks above the surface are about 500 metres long, but the kelp on the reef's boulders can be seen just below the surface for around a further 250 metres seawards. There is so much shallow ground well offshore that it is very easy to run aground at low tide, even with a small RHIB, so extra care should be taken when navigating around this position.

There is a good selection of marine life about with some good edible brown crabs, wolf fish and cod. Because of the shallow depths and fairly strong currents, any groundswell badly affects this dive site and the current gets worse the further out you swim.

Cydonia

(9) ✯ ✯ ✯

55 41'.652 N 001 47'.355 W approximately

This is the site where the SS *Cydonia* was wrecked in September 1916. The remains of the *Cydonia* are well dispersed across a wide area among the rocks and boulders, some 200 metres out, on the north side of Castlehead Rocks. Her two boilers are still there just off the reef, standing upright among twisted steel framework, steel plates and masses of iron pipes. The wreck belonged to Peter McCrieth, who was one of the Berwick Fisheries Officers until he moved down south a few years ago. Peter was also a diver and, before he retired from his sport diving, he spent some time over a number of years salvaging the wreck with one of his buddies. Quite a substantial amount of it still remains, even though it is well broken up and hidden under a thick covering of kelp It makes an excellent rummage dive, especially at low, slack water, because, although the site is fairly shallow, the tidal streams are very strong and become even stronger the further out you go.

(10) ★ ★ ★

55 41'.463 N 001 47'.495 W

A small ship's boiler lies on top of the reef, halfway along Castlehead Rocks, which possibly belonged to the steam trawler *James B. Graham*. There are other small pieces of wreckage here and there, but nothing to indicate that this is a wrecksite, because the boiler is nearly certain to have been rolled in by the sea. The reef itself is very big and has numerous large boulders lying up against the northern edge. Some good cod and large colourful ballan wrasse can be seen under the reef's overhangs and there is the occasional crustacean for the pot. Visibility is never very exceptional in the shallow depths and the tidal stream is fairly strong, especially on the spring flood, but there is plenty of shelter behind the reefs. A surface marker buoy should be used, because you can end up a long way from the boat at the end of a dive.

Black Skerrs

(11) ★ ★ ★

55 41'.524 N 001 47'.849 W

This reef is the end of the Black Skerrs, which runs out from the land at Snipe Point and is parallel to Castlehead Rocks; it is, though, much shorter than they are. On the northern side of the reef there is a high underwater cliff face leading down onto huge boulders with lots of long deep crevices, tunnels and overhangs, many of them so long and deep that it is impossible to reach anything inside. Large cod, conger, ling and ballan wrasse are commonplace, along with lots of squat lobsters, a few crabs and the occasional lobster. Where the reef submerges below the surface at low tide, it splits into two reefs, one going straight out to sea and the other curving southeast. The highest and longest reef is the one going straight out, about 300 metres long. It remains a cliff face most of the way but the current is a lot more noticeable at the end of the reef. On this dive, as on the one above, a surface marker buoy should be used.

(12) ✯ ✯ ✯

55 41'.528 N 001 48'.210 W

About 250 metres off the rocky dolorite shoreline of the Black Skerrs, three large rocks dry to 1.2 metres at low spring tide and form mini-islets. They are surrounded by other submerged rock mounds, all covered in dense kelp and minute mussels. The seaward side of the islets is the deepest and most interesting with a number of deep overhangs and small caves, too little to enter, but often harbouring a blue creepy-crawly, even if it is usually well out of reach of the longest crab hook.

On one diving trip to Holy Island, we rounded False Emmanuel Head to discover a 12-metre Berwick lobster boat stranded high and dry on top of the highest of the three islets, its bow and stern sections protruding almost two metres over the ends of the big flat rock. After our laughter had subsided we motored across to see if they needed any kind of assistance, but were greeted with an embarrassed stony silence, then a voice mumbled: 'We're jus' waitin' fir the witter tae cum back!' If only I had taken my camera with me: it would have been a gem of a picture.

One hundred metres inshore of the three islets, which incidentally have a large resident colony of grey seals on and around them, there are a number of long low reefs with big overhangs, caves and deep crevices, many covered with soft corals. Fifty metres to the north of these is a long L- shaped reef, standing up to 4 metres high in places, and at low water the kelp over the top is visible on the surface. The surrounding seabed has large patches of sand and craggy rocks, all coated in a thick carpet of minute mussels which often attract some large plaice. Tidal streams on the flood run in an easterly direction around the long stretch of Castlehead Rocks and are quite strong on the top half of the tide. Inside the three islets, where the reefs are at low ebb tide, especially during springs, the water is often crystal clear and like a millpond during the summer. A number of large, boulder-like mounds, many with long crevices and overhangs covered in heavy kelp and tangleweed, lie just to the west of the three islets. Two hundred metres further to the northwest of these, another long, high reef commences close inshore and leads out to sea for about 300 metres. The top of this reef and the boulder- and rock-strewn ground just to the northwest is covered in heavy kelp, but the seabed then becomes much, more shallow and gradually leads onto fine sand for the next 1½ miles towards Berwick.

Wingate Reef

(13) ✯ ✯ ✯

55 42' 459 N 001 50'.533 W

Wingate Reef should not be confused with the Wingate next to the Plough Seat on

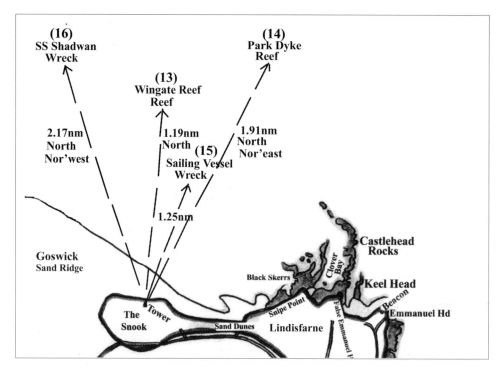

Wingate and Park Dyke reefs

the other side of Holy Island. The location of this site is 1.58 miles north from the Snook on Lindisfarne and WNW of dive site (12). The reef begins about a quarter of a mile off the shore at low tide and is half a mile long. It comes up from the sandy sea-bed at 12 metres to about 4 metres and has a considerable amount of current running over it. There are lots of interesting overhangs and crevices where large cod shelter from the tidal flow. Thick tangleweed and kelp fronds grow from the top of the higher ridges and you often see big pollack hovering over the edges. A nice dive site, but very exposed and involving a long journey unless you can find a launch site at Berwick.

Park Dyke

(14) ✩ ✩ ✩

55 42'.893 N 001 49'.166 W

Park Dyke is even further out to sea and very exposed during a northerly swell. The position is 20° north of east and three quarters of a mile further out to sea from the end of Wingate Reef, or 13° west of north and exactly 1.47 miles from the three rocks on dive site (12). The Park Dyke is a rocky shad, a quarter of a mile wide and three quarters of a mile long. The shad is carpeted in kelp and rises from the sandy seabed at 13 metres to between 3 and 5 metres. The steep walls on the north and south sides are covered in soft corals and different kinds of anemone and there are numerous overhangs and long crevices containing shellfish. The tidal streams are very strong and it is recommended that surface marker buoys be used, because a diver surfacing can very quickly disappear into the distance. The site is very exposed to the wind and sea from the north and 'white horses' often develop on the surface. As with dive site (10), you will have a long journey to get to it and there is no passing boat traffic if assistance is required.

To the northwest of Park Dyke, the seabed is very undulating, with shallow and deep channels, rolling hills and valleys that criss-cross one another for about 3 miles.

Sailing vessel wreck

(15) ✷ ✷

55 42'.379 N 001 49'.686 W

This is all that remains of a large wooden sailing vessel and its cargo of ferrous metal, which looks just like a flattened double-decker bus about 1.5 m high. It lies in about 15 metres on a low spring tide and the block of metal is about 12 metres long and 9 metres across. Nothing else remains and the surrounding seabed is undulating with boring rocks and boulders.

SS *Shadwan*

(16) ✷ ✷ ✷

55 43'.212 N 000 51'.190 W

The wreck of the 1,538-ton steamer *Shadwan* is located 2.17 nautical miles NNW of the tower at the Snook on Lindisfarne, or/and 5.18 nm SE of Berwick lighthouse and 1.96 nm NE of Goswick Tower.

On her final voyage, in mid-November 1888, the *Shadwan* took on a full cargo of wheat, barley and flour at Fiume (later to become Rijeka, Yugoslavia's largest port) for passage to Leith. The weather remained pleasant until she was approaching Berwick, when a violent northeast-

The Shadwan *bell, recovered 2005*

erly gale developed. Huge, eight-metre breaking waves pounded the ship and Captain Willis must have known he would have trouble reaching the shelter of the Firth of Forth. On Wednesday, 28 November 1888, the red-funnelled steamer was driven into shallow water, dismasted and lying beam ends to the sea, when her flag of distress was seen off Berwick. The steam trawler *Sir George Elliot* went to her assistance and a steamship travelling south also bore down on her. The crew of the stricken ship were observed on deck. It was intended, if possible, to take her to the Tyne, but she foundered. Local newspapers claimed that the crew were rescued and the stricken ship then plundered.

The *Shadwan* (Official No.77013) was an iron-hulled 1,538-ton schooner-rigged steam cargo ship that measured 78.02 m in length, with a 10.05-m beam and a 7.01-m draught. C. S. Swan and Co. at Wallsend-on-Tyne built and completed her as Yard No.31 in August 1877 for Watson and Pigg of London, with Captain Kennedy the master. The single iron screw was powered by a 150-nhp, two-cylinder compound steam engine that used one boiler. The cylinders measured: 78.74 cm and 147.32 cm, with a 76.2 cm-stroke (31 in. and 58 in. with a 36-in. stroke). T. Clark manufactured the engine and ancillary machinery at Newcastle. She had one deck, five bulkheads, water ballast and an amidships bridge deck.

On 20 May 1879, the *Shadwan* had arrived at Plymouth with a cargo of maize from Sulina and at 0600 hrs on the 22nd she was involved in an incident and grounded in the Channel outside the Great Western Docks, at supposedly high water. The ship was damaged, although no blame was attached to the steamer, but she was out of action for 45 days.

In 1880, Nelson, Donkin and Co., London was the owners and Captain Watson the master.

In 1881, she had the same owners with the Official No.77012 and designated code recognition signal letters: RBNC.

At between 0100 hrs and 0200 hrs on 21 March 1881, the *Shadwan* was involved in a collision in the River Thames with the Russian schooner *Nora*. Both vessels were being towed by tugs, the *Shadwan* being towed down the north side by the steam tugs *Contest* and *Lioness*. The owners of the Russian schooner took legal action against the steamer's owner Nelson, Donkin and Co., but the court found in favour of the *Shadwan*, because the tug towing the *Nora* did not take proper precautions.

From 1886, the registered owner was Duncan and Co. and Captain John Willis was the master until she was wrecked.

The *Shadwan* crossed the Atlantic a number of times, being seen in Philadelphia and New York; she also visited many European and Mediterranean ports on her voyages.

On 27 July 1888, the *Shadwan* had arrived at Greenock following a voyage from Barcelona to Pretoria, according to Lloyd's Shipping Intelligence.

Register of American and Foreign Shipping, 1857–1900; Miramar Ship Index; Starke/Schell.

Wrecksite

The wreck is orientated in an ENE to WSW direction, with the bow to the ENE. It is upright, but totally broken up and largely buried, covering an area of 31 metres in length by 7 metres across, with the highest part standing no more than 1.8 metres and surrounded by large reefs. The starboard side is collapsed outwards, while the port side is collapsed inwards. The single boiler is well broken up on its side, next to the engine, which also lies over on its side. A four-bladed screw is also visible amongst the wreckage. In August 2003 the wreck was identified when the ship's bell was recovered, then, soon after, three beautiful bronze dolphins in an arched position were found; these were the supporting legs of the ship's steering binnacle.

MORE DISTANT WRECKS TO VISIT

Fingal

Date of loss: 15 March 1915

Wreck: ✴ ✴ ✴ ✴

Depth: 56 m

Reference: 55 20′.720 N 001 20′.562 W

Location: 6.62 nm ENE of Coquet Island

The *Fingal* (Official No.99246) was a steel-hulled 1,548-ton British passenger/cargo steamer measuring 85.34 m in length, with a 10.66-m beam, a 5.48-m draught and 5.86-m moulded depth. W. B. Thompson and Co. Ltd, Dundee built and completed her as Yard No.121 in May 1894; she was launched on 22 March 1894 for the London and Edinburgh Shipping Co. Leith, who was also the owner at the time of loss. The single screw was powered by a 616-nhp three-cylinder triple expansion steam engine tthat used two double-ended boilers and gave 17 knots. The cylinders measured 81.28 cm, 124.46 cm and 203.2 cm with a 121.92-cm stroke (32 in., 49 in. and 80 in. with a 48-in.stroke). W.B. Thompson and Co. Ltd also manufactured the engine and ancillary machinery at Dundee. She had a 21.03-m poopdeck, a 21.03-m bridge deck and 22.25-m forecastle.

Final voyage

The *Fingal* was torpedoed and sunk at 1050 hrs on 15 March 1915, 6 miles east by south of Coquet Island, by SMU *U 23*, a KDM submarine, commanded by Oblt.z.S.Hans Schultheß. The steamer was on passage from London for Leith with a general cargo. Twenty one of her crewmen were picked up by the fishing vessel *Ayacanora* and landed at North Shields, but six others, including a stewardess from Leith, were lost:

Gray, Thomas, 19 yrs, Ordinary Seaman MM

Hogg, Walter Lumsden, 31 yrs, Able Seaman MM

Laurenson, John, 48 yrs, Able Seaman MM

McPherson, Nellie, 26 yrs, Stewardess MM

Reibelt, Walter, 28 yrs, Fireman MM

Smith, John Harper, 54 yrs, First Mate MM

On 20 July 1915, SMU *U 23* was torpedoed and sunk by the British submarine HM S/M *C27*, at position 58.55'. N 00 14' E. The British boat was working in connection with decoy trawler HMT *Princess Louise*; 24 of the U-boat's crew were killed, but ten survived.

LCWLR 1914–1918, p. 9; BVLS 1914–1918, p.5; CWGC; *The Cross of Sacrifice*, Vol. V; Starke/Schell; BMS 1914–1928, p.156.

Wrecksite

The wreck is orientated in a SSE to NNW direction. It lies on a seabed of sand and shingle, in a general depth of 56 metres (LAT). The wreck is upright and intact, stands 6.3 metres high and covers an area of 87 metres in length by 15 metres across, with lots of nets covering much of it. Large cod have been observed all around the wreckage and a shoal of bib have adopted the engine area. The ship's bell identified the wreck in May 2005 and items of crockery bearing the company's motif have also been recovered. Sadly, one of the divers who identified the wreck was lost on it soon after; his body has never been found, despite rigorous searches by friends and the police.

Morlaix, Ex *Edmond Troppey*, Ex *Fedalah*, Ex *Oran*

Date of loss: 5 May 1942

Wreck: ✰ ✰ ✰ ✰

Depth 58 m

Reference: 55 22'.785 N 001 22'.095 W

Location: 8.48 nm NE of Coquet Lighthouse

The *Morlaix* (Official No.167815) was a steel-hulled 419-ton British steam cargo vessel measuring 53.34 metres in length, with an 8.5-m beam and a 2.8-m draught. Goole Shipbuilding and Repairing Co. Ltd built and completed her at Goole as Yard No.138 in May 1911; she was launched as the *Oran* on 18 March 1911 for M. Camuyrano, Buenos Aires, Argentina. The single steel screw was powered by an aft-positioned 85-nhp, three-cylinder triple expansion steam engine that used one single-ended boiler with three plain furnaces, 4.73 sq. m (51 sq. ft) of grate surface and 148.64 sq. m (1600 sq. ft) of heating surface. The cylinders measured 34.29

cm, 53.34 cm and 88.9 cm with a 60.96-cm stroke (13½ in., 21 in. and 35 in. with a 24-in. stroke). Richardson and Westgarth and Co. Ltd manufactured the engine and ancillary machinery. She had one steel deck, three bulkheads cemented, a 5.48-m bridge deck and 7.63-m forecastle; she also had a 50-ton (141.58-cubic m) fore-peak tank, a 16-ton (45.30-cubic m) aft-peak tank and Lloyd's classed her as 100 A1.

In 1917, the vessel was renamed *Fedalah* by Cie. Chérifienne de Navigation, Casablanca (France), who purchased her. L'Union Cie. Française de Commerce and de Transp. Maritime, Bordeaux, France, purchased and renamed her *Edmond Troppey* in 1921.

Soc. de Remorq. and de Transp. par Chalands et Allèges de Mer Remorqués, Le Havre, France, was the registered owner in 1923. In 1925 she was renamed *Morlaix* by Soc. Havraise de Transp. and de Transit, Le Havre, France, who was then the registered owner.

In 1934–1935 the designated code recognition signal letters were: TSQO.

The Admiralty seized the vessel at Milford Haven in June 1940 and placed her under the control of the Ministry of War Transport (MoWT) at Cardiff; C. F. Cuthbert Brown and Co. Ltd was appointed Crown nominee manager. The designated code recognition signal letters then became: MKXS.

Final voyage

On 5 May 1942, the *Morlaix* sank following a collision with the 1,344-ton (ex-French) steam trawler *Finlande* (1937 - Ministry of War Transport), at 55 25'.30 N 01 22'.30 W. The *Morlaix* was in ballast and on passage from Macduff for Sunderland, was sailing independently and none of the crew was lost.

On 18 December 1944, the *Finlande* was wrecked off North Head at Peterhead while voyaging from Iceland to Hull.

LCR 1942, p. 9 (f); Starke/Schell.

Wrecksite

The wreck is orientated in an ESE to WNW direction and lies on a seabed of hard sand and gravel, in a general depth of 58 metres (LAT). It is upright, intact and fairly substantial, standing 5.2 metres high at the stern to midships section, with decking and some superstructure visible, but her bows to the east are reported to be broken off. The wrecksite covers an area of 55 m in length by 10 m across, with the upper structures coated in a beautiful array of soft corals and large plumose anemones. The ship's bell, which may still be around, will most probably be inscribed *Oran 1911*. Shoals of various fish have adopted the wreck so it will make a reasonable boat-angling venue.

Hornchurch

Date of loss: 3 August 1917

Wreck: ✩ ✩ ✩

Depth: 42 m

Reference: 55 22'.132 N 001 28'.567 W

Location: 3 nm NE of Coquet Lighthouse

The *Hornchurch* (Official No.139154) was a steel-hulled 2,159-ton British steam cargo ship measuring 85.34 m in length, with a 12.31-m beam, a 5.61-m draught and a moulded depth of 8.45 m. Osbourne, Graham and Co. at North Hylton, Sunderland built and completed her as Yard No.200 in September 1916; she was launched on 17 May 1916 for J. Hudson and Co. Ltd, London, who was also the owner at the time of loss. The single steel screw was powered by a 225-nhp, three-cylinder triple expansion steam engine that used two single-ended boilers working at a pressure of 180 psi, with six corrugated furnaces, 9.75 sq. m (105 sq. ft) of grate surface and 308.43 sq. m (3320 sq. ft) of heating surface, which gave 10 knots. Clyde Shipbuilding and Engineering Co. Ltd, Port Glasgow, manufactured the machinery. She had one deck, a well deck, a 28.65-m quarterdeck, a 7.01-m poopdeck, 15.84-m bridge deck and an 8.22-m forecastle. The *Hornchurch* was also armed for defence on completion.

Final voyage

On 3 August 1917, the *Hornchurch*, with Captain J. W. Gagen in charge, detonated a mine and sank 3.5 miles off Coquet Island. The KDM submarine SMU *UC 29*, commanded by Oblt.z.S. Ernst Rosenow, had laid the mine on 25 April 1917. The steamer was en route from London to Methil with a cargo of coal; two crewmen were lost.

> Harrigan, Michael, 48 yrs, Lamp Trimmer
>
> Nilsson, Oscar, 38 yrs, Fireman

On 7 June 1917, SMU *UC 29* was south of Ireland at position 51 50' N 11 50' W when the Q-ship *Pargust* sank her by gunfire; 23 of the crew, including Oblt.z.S. Rosenow, were killed but two men, the watch officer and a seaman, survived.

LCWLR 1914–1918, p.161; CWGC; *The Cross of Sacrifice* Vol. V; BVLA 1914–1918, p.61.

Wrecksite

The wreck is orientated in a S by W to N by E direction. It lies on a firm seabed of sand, stone and shells, in a general depth of 42 m (LAT). The wreck is broken into two main sections and is well smashed up and decayed, but still very substantial, with the highest parts standing over 8 m from the seabed. The wreck covers an area 90 m long and 23 m across and lots of flattened pipes, brass valves, iron/steel wheels and cogs, an anchor windlass, lengths of chain and two anchors lie intermingled with the mound of broken machinery and twisted steel plates. Soft corals adorn the highest sections around the boilers and shoaling fish, mainly bib and pollack, are fairly common during the summer months.

Driebergen

Date of loss: 28 August 1940

Wreck: ★ ★ ★ ★ ★

Depth: 54 m

Reference: 55 24'.142 N 001 24'.345 W

Location: 6.10 nm northeast of Coquet Lighthouse

The *Driebergen* was a steel-hulled 5,231-ton Netherlands steam cargo ship measuring 122.53 m in length, with a 17.67-m beam and an 8.22-m draught. New Waterway Shipbuilding Co., Schiedam built and completed her as Yard No.116 in November 1923; she was launched on 25 August 1923 for N.V. Furness Scheepvaart and Agentuur Mij., Rotterdam. The single screw was powered by a 343-nhp, D.R.-geared steam turbine that used three boilers and gave 12.5 knots. Metropolitan Vickers Electrical Co. Ltd, Manchester manufactured the engine and ancillary machinery. She had two decks, water ballast and an 11.37-m forecastle and was later equipped

SS Driebergen *loading, circa 1934*

with wireless, D.F. and electric lights. Her designated code signal recognition letters were: PDTD.

From 1926, N.V. Zuid Hollandsche Scheepv. Mij., Rotterdam was the registered owner and Furness, Rotterdam became the manager.

Final voyage

On 28 August 1940, the *Driebergen* sank near Alnmouth following a collision with the 10,365-ton British motor vessel *Port Darwin* (1918 - Commonwealth and Dominion Line Ltd, London). The *Driebergen* was sailing as a part of the southbound 47-ship convoy FS 265 (Methil - Southend) and was transporting wheat from Bahia-Blanca via Methil to the Tyne; none of her crew was lost.

LCR 1940, p.7 (f); Starke/Schell.

Wrecksite

The wreck, which is probably that of the *Driebergen*, is orientated in a SE to NW direction, with the bows detached. It lies on a seabed of sand, mud, black shells and rock in a general depth of 54 metres (LAT). The wreck is uptight and mostly intact, standing over 6.5 m high amidships around the partially collapsed superstructure. The bows lie to the SE, are broken off and lying intact close by the main wreckage. It is very substantial and covers an area 81 m long and 19 m across, with lots of broken debris strewn around nearby. The upper and most exposed structures are covered in an array of soft corals that light up the eerie dark green water when the sun's light is able to penetrate. Large cod, ling and conger have been observed and shoals of bib swim over the wreck.

Lady Eleanor

Date of loss: 26 April 1895

Wreck: ✯ ✯ ✯

Depth: 64 m

Reference: 55 25'.360 N 001 20'.658 W

Location: 8.32 nm NE of Coquet Island

The *Lady Eleanor* (Official No.68929) was an iron-hulled 764-ton schooner-rigged steam cargo vessel measuring 60.96 m in length, with an 8.6-m beam. John G. Gulston of Sunderland built and completed her as Yard No.3 in 1875 and launched her in September 1875 for the 2nd Earl of Durham, George Frederick d'Arcy Lambton, Sunderland; the ship was also registered at Sunderland. The single iron screw was powered by a two-cylinder compound steam engine that used one boiler.

From 1891, the registered owner was the Rt. Honourable Charles Robert Grey, 5th Earl of Howick, at Sunderland.

Final voyage

During thick fog on 26 April 1895, the *Lady Eleanor*, a well-known Wear trader, sank following a collision with the 1,242-ton passenger/cargo steamer *Iona* (1883 – London and Edinburgh Shipping Co., Leith), 10 miles NE of Coquet Island. Of *Lady Eleanor*'s crew of 16, three men were lost: Mr Anderson, the chief engineer, William Todd, the steward, and a fireman, but the *Iona* rescued the other 13 crewmen and took them back to Sunderland. Captain J. Robinson from the stricken ship had a very narrow escape, as his vessel, which had been cleft almost in two by the force of the collision, went down; he fortunately seized hold of some wreckage and kept afloat for nearly half an hour before being picked up. The crewmen that drowned were last seen standing next to the rail of the sinking steamer. The *Lady Eleanor* had been on passage from Sunderland for Aberdeen with a cargo of coal when she was struck in the port side at about 2215 hrs by the bow stem of the *Iona*. *Lady Eleanor* was a well known Wear trader. The *Iona*, which was carrying a crew of 28 and 6 passengers from Leith to London, was left badly damaged.

BoT Wreck Return 1895, Appendix C, Table 1, p.147 (669); Miramar Ship Index; *The Times*, Monday, 29 April, 1895, p.6; Starke/Schell.

Wrecksite

This wreck, probably that of the *Lady Eleanor*, is orientated in a SE to NW direction. It lies on a firm seabed of sand and gravel in a general depth of 64 m (LAT). The wreck is upright but totally collapsed and well broken up, standing just 2 m high and covering an area 61 m long and 17 m across. Quite a number of crustaceans but not many fish have been observed around the wrecksite.

Sophie Annet, Ex Belair

Date of Loss: 25 September 1903
Wreck: ✶ ✶
Depth: 43 m
Reference: 55 26′.418 N 001 28′.263 W
Location: 4.24 nm NE of Seaton Point

The *Sophie Annet* was an iron-hulled 1,369-ton Netherlands schooner-rigged steam cargo ship measuring 74.62 m in length, with a 9.93-m beam and 5.02-m draught. J. and G. Thomson at Clydebank, Glasgow built and completed her as Yard No.175;

she was launched as the 1,419-ton *Belair* (Official No.82273) on 16 October 1879 for D. Caw and Co, Glasgow. The single iron screw was powered by a 150-hp, two-cylinder compound steam engine that used one boiler. The cylinders measured 68.58 cm and 132.08 cm with a 91.44-cm stroke (27 in. and 52 in. with a 36-in. stroke). She had five bulkheads and water ballast. The designated code recognition signal letters were: SVDH.

Caw, Prentice, Clapperton and Co., Glasgow was the registered owner in 1887. In 1890 she was sold to Belair S.S. Co. Ltd, Cardiff with Jugo and Co. the manager. The Lloyd's registered tonnage was 1,369 tons gross in 1891. In early 1893, she was sold to William Stoker, Cardiff (South Shields).

Later in 1893, J. E. Guthe and Co., Cardiff (West Hartlepool) purchased her. West Hartlepool Steam Navigation Co. Ltd, Cardiff was the registered owners in 1898.

Noord Nederl. Scheepvaart Maat at Harlingen, Netherlands, was the registered owner in 1900 and they renamed her *Sophie Annet*.

Final voyage

On the morning of Friday, 25 September 1903, the *Sophie Annet*, with Captain Khart in charge, was proceeding in ballast and on passage from Zaandam in the Netherlands for Grangemouth, when, during dense fog, she struck some rocks at the south end of Longstone in the Outer Farne Islands. The ship was badly holed but managed to pull herself clear. Six of the crew put off in a boat, with instructions from the master to stand by, but the *Sophie Annet*, with ten feet of water in the holds, slipped off and set away in a southerly direction towards Alnmouth. Meanwhile, the Scottish steam trawler *Isabella* of Montrose found the six crewmen in the boat and took it in tow; the men were later landed at Berwick. As the *Sophie Annet* proceeded south she met the Leith steamer *Warsaw* sailing from Sunderland to Leith and after a discussion between the two masters, it took her in tow. After travelling for some time, the *Sophie Annet* signalled to the Leith ship that she sinking rapidly, so the remaining 14 crewmen were immediately taken onboard the *Warsaw*. The wire hawser was let go and the *Sophie Annet* sank almost at once, going down bows first. The crew was landed at Leith on the Saturday, but their luggage and personal effects went down with the ship. The Netherlands Consul at Leith, Mr Turnbull, then arranged the return journey home for all 20 Dutch seamen.

On the day the crew was landed at Leith, Lloyd's agent at Beadnell also telegraphed *The Times*, alleging that 'the *Sophie Annet* had been involved in a collision with the Scottish herring boat *M.E. 606* off the Longstone', but this was a misunderstanding on the part of the agent.

The Times, Monday, 28 September 1903, p. 4; Starke/Schell; Register of American and Foreign Shipping, 1857–1900.

Wrecksite

The wreck, possibly that of the *Sophie Annet*, is orientated in a S to N direction and lies on a seabed of sand in a general depth of 43 m (LAT). It is now collapsed and well broken up, covering an area 43 m long and 15 m across, with the highest structures standing no more than 3 m from the seabed. A number of crustaceans but very few fish have been observed. If these are the remains of *Sophie Annet*, the bell if located, will be inscribed: *Belair* 1879.

Peik, Ex Regulus

Date of loss: 21 April 1917
Wreck: ✳ ✳ ✳ ✳
Depth: 36 m
Reference: 55 27'.647 N 001 30'.132 W
Location: 3.56 nm SE of Dunstanburgh Castle Point

The *Peik* was a steel-hulled 701-ton Norwegian cargo steamship that was registered in Sandefjord and measured 62.5 m in length, with a 9.1-m beam and a 4.2-m draught. Porsgrund Mekaniske Verksteder, Porsgrunn built and completed her as Yard No.56 in November 1910; she was launched as the *Regulus* on 10 October 1910 for Aktieselskapet 'Regulus', Kragerø; A.O. Lindvig was the manager. The single screw was powered by a 91-nhp, three-cylinder triple expansion steam engine that used one boiler and two furnaces. The cylinders measured 38.1-cm, 60.96-cm and 93.98-cm with a 66.04-cm stroke (15 in., 24 in. and 37 in. with a 26-in. stroke). Porsgrund Mekaniske Verksteder, Porsgrunn manufactured the engine and ancillary machinery. She was classed as 100 A1. The designated code recognition signal letters were: MGJB

In 1915, she was sold to Aktieselskapet 'Peik', Kragerø and renamed *Peik*; the manager was E. Jüel.

From 1916, Dampskipsselskapet Aktieselskapet Asnæs, Sandefjord was the registered owner and she was renamed *Peik*; Ole Drolshammer became the manager. Later in 1916, Håkon Rachlew became the manager.

Final voyage

On 21 April 1917, the KDM submarine SMU *UC 44*, commanded by Kapitänleutnant Kurt Tebbenjohanns, torpedoed and sank the *Peik*. The *Peik* had left the Tyne at 1130 hrs under the command of Captain Alfred Olsen, for passage to Arendal in Norway with a general mixed cargo, including aluminium. At 1600 hrs she was reported as having passed Coquet Island and was four miles from land when two of her crew, Thorvald Olsen (Second-in-Command of Pilots), who was on the gangway, and seaman Ivar Gabrielsen, on watch at the time, observed the white trail of a torpedo heading towards their ship on the starboard side. There was no time to take evasive action before it detonated against the machine room at the stern end, causing a violent explosion that knocked the crew off their feet and fractured the pilot's leg in two places. The pilot and seaman Gabrielsen both jumped into the sea. The port lifeboat, which was undamaged, was lowered down and the two men were picked up within ten minutes. All 15 crewmen were rescued by a British steam trawler and landed at the North Shields quay at 1930 hrs. The *Peik* went down by the bows and sank in between two and a half and three minutes, taking confidential papers with it. After the vessel had gone down, Captain Olsen, who was by this time in the lifeboat, noticed the submarine's periscope, later identified as belonging to *UC 44*, alongside the position of sinking. Fortunately none of the crew was lost, but the submarine gave no prior warning of the attack, even though the vessel was clearly marked as Norwegian.

Sjøforklaringer over norske skibes krigsforlis, 1914–1919; ANCL 1914–1918, p.95; LCWLR 1914–1918, p. 121.

Wrecksite

The wreck, which is probably that of the *Peik*, is orientated in an E to W direction. It lies on a seabed of fine sand, mud, broken shells and rock, in a general depth of 36 m (LAT). The wreck – referred to by local divers as 'the upside down wreck' – is reasonably intact but inverted and collapsed, with the highest part standing just over 3 m from the seabed. It covers an area of 64 m in length by 14 m across. Lying beneath the wreckage are large aluminium castings that appear to be part of a cargo.

Acclivity

Date of loss: 20 January 1952
Wreck: ✮ ✮ ✮
Depth: 26 m
Reference: 55 28'.118 N 001 32'.792 W
Location: 1.55 nm E of Craster and 2.06 nm SSE of Castle Point, Dunstanburgh

The *Acclivity* (Official No.162667) was a steel-hulled 389-ton British motor tanker measuring 49.98 m in length, with a 7.46-m beam and a 2.76-m draught. George Brown and Co. at Greenock built and completed her over 12 months as Yard No.182 in December 1931; she was launched on 29 October 1931 for F. T. Everard and Sons Ltd, London, who also owned her at the time of loss. The single bronze screw was powered by an aft-positioned 112-nhp, two-stroke single acting four cylinder diesel

The *Acclivity*

oil engine and a donkey boiler working at a pressure of 180 psi. Newbury Diesel Co. Ltd, Newbury manufactured the machinery. She had a flat keel, nine bulkheads cemented, one deck, a 13.10-m poop deck and a 6.09-m forecastle. The vessel also had 123 tons of cellular double bottom, a 46-ton deep-tank aft and a fore-peak and aft-peak tank. The designated code recognition signal letters were: MQDK.

The *Acclivity* was something of an innovation in her day as she was a low air draught tanker, designed to negotiate the bridges on the River Seine during her voyages with edible oil from Zwijndreche to Paris.

The tail shaft was inspected in May 1950 and fitted with an approved oil-retaining gland.

In January 1951 she was certified as 100A1 for carrying petroleum in bulk.

Final voyage

On 20 January 1952, the *Acclivity*, commanded by Captain C. Gould and transporting a cargo of linseed oil from Thames Haven to Newburgh in Fife, struck a submerged object which the master believed to be a wreck. When the vessel took on a heavy list to port, Captain Gould sent out a message saying his vessel was sinking and the crew took to the lifeboat. About one hour later, the 454-ton steam collier *Magrix* (1938 – R. Rix and Sons, Hull) picked them up, but the lifeboat broke up in the heavy swell just as it reached the collier's side. The *Acclivity* was then taken in tow by the *Magrix*, but after an hour the line parted and, soon after, at around dawn, the tanker foundered, 1.55 nm E of Craster. The crew were all safely landed at Amble.

LCR 1952, p. 4; Starke/Schell; *The Times*, Monday, 21 January 1952, p. 6; BoT Wreck Return, 1952.

Wrecksite

The wreck is orientated in a N by E to S by W direction and lies on a seabed of hard sand and gravel, in a general depth of 26 m (LAT). It is intact and leans over on its port side with the deck vertical against a small reef. The aft bridge structure has now fallen onto the stony seabed. There is a lot of debris lying in the small area between the decks and the reef. The bell has so far not been recovered and is very likely to have fallen into the silt and debris that has built up around the bow section.

The general layout is similar to any other small tanker, with few portholes and much of the forefront taken up with pipework. Steel railings still run the whole length of the vessel from the bridge to the small hatch at the bows. The stern section is well worth a visit, as the decking is now well deteriorated, making it reasonably easy to penetrate the open spaces below the decks. From this point, you can swim around to see the large rudder hanging from the pintles and the bronze screw still attached to the shaft above it. Plumose anemones cover the entire wreck, making it very pretty.

Buka, Ex Tika, Ex Henja, Ex Eben Haezer

Date of loss: 7 April 1970

Wreck: ✭ ✭ ✭

Depth: 36 m

Reference: 55 28'.782 N 001 30'.392 W

Location: 3.93 nm ESE of Castle Point, Dunstanburgh

Silhoutte of what Buka *would look like*

The *Buka* was a steel-hulled 198-ton Netherlands Skute-type motor cargo vessel measuring 32.24 m in length, with a 6.31-m beam and a 2.47-m draught. She was specifically designed to navigate the shallow channels of the Netherlands. N.V. Noord Nederlandsche Scheepswerven, Groningen built and launched her as the *Eben Haezer* in 1930 for J. H. Timmer, Groningen; B. Oeseburg was the manager. A 44-nhp, four-stroke single-acting four-cylinder diesel oil engine powered her single screw. The cylinders measured 26.99 cm (10⅝-in.) and 34.61 cm (13⅝ in.) Appingedammer Brönz, Motorenfb. N.V. manufactured the engine and ancillary machinery. She had one deck, an 8.8-m quarterdeck and 3.3-m forecastle. The designated code recognition signal letters were: PDUE.

On 11 August 1942, the Kriegsmarine Office at Rotterdam requisitioned the *Eben Haezer* as a substitute for the coastal motor vessel *Deni*, as the *Deni* had insufficient horsepower and was returned to the owner. The *Eeben Haezer* was then used as a transporter in the Speer Flotilla, Wiking, Norway. (Albert Speer was Hitler's Minister of Armaments and War Production during World War Two and was the mastermind of the Speer Flotilla, a large transport company under German military and civilian administration in the occupied areas. It operated hundreds of civilian-manned vessels in European and even African waters, the vessels very often being no more than converted barges.)

In August 1943, the *Eben Haezer* became a guardship in the West Baltic Coastal Protection Flotilla. On 9 May 1945 she was seen at Salangsverket, Norway. The *Eben Haezer* left Drontheim on 4 August 1945 and was taken over by representatives of the Netherlands Government at Kristiansand on the 13th. On 15 August 1945 she left Kristiansand for Copenhagen, where she arrived on the 19th, then arrived at Rotterdam on 20 September 1945. She was renamed *Henja* in 1958 when she was purchased by Henja. H. Prins at Groningen. Fa. W. F. Kampman, Amsterdam, purchased and renamed her *Tika* in 1962. From 1963, H. Buitenwerf at Groningen became the registered owner and renamed her *Buka*.

Final voyage

On the evening of 7 April 1970, the *Buka* left St. David's in Fife, bound for London with a 238-ton cargo of roadstone. The following morning, however, she was reported as having sprung a serious leak while 3.5 miles east of Castle Point, Dunstanburgh, Northumberland. The four crewmen were said to have abandoned ship because the *Buka* immediately filled up with water. Within 30 seconds she had disappeared and a passing coaster, the *Eleanor Dawson*, picked up the four men and landed them at Craster, three miles away.

LCR 1970, p. 20; LR 1969–1970, no.5415145 (B); Starke/Schell.

Wrecksite

The wreck is orientated in a SSE to NNW direction and lies on a seabed of firm sand, stone and rock in a general depth of 36 m (LAT). In 1997, this wreck was totally intact but the elements have taken their toll in recent times. Explosives were used on the wreck in around the year 1999 and it was reported to be lying partly on its side. It is now quite badly broken up, with the stern, which stands around 4.6 m from the seabed, listing about 45º to starboard. The bridge/wheelhouse is slowly collapsing and the hull sides of the hold have fallen over. The bows, however, are still intact and upright and stand 5 m high. The hold was supposed to have contained the 238 tons of roadstone, but that area has always been largely empty, apart from some deposits of silt. It seems unlikely that such a heavy cargo should disappear unless, of course, it was not there when the vessel sank.

Nidelven

Date of loss: 27 April 1917

Wreck: ✮ ✮ ✮ ✮

Depth: 39 m

Reference: 55 28′.647 N 001 29′.962 W

Location: 3.24 nm ESE of Castle Point, Dunstanburgh

Left: Painting of Nidelven
Right: Norwegian steamer Nidelven, *circa 1912*

The *Nidelven* was a steel-hulled 1,262-ton Norwegian steam passenger/cargo ship measuring 70.43 m in length, with a 10.13-m beam and a 4.11-m draught. Trondhjems Mekaniske Verksteder at Trondheim built and completed her as Yard No.134 in November 1908; she was launched on 23 September 1908 for Det Nordenfjeldske Dampskibsselskap, Trondheim, who was the owner at the time of loss. The single screw was powered by a 132-nhp, three-cylinder triple expansion steam engine that used one boiler. The cylinders measured 43.18 cm, 72.39 cm and 121.92 cm with an 83.82-cm stroke (17 in., 28½ in. and 48 in. with a 33-in. stroke). Trondhjems Mekaniske Verksteder, Trondheim manufactured the engine and ancillary machinery. She had one deck, an 84-ton (237.86-cubic m) quarterdeck, a 41-ton (116.09-cubic m) deckhouse and a 29-ton (82.11-cubic m) forecastle. Her designated code recognition signal letters were: MFKR.

Final voyage

At 1145 hrs on 27 April 1917, the *Nidelven*, with Captain Agnar Bjarne Aas in charge, struck a mine on the starboard side and sank 6 miles NE of Coquet Island; the mine having been laid the previous day by the KDM submarine SMU *UC 29*, commanded by Oblt.z. S. Ernst Rosenow. The steamer was on passage from the Tyne for Svolvær in Norway with a cargo of coal and passengers. Two of the crew were picked up from the sea by a steam trawler, the rest were rescued by the destroyer HMS *Test*. Later on that evening the whole crew were put on board the destroyer HMS *Penn* and taken to Leith, where they were put ashore the next morning. Eleven were taken to the naval hospital, with the rest of the crew going to the sailors' home. The three people who died were:

> Handberg, Arne, Mess Boy from Trondheim
>
> Lapaychuk, a passenger from Russia
>
> Svendsen, Gunnar, Sailor from Bod

Sjøforklaringer over norske skibes krigsforlis 1914–1919; LCWLR 1914–1918, p.125; ANCL 1914–1918, p. 93; LR 1915–1916, no.463 (N); Starke/Schell.

Wrecksite

The wreck is very substantial, sitting upright in a general depth of 39 m (LAT). The hull and outline is quite distinguishable all around and is intact up to about half way, to just below the deck, where it has collapsed down along with the superstructure and decking. These have collapsed down onto the boiler and engine, making access to anything rather difficult, but portholes and other artefacts are still recovered from time to time. Cod and other species of fish can sometimes be observed around the wreck, which should make an interesting boat-angling venue.

Hesvik, Ex Eduardo Grothmann, Ex Norderney

Date of loss: 23 September 1914

Wreck: ✳ ✳ ✳

Depth: 34 m

Reference: 55 28'.182 N 001 29'.673 W

Location: 3.54 nm SE of Castle Point, Dunstanburgh

The *Hesvik* was a steel-hulled 1,232-ton Norwegian steam cargo vessel measuring 71.09 m by length, with a 10.74-m beam and a 4.31-m draught. Act. Ges. Neptun, Rostock, Germany built and completed her as Yard No.164 in January 1898; she was launched as the *Norderney* at the end of 1897 for Nord-Ostsee Rhederei, Hamburg. Her steel propeller was powered by a three-cylinder, 93-hp triple expansion steam engine that used one boiler and gave 10 knots. The shipbuilders manufactured the machinery. She had one deck, a 21.33-m quarter deck, an 18.28-m bridge deck and 7.92-m forecastle.

In 1901 she was renamed *Eduardo Grothmann* by her new owners Richard Grothmann, Hamburg, Germany.

In 1913 she was sold to A/S Hesvik (Carl Bech and Co.), Tvedestrand in Norway and renamed *Hesvik*.

Final voyage

On 23 September 1914, the SS *Hesvik* was in ballast and on passage from Arendal, Norway for Grimsby when she detonated a mine and sank at about 2300 hrs. The crew was picked up by the British motor torpedo boat HMS *Itchen* at 1800 hrs the following day and were put ashore in North Shields. Two people were either killed in the explosion or drowned:

> Andersen, Oscar, First Engineer from Kristiansand
>
> Karlsen, Arnold, Donkeyman from Arendal

Captain Sven Marcussen, master of the *Hesvik*, wrote in the ship's log book and said in the Maritime Declaration that he believed his ship was 15 nm SSE of Longstone light when the mine detonated and it began to sink. Lloyd's, however, says that she was 8 miles south.

LR 1915–1916 no.62 (1); Starke/Schell.

Wrecksite

The wreck, which is now believed to be the *Hesvik*, is orientated in a SSE to NNW direction. It lies on a seabed of dark sand, gravel and rocks, in a general depth of 34 m (LAT). The hull is made from riveted iron and the remains are well and truly collapsed and broken up. Beginning at the iron screw, it is possible to swim along the prop shaft tunnel leading to the engine, which is still intact. All of the superstructure has fallen away and lies in a flattened tangle of rubble on either side, making it very low to the seabed. The engine and boiler, which stand upright, are still recognisable, with a donkey engine and boiler to the fore. Towards the bows, loose fittings, ribs and girders lie in a jumbled mass. Unlike many wrecks in this part of the sea, no nets have yet become entangled with the remains, making it a relatively safe dive, especially if the visibility is good. The wreck covers an area 80 m long and 22 m across and stands up about 3.2 metres off the seabed. The bow itself has deteriorated but still stands up about 3.5 m off the seabed. Off to the starboard of the bows are a lot of jumbled steel plates and framework, which may be the remains of the superstructure. To date, no bridge instruments have been found and it appears never to have been salvaged, although divers have recovered a number of portholes.

If this is the wreck of the *Hesvik*, the bell will be inscribed *Norderney* and, either *1897* or *1898*.

This wreck has always been considered to be that of the *Hogarth*, but about ten year ago a bell was located inscribed *Gaelic 1898*. A lot of serious research by the author and his friends, Andy Anderson and Ian Wright from Bishop Auckland diving club, has shown, however, that no ship of that name was lost off the northeast coast.

One other interesting theory is that 3.15 nm NE of this wreck, at 55 30'.175 N 001 25'.317 W, there is a wreck called the *Igor*, which was owned by the Gaelic Steam Ship Company in 1898. Although they renamed the ship *Cairnbahn*, it is possible that when they acquired the ship in 1898, they also made a bell called *Gaelic* after the company. Could this be her wreck? The only problem with this theory is that she had two boilers, while this wreck has only one.

Bonheur

Date of loss: 23 December 1918
Wreck: ✵ ✵ ✵ ✵ ✵
Depth: 103 m
Reference: 55 28'.452 N 000 54'.586 W
Location: 23.04 nm ENE of Coquet light and 25.83 nm SE of Longstone light

The *Bonheur* was a steel-hulled 7,133-ton Norwegian motor cargo vessel measuring 129.66 m in length, with a 16.84-m beam and an 8.40-m draught. A/S Burmeister and Wain, Copenhagen, Denmark built and completed her as Yard No.308 in June 1918; she was launched on 1 March 1918 for Aktieselskapet Dampskipsselskapet Bonheur, Kristiania, and Fred. Olsen and Co. was the manager. The twin steel screws were powered by two six-cylinder diesel engines that gave 11 knots. A/S Burmeister and Wain, Copenhagen manufactured the machinery.

Final voyage

On 23 December 1918, this big new ship detonated a mine during a raging gale, 23 miles from Coquet Island, and she very quickly began to founder. The *Bonheur* had left Kristiania on her maiden voyage, carrying a crew of 37 and a general cargo to Hull and South American ports. The master gave the order to abandon ship and 21 of the crew got away in one boat, while the others were busy lowering another. The first boat was carried away from the stricken vessel by the heavy seas and the men in it, being scantily clad with very little food, spent a dreadful time from the Monday evening to Thursday afternoon. One of the men died from exposure on Christmas morning and another succumbed in the afternoon. A donkeyman, a cook and the cabin boy were almost frozen to death by the time they were sighted by the 138-ton steam trawler *Ostero* (built in 1897 by Edwards Bros., North Shields) which picked up the remaining ten men and took them to Grimsby. On arrival, several of them were taken to hospital suffering from frostbite and exposure. The following 16 crewmen died in the sea:

Andersen, A.J.M., Boatswain, Copenhagen

Andersen, Emil, Sailor, Grandøse, Denmark

Andersen, Magnus, Cook, Kristiania

Brunstrøm, O.A., Sailor, Åbo, Finland

Drangseid, B, Assistant Engineer, Flekkefjord

Haakonson, Nils, Sailor, Sweden

Holther-Sørensen, R. Master, Kristiania

Holm, Karl, Second Engineer, Drammen

Knutsen, Sverre, First Engineer, Hvidsten

Larsen, A.J.Fr., Oiler, Denmark

Marthinsen, E., Fourth Engineer, Kristiania

Petterson, Karl, Sailor, Sweden

Pedersen Parkes, H., Sailor, Nakskov, Denmark

Schultz, Nils, Assistant Engineer, Fredrikstad

Steen, Adolf, Oiler, Kristiania

Teilman, Gunnar, Second Mate, Kristiania

LCWLR 1914–1918, p. 375; Starke/Schell; *The Times*, Saturday, 28 December 1918, p.3.

Wrecksite

The wreck, most probably that of the *Bonheur*, sits in a half-metre scour and is orientated in a SSE to NNW direction. It lies on a seabed of mud, sand and gravel, in a general depth of 103 m (LAT). The wreck is intact, except that it is broken in two amidships. It stands almost 9 m high and covers an area of 90 m in length by 15 m across, with several areas of loose debris.

Sphynx, Ex St. Philippe, Ex Sphynx, Ex Swansea

Date of loss: 29 January 1919

Wreck: ✷ ✷ ✷ ✷

Depth: 63 m

Reference: 55 29'.690 N 001 24'.753 W

Location: 5.97 nm E of Castle Point, Dunstanburgh

The *Sphynx* was an iron-hulled 1,698-gross ton Swedish steam cargo ship measuring 79.60 m in length, with an 11.09-m beam and holds 5.54 m deep. Blyth Shipbuilding and Dry Docks Co Ltd, at Cowpen Quay, Blyth built and completed her as Yard No.48 in September 1883; she was launched as the *Swansea* (Official No.91226) in September 1883 for Mesnier and Cie., Le Havre, in France. The single screw was powered by a 168-hp, two-cylinder compound steam engine. The cylinders measured 81.28 cm and 157.48 cm with a 106.68-cm stroke (32 in.and 62 in., with a 42-in stroke). R. and W. Hawthorn at Newcastle manufactured the engine and ancillary machinery. She had one deck, two tiers of beams, four cemented bulkheads, a 28.04-m quarter-deck, a 7.06-m bridge deck and 10.05-m forecastle. The ship was originally 1,493-tons but was altered some time later.

She was renamed *Sphynx* by Moss Steam Ship Co. Ltd at Liverpool in 1885.

Soc. Navale de l'Ouest, Le Havre purchased and renamed her *St. Philippe* in 1896.

Welfare Shipping Co. Ltd, Sunderland purchased and renamed her *Sphynx* in 1909; C. J. Welch and Co. was the manager.

In 1912, Ångfartygs A/B Sphynx, Helsingborg bought her and B. O. Börjesson was the manager. Her official number then became 5332.

She had the same owners in 1917, but F. Börjesson became the manager.

In 1918 the ship was requisitioned by the Shipping Controller in London and H. Cail and Co. was appointed as the Crown nominee manager.

At the end of 1918 she was returned to the Swedish owners, Ångfartygs A/B Sphynx. The designated code recognition signal letters were: JWNT.

Final voyage

On 29 January 1919, the *Sphynx* left Sunderland for Malmö, Sweden with a cargo of coal, but detonated a mine at 2200 hrs and sunk in the North Sea near Coquet Island. From her crew of 18 men, only one survived. Those that died were:

Andersson, Karl August Leonard, 37 yrs

Backe, Birger Pontus, 25 yrs

Bengtsson, Hugo Benjamin Palander, 19 yrs

Eriksson, Benjamin, 29 yrs

Gitkewitch, S., from Russia, 45 yrs

Ivanoff, Vladimir, from Poland, 21 yrs

Johansson, Axel Fredrik, 40 yrs

Johansson, O.V., from Finland, 46 yrs

Johansson, Ola, 46 yrs

Knutsson, Kristian, Master, 42 yrs

Lundgren, Johan Edvin, 32 yrs

Olsen, S., from Norway, 18 yrs

Pålsson, Emil Filip, 29 yrs

Roslund, Axel Wilhelm, 32 yrs

Sandgren, J.G. from Finland, 32 yrs

Stengård, Carl Emil, 34 yrs

Svensson, Karl Johan Ivan, 28 yrs

Starke/Schell; LCWLR 1914–1918, p. 375.

Wrecksite

The wreck, probably that of the *Sphynx*, is orientated in a NNE to SSW direction, with the bows to the NNE. It sits in a very long one-metre deep scour and lies on a seabed of mud, sand, black shells and gravel, in a general depth of 63 m (LAT). It is upright, appears intact, stands 6.7 m high and covers an area of 62 m in length by 11 m across. 140 m to the NE, however, there is also a large amount of wreck debris that could be from this wreck and is worth investigating. There are reported to be four holds that are still full of hundreds of tons of coal. If this is the *Sphynx*, the bell, if located, will be inscribed: *Swansea 1883*.

Bør

Date of loss: 21 February 1918
Wreck: ✶ ✶ ✶
Depth: 95 m
Reference: 55 29'.147 N 001 09'.585 W
Location: 15.66 nm NE of Coquet Island

The *Bør* was a steel-hulled 1,149-ton Norwegian steam cargo ship measuring 69.72 m in length, with an 11.02-m beam and a 4.77-m draught. Nylands Verksted built and completed her at Kristiania as Yard No.239 on 27 July 1914; she was launched for Aktieselskapet 'Ganger Rolf' (Bonheur), Kristiania, who was also the owner at the time of loss; Fred Olsen and Co., Kristiania was the manager. The single steel screw was powered by a 148-nhp, three-cylinder triple expansion steam engine that used one boiler. Nylands Verksted also manufactured the engine and ancillary machinery at Kristiania. She had one deck, a 6.7-m poopdeck, a 20.4-m bridge deck and 8.2-m forecastle. Her designated code recognition signal letters were: MKLT.

Final voyage

On 21 February 1918, the KDM submarine SMU *UC 49*, commanded by Oblt.z. S. Hans Kükenthal, torpedoed and sank the *Bør* off Coquet Island. The *Bør*, which had Captain John Sundby as the master, was on passage from the Tyne for Kristiania with 883 tons of coal and 520 tons of aluminium powder. Without any warning, she was struck at 1500 hrs in front of the no.3 hatch and the First Engineer, Leif F. Dæhlin from Kristiania, was killed. The remaining 17 crew members were picked up by an armed escort trawler and landed at Leith the following day. The position, according to the Maritime Declarations of Norwegian Ships, was sunk at 55 27′ N 01 09′ W.

Sjøforklaringer over norske skibes krigsforlis 1914–1919; LCWLR 1914–1918, p. 202; ANCL 1914–1918, p. 76.

Wrecksite

The wreck, which is probably that of the Norwegian steamer, is orientated in a SE to NW direction. It lies on a seabed of mud and fine sand in a general depth of 95 m (LAT). The wreck sits in a one-metre deep scour that extends over 55 m in length, but the wreck itself covers an area 53 m long and 14 m across and stands 3.6 m high. It is probably intact, but appears to be inverted.

Caledonia, HM Trawler

Date of loss: 17 March 1917
Wreck: ✳ ✳ ✳
Depth: 69 m
Reference: 55 30′.793 N 001 16′.458 W
Location: 10.86 nm ENE of Castle Point, Dunstanburg

Silhouette of HM steam trawler Caledonia

The *Caledonia* was a steel-hulled 161-ton ketch-rigged steam trawler measuring 34.18 m in length, with a 6.42-m beam and a 3.37-m draught. Hall, Russell and Co. Ltd, Aberdeen built and completed her as Yard No.409 in September 1906; she was launched on 22 August 1906 for Thomas L. Devlin at Granton. The single screw was powered by a 65-hp, three-cylinder triple expansion steam engine that used one boiler. She had one deck. Port reg: GN.34.

In 1915, the vessel was requisitioned and in March 1917 was designated for Special Service.

Final patrol

On 17 March 1917, HMT *Caledonia* was off Newton Point, Northumberland, on her way from Aberdeen to Lowestoft for fitting out as a Special Service vessel, when the KDM submarine SMU *UC 50*, commanded by Kapitänleutnant Rudolf Seuffer, captured her.

At 1500 hrs and 20 miles E by S of Longstone, *UC 50* had stopped and sunk the 181-ton British trawler *Kestrel*; the crew was ordered into the lifeboat but her skipper was taken prisoner. Then, at 1600 hrs, the *Caledonia* was sighted. She was flying the White Ensign, but quickly hauled it down and surrendered and the crew was taken on board the submarine. The circumstances probably did not allow for a closer inspection of the trawler. The *Caledonia* was then scuttled using explosive charges/grenades.

The 25-ton drifter HMS *Gowan*, which was also on her way from Aberdeen to Lowestoft for fitting out, was intercepted 15 miles SE of Longstone. The crew was ordered into the lifeboat and the drifter was sunk with one 88-mm shell hit. The skipper of the *Kestrel* joined the bulk of the crews of the *Caledonia* and *Gowan* in the lifeboats, where one of *Gowan's* crew, George Holdsworth Moat, a deckhand in the RNR, later died of exposure.

Rudolf Seuffer took as prisoners of war the skipper of *Caledonia* (described as a warrant officer in the RNR) and a leading machinist. Initial interrogation by the U-boat's crew suggested that the purpose of the *Caledonia* was tending to the harbour defence minefields. Other sources claim that the *Gowan* was being towed by the *Caledonia*.

Lloyd's War Losses 1914–1918, p.106; *British Fishing Vessels Lost at Sea Due to Enemy Action*, 1914–1918; ADM 137/339; ADM 137/390.

Wrecksite

The wreck, possibly that of the *Caledonia*, is orientated in a SE to NW direction, with the bows to the southeast. It lies on a seabed of fine sand, mud and black shells in a general depth of 69 m (LAT). The wreck is intact and stands over 4 m high with some debris close by. It covers an area of 32 m in length by about 6 m across, with larege numbers of fish swimming over the wreck.

Igor, Ex Cairnbahn, Ex Trevider

Date of loss: 17 September 1918
Wreck: ✫ ✫ ✫ ✫

Depth: 58 m

Reference: 55 30'.175 N 001 25'.317 W

Location: 5.77 nm ENE of Castle Point, Dunstanburgh

The *Igor* (Official No.81677) was an iron-hulled 1,534-ton Swedish steam cargo ship measuring 79.07 m in length, with a 10.99-m beam and a 5.3-m draught. John Readhead and Co. at South Shields built and completed her as Yard No.200 in October 1883; she was launched as the *Trevider* on 29 October 1883 for E. Hain and Son, St. Ives. The single steel screw was powered by a 161-nhp, two-cylinder compound steam engine that used two single-ended boilers with four furnaces, 6.03 m (65 sq. ft) of grate surface and 251.39 m (2706 sq. ft) of heating surface. The cylinders measured 76.2 cm and 147.32 cm with a 91.44-in. stroke (30 in. and 58 in. with a 36-in.stroke). John Readhead and Company manufactured the engine and ancillary machinery at South Shields. She had one deck, a well deck, a 31.1-m quarterdeck, a 19.3-m bridge deck and an 8.5-m-forecastle.

In 1885, Trevider SS. Co. Ltd, St. Ives was the registered owner and E. Hain and Son was the manager.

Gaelic S.S Co. Ltd at Newcastle purchased the ship in 1898 and and renamed it *Cairnbahn*; Cairns, Young and Noble was the manager. A new donkey boiler was fitted in 1900.

In 1904 she had the same owner but Cairns, Noble and Co. became the managers.

In 1912, Cairn Line of Steamships, Ltd was the registered owner using the same managers.

She was renamed *Igor* in 1913 by Rederi A/B Hebe, Helsingborg and G. W. von Liewen was the manager. In February/March 1916, the registered owner was Rederi A/B Igor, Sundsvall and L. Norström was the manager.

From July 1917, AB Svenska Amerika-Mexico-Linien, Göteborg in Sweden was the registered owner and Dan Broström became the manager.

Final voyage

At 1845 hrs on 17 September 1918, the *Igor*, commanded by Captain O. T. Christianson, reportedly developed a serious leak and sank ten miles south of Longstone light. Lloyd's and a Swedish source stated that she was either torpedoed or struck by a mine. The steamer was part of a convoy and on passage from Göteborg for the Tyne with a general cargo, including wood. All of her crew safely abandoned ship in the boats and an escort vessel picked them up.

LR 1915–1916, no.62 (1); Starke/Schell.

Wrecksite

The wreck, probably that of the *Igor*, is orientated in an ESE to WNW direction. It lies on a firm seabed of dark sand and black shells in a general depth of 58 m (LAT). The wreck is upright and intact, covering an area 63 m long and 15 m across and stands about 7 m high around the collapsed bridge superstructure. Plenty of marine life has been observed, including some very large cod, making this an excellent boat-angling venue. If the bell is recovered it will almost certainly be inscribed *Trevider 1883*. Interestingly, though, a ship's bell inscribed *Gaelic 1898* was recovered from a wreck, thought to be the *Hesvik*, at 55 28'.188 N 001 29'.677 W. As mentioned above, the *Igor* was purchased by the Gaelic Steam Ship Company in 1898.

Patia, HMS

Date of loss: 27 April 1941
Wreck: ✮ ✮ ✮ ✮ ✮
Depth: 57 m
Reference: 55 31'.420 N 001 26'.098 W
Location: 6.54 nm SE of Beadnell Point

Elders Fyffes steamer, Patia

HMS *Patia* (Official No.145920) was a steel-hulled 5,355-ton British steam catapult ship measuring 123.05 m in length, with a 16-m beam and a 9.24-m draught. Camel Laird and Co. Ltd, Birkenhead built and completed her as Yard No.885 in March 1922; she was launched on 14 January 1922 for Elders and Fyffes Ltd, Liverpool and registered there. The single screw was powered by a 447-nhp, three-cylinder triple expansion steam engine that used three single-ended boilers and gave 13.5 knots. The cylinders measured 69.85 cm, 118.11 cm and 198.12 cm with a 137.16-cm stroke (47.5 in., 46.5 in. and 78 in. with a 54-in. stroke). Camel Laird and Co. Ltd manufactured the engine and ancillary machinery at Birkenhead. She had two decks, two part decks, water ballast, a 12.89-m poop deck, a 47.85-m bridge deck and a 13.41-m forecastle. The *Patia* was fitted with a wireless direction finder. From 1934 the designated code recognition signal letters were: GDCY.

The Admiralty requisitioned the ship as an Ocean Boarding Vessel in October 1940.

In March 1941, *Patia* was rebuilt to a Pegasus Class Auxilliary Fighter Catapult Ship, capable of launching Hurricane aeroplanes. She was armed with two 6-inch guns, three H.A. quick-firing guns, two Hotchkiss, two pom-poms and three of the newly-invented Harvey three-inch rocket-missile projectors, to use against enemy aircraft. This class, consisting of *Ariguani*, *Patia*, *Maplin*, *Springbank* and *Pegasus*, were converted from merchant cargo ships in an effort to try and combat the long-range German Folke Wulf 200 Condor reconnaissance aircraft that were exploiting the gap in the mid-Atlantic, beyond the range of Allied aircraft. The reconnaissance aircraft used this lack of air cover to guide their U-boat wolf packs towards Allied convoys.

For a Hurricane Catapult pilot, though, it was a one-way journey once he had left the ship, because there was nowhere to land but the sea.

After her completion by Brigham and Cowan at South Shields, *Patia* was commissioned on 26 April as a Fighter Catapult Ship and the following day proceeded out of the Tyne for gun trials, returning at 1600 hrs.

Final voyage

At 1825 hrs on 27 April 1941, HMS *Patia* left her berth and sailed down the River Tyne, bound for Belfast, where she was to pick up the Hurricane aircraft. Thousands of people lined the river to see her off on her maiden voyage. From South Shields she headed north, accompanied by a single Blenheim aircraft, which left her when darkness set in. *Patia* was about 4 miles off Boulmer, Northumberland and the crew was looking for the 20F buoy when she was attacked by an Aalborg-based German Heinkel III, coming in from the eastward, bearing Green 130°. The ship was at cruising stations and her radar (RDF) set was faulty.

Lt. D.A. Chantler RNR, one of the survivors, stated at the Inquiry:

We passed 20G Buoy at 2117 hrs and about three minutes later I spotted this attacking plane and we were taken by surprise, as it was flying at a height of 70 feet. On approaching, the aircraft dropped one bomb about one mile away – it was a bad miss. The plane then flew over the ship and dropped a second bomb, which was a near miss on the port side. Action Stations were sounded after the first bomb dropped. Unfortunately we were taken by surprise and no guns were brought into action on the first attack. She flew to the north and west and attacked again from the northward about five minutes later. At the time of the first assault, the commander put the helm hard to starboard.

In the second strike everyone held their fire until the plane was within range. All AA armament was brought to bear. In that attack the aircraft opened fire with machine guns and dropped two more bombs, which fell well clear of the ship, slightly on port quarter, at masthead height. In that attack the starboard pom-pom and after port Hotchkiss jammed; Lieutenant Webb was on the gun. After flying over the ship she flew away to the southward and then attacked again from aft, this time raking us with machine gun fire. I think Lt Nicholls met his death on the Harvey Projector, amidships aft. The aircraft passed over the ship over port bow and flew out of sight and was again seen later to be flying east and south. We rested the gun crews; she made a final attack from port quarter. In that attack she opened fire with machine guns at a very low altitude and also dropped three bombs. All AA armament we could bring to bear opened fire. The first bomb was a near miss astern, the second hit the ship, holing either the after starboard side of the engine room or forward side of no.3 hold. The third dropped on the starboard side, a near miss that damaged the bridge. The plane dropped a flare and opened fire with after machine guns. Immediately flames burst from the tail of the plane and she seemed to disappear into the sea, close by. I went round the ship seeing boats away. I was with the captain just before I jumped overboard with the Carley float. The ship had righted herself after heeling over to port, but was beginning to founder. The sea came up on the boat deck and Lt Menhinick threw over the Carley float and Lt Cdr Robbin jumped over together with Lt Menhinick, an AB and myself. We nearly went down with the ship, but fortunately her stern stuck in the mud and we drifted with the tide clear of her.

Temporary Lt A. Menhinick RNVR was not part of the ship's company but was on passage with her to train the crews on the use of the Harvey Projector. He was rescued by the *Chassiron* at 0230 hrs.

Lt Chantler also said it was a fine twilit night at the time and he thought it was the Hotchkiss or pom-pom that brought the plane down as it was too short a range for the Harvey Projector. When asked if they were able to take any avoiding action, Lt. Chandler said: 'We could have, but we did not take it because Commander Baker said that he did not agree to the taking of avoiding action, we could bring more to bear when attacking from forward or aft.'

HM Trawler *Chassiron* picked Lt Chandler up, along with the German flight crew and Chief Petty Officer Prior.

When asked about the aircraft being shot down, Mr S.V. Gibbs, a Commissioned Gunner RN, said: 'I saw it actually on fire which was caused by 3-inch or by the Harvey Projector. Firing was effective all round.'

The following is an extract from an account written later by Chief Engineer Lt Cdr A. E. Robbin RNR, who was a survivor on *Patia* and was also a witness at the inquiry:

> During the action I was in the engine room with the second, fourth, sixth and seventh engineers, electrical engineer, donkeyman, storekeeper and greasers. One bomb hit no.3 hold, adjoining the engine room. The shock of the explosion fractured the main steam pipe, the engine room being filled with live steam and all the lights failing. The engine room had to be abandoned immediately. Of the engine room staff, the second engineer was in hospital for more than four months, recovering from burns and shock. The seventh engineer and electrical engineer died in hospital. The fourth engineer's body was picked up on a Carley float, badly scalded. The donkeyman and storekeeper's bodies were never recovered.
>
> After making our way to the upper deck, the sixth engineer and myself assisted in shutting steam off the engine room, after which I reported to the commanding officer. By this time the ship was settling, the after deck being underwater. Some of the boats were badly damaged, the last being lowered away at this time. The C.O. and I decided that as this boat was overloaded, we could stay on board as long as possible, together with two officers, one seaman and a Carley float.
>
> The C.O. left me to go to his cabin to destroy some confidential papers. This was the last time he was seen alive, his body being picked up on a float the following day, dead from exposure. A few minutes after the C.O. left me, at about 2150 hrs, the ship began to sink rapidly and the two officers, the seaman and myself jumped overboard with the Carley float.
>
> Unfortunately, when the *Patia* sank, the last boat to be lowered capsized, throwing the occupants, including several wounded, into the water. We on the float paddled around and picked up about a dozen of these men. After being in the water for some time we found great difficulty in keeping conscious, the sea being so cold. Before being picked up by the French trawler HMT *Chassiron*, three of the men on the float had died from exposure. It picked us up at about 0230 hrs. We had then been in the water approximately 4½ hours

and were landed at North Shields at about 0800 hrs. After being there five days, I proceeded on survivor's leave.'

This report is courtesy of Lt. Cdr. (E) A.F. Robbin's daughter, Mrs Nena Murstad, and Tel/Radar Officer William H. Pope.

Thirty one of the bedraggled and exhausted crew, many with their clothes burnt off and suffering from terrible burns, broken bones and serious wounds, managed to drift and scramble the four miles to shore in a lifeboat, where a policeman and soldiers directed them towards the little village of Boulmer. Some of the sailors, no more than boys who had lied about their ages to enlist in the navy, were crying in despair. While the ship's crew was arriving on shore, the local lifeboat was called out with an armed escort to pick up three of the survivors from the German plane (one crewman had been killed in the attack) and it was only when they found themselves in the midst of a great deal of wreckage that the lifeboat crew realised that a British ship had gone down. Local people rallied round and gave the sailors dry clothes, towels and treated their wounds; then they were given wine and spirits that were set up in the Fishing Boat Inn. All the children at the village school were sent home a few hours early to allow them to see the ship's crew leave for North Shields in a bus. The men were given 14 days leave after being shipwrecked, but sadly – and some would say disgracefully – their pay was stopped the moment the ship went down. A Board of Inquiry decided that because the ship was at cruising stations when she was attacked, they were at fault for being taken by surprise. Following that tragedy, the whole of the British Fleet was reminded and instructed to stay on the alert while off the northeast coast.

Commander Baker had been Chief Officer with Elder and Fyffes during peacetime.

Rumours abounded that a German spy had been on board the *Patia*, but there was never any proof or evidence of this.

Commander David Marion Burton Baker RNR, seven officers and 31 ratings were reported missing or killed:

Commander David Marion Burton Baker RNR, seven officers and thirty-one ratings were reported missing or killed:

> Baker, David M. B., Commander RNR, killed
> Bartram, Norman, Petty Officer Steward NAP, killed
> Cook, William Charles, Able Seaman RN, missing
> Davis, Reginald, Acting Leading Signalman RN, missing
> Day, Morris Nathanial, Fireman, NAP, missing
> Doherty, John, Greaser NAP, killed
> Downs, James Robert, Fireman NAP, killed

Ferguson, John, Donkeyman NAP, killed

Godley, Albert William, Ordinary Seaman RN, killed

Gray, William, Carpenter NAP, killed

Hengler, Sidney J, Storekeeper NAP, killed

Hughes, George, Butcher 2nd class NAP, killed

Huzzey, William Alfred, Assistant Storekeeper NAP, killed

James, John Edward, Ordinary Seaman RN

Jewers, William, Greaser NAP, missing

Jones, Alfred, Ordinary Seaman RN, killed

Lawence, Leonard, Greaser NAP, killed

Matcham, Arthur, Storekeeper NAP, missing

Minten, Leonard Alfred, Ordinary Seaman RN, missing

Neuling, Julius Peter, Greaser NAP, killed

Nicholls, Cyril Sydney, Temp. Lieutenant RNVR, killed

Orman, William Frank, Fireman NAP, killed

Owen, Frederick Joseph, Lieutenant RNR, missing

Owen, Royston William Henry, Second Writer NAP

Parish, Frederick Arthur, Able Seaman RN, missing

Pelling, Henry, Fireman NAP, missing

Phillips, Godfrey Sidney Philip, Ordinary Seaman RNVR

Prim, Benjamin K., Temp.Sub Lt. (E), RNVR, killed

Riley, Edward Lawrence, Lieutenant RNVR, missing

Rogers, Douglas, Fireman NAP, killed

Short, Cyril, Ordinary Seaman, killed

Smith, John, Ordinary Seaman RN, killed

Smith, Wilfred Stennentt, Ordinary Coder RN

Stafford, George, Fireman NAP, killed

Tompkins, Frederick E, Petty Officer Steward NAP Vowles, Raymond
Hubert Ray, First Writer NAP, missing

Williams, Bertram Erskine Thomas, Py/Ty/Lt RNR, missing

Died later from wounds:

Jennings, Neville, Electrician NAP, 28/4/41
Kirkham, W., Temp. Act. Sub Lt. (E) RNVR, 28/4/41

Wounded:

Connor, Walter, Telegraphist RNV (W) R
Cousins, Desmond A., Ordinary Coder RN

Downs, Robert, Fireman NAP

Edmond, John, Fireman NAP

Forster, Richard T., Fireman NAP

Gervause, Walter L., Fireman NAP

Gilbertstedt, Robert V., Able Seaman RN

Goodman, Alfred S., Assistant Steward NAP

Johnson, Raymond, Ordinary Seaman RN

Jones, Charles E., Assistant Steward NAP

Jones, E., Temporary Lt. Engineer RNR

Kilbride, John, Ordinary Seaman RN

Maddock, E. H., Temporary Sub.Lt. Engineer RNR

McDonald, J., Temporary Paymaster Sub.Lt. RNR

McDonald, Leslie, Fireman NAP

Moor, George, Ordinary Seaman

Pawley, Richard J., Able Seaman RN

Ryan, David J., Ordinary Seaman RN

Sadler, A., Ordinary Seaman RN

Shields, John R., Able Seaman RN

Swinney, Dixon, Ordinary Seaman RN

Wade, Stanley, Ordinary Seaman RN

Watt, A., Temporary Surgeon Lt. RNVR

ADM 1/11290; N.L. 9782; LCWLR 1939–1945, p. 232; BVLS 1939–1945, p. 12; SRN Vol. 2, p. 271; CWGC.

Wrecksite

This large naval vessel is orientated almost N to S and lies on a seabed of firm sand in a general depth of 57 m (LAT), with her decks at 48 m and a least depth 43 m. It sits upright all the way back to no. 3 hold, where it was broken by the bomb's direct hit. From this point to the stern, it is twisted through 90°, leaving the decks lying nearly vertical. Starting near the bridge and swimming over to the bow on the port side, the diver can still see the railway track-like structure, which was used to launch the Hurricane fighter plane. Halfway back from this ramp stands the large derrick that was used to lift the Hurricane onto the tracks, still standing erect and pointing towards the surface like some weird sentinel. The derrick is now festooned in masses of trawl net and is held aloft by dozens of floats. When descending down through the eerie gloom the net makes a strange but very spectacular sight. Moving back to the bridge, the main body is still recognisable, although there has been some collapse of the bridge roof, making the main bridge compartment only 1.5

m high. Inside are the remains of the bridge operating systems, with the wooden wheel, although badly worn, still intact and within arm's reach, while behind the wheel is the doorway leading into Captain Baker's cabin. The door has long since rotted off, leaving a black, cold and uninviting void. The bridge wings still have anti-aircraft guns defiantly pointing towards the surface with empty shells lying scattered around the base, testifying to the brave and heroic fight the crew put up against the Heinkel bomber. Moving away back from the bridge to the engine room, skylights allow the diver to see right down the stairwell to the engine room and further back still, revealing the gaping hole where the funnel once stood, flanked on four sides by ventilation shafts that supplied air to the engines. Close by are the davits that had been left outboard, providing the means of escape for the ship's crew. A little further back, the wreck is twisted and broken, with the decks changed from horizontal to vertical. Caution is required at this point, because a very large trawl net is suspended from the bottom of the deck and lies like a huge curtain, nearly parallel with the decks. The net is also suspended on floats and is a considerably danger to the diver in the very dim light and murky conditions. The ship's main bell lies someway off the wreck, left there when a lifting bag to which it was tied broke loose and fell back to the seabed. Large cod, bib, pollack, ling and probably conger can be found all around the wreck, making it an excellent boat-angling venue.

Patia is one of the most spectacular wrecks off the northeast coast but because of her size and the depth involved, she presents the diver with much more of a challenge than do many other wrecks in similar depths. It should also be remembered that she is a war grave. As recently as September 1997, some of the ship's brave survivors visited the area to meet local people who helped them in their time of need.

Storfors

Date of loss: 27 February 1940
Wreck: ✭ ✭ ✭ ✭ ✭
Depth: 75 m
Reference: 55 32'.075 N 001 19'.898 W
Location: 9.99 nm ESE of Beadnell Point

The *Storfors* (Official No. 5957) was a steel-hulled 550-ton Swedish steam cargo vessel measuring 50.08 m in length, with an 8.3-m beam and a 3.27-m draught. Göteborgs Mekaniske Verkstader AB, Göteborg, Sweden built and completed her as Yard No. 350 on 18 March 1918; she was launched on 19 December 1917 for Uddeholms AB, Uddeholm in Sweden, who was also the owner at the time of loss; A. Herlenius was the manager. The single steel screw was powered by an aft-positioned 68-nhp three-cylinder triple expansion steam engine that used one single-ended boiler and gave 8.5 knots. The cylinders measured 13⅜ in., 22¼ in. and 37⅜ in. with a 23⅝-in. stroke. Göteborgs MV.Altieb., Göteborg in Sweden manufactured the machinery. She had one deck, a 14.9-m poop deck, a 49-ton (138.75-cubic.m) house deck and a 7-m forecastle and was fitted with electric lighting. The designated code recognition signal letters were: SGOW.

In 1930, Fritiof Olsson was the manager.

Final voyage

On the night of 27 February 1940, the *Storfors* foundered following a collision with the 1690-ton destroyer HMS *Jackal*, 12 miles from Beadnell Point. The *Storfors* was sailing as part of the northbound 26-ship convoy TM.15 (Tyne to Methil) and was transporting a cargo of coal from Hull to Gothenburg. The crew of 14 abandoned the vessel, which was in danger of sinking, were picked up by the warship and landed at a northeast port the next day, although a local lifeboat had spent three hours searching for the men.

LCR 1940 p. 9 (f); LR 1919–1920, no. 27121 (S); IDNS p.144; Starke/Schell; Miramar Ship Index.

Wrecksite

The wreck is orientated in a NE to SW direction and lies on a firm seabed of gravel and sand in a general depth of 75 m (LAT). It is upright and intact and stands almost 7.5 m at the stern end, which faces to the southwest, where the bridge/wheelhouse superstructure is still almost complete and covered in a profusion of soft corals. All of the vessel's interesting bridge equipment, lifeboat davits, winches, doors and portholes are still in place. Lots of large fish, mostly cod, have been observed all over the wreck so it will make an excellent boat-angling venue.

Lunesdale

Date of loss: 12 March 1929
Wreck: ✮ ✮ ✮ ✮
Depth: 70 m
Reference: 55 32'.817 N 001 23'.397 W
Location: 7.81 nm E by S of Beadnell Point

The *Lunesdale* (Official No. 127934) was   *Silhouette of British steamer,* Lunesdale
a steel-hulled 216-ton British steam cargo
vessel measuring 35.07 m in length, with a
6.57-m beam and a 2.57-m draught. Thomas Dobson and Co. Ltd at Hessle, Hull built and completed her as Yard No.151 in October 1908; she was launched in the

third quarter of 1908 for Lancaster and Liverpool S.S. Co. Ltd at Liverpool. An aft-positioned 60-hp, two-cylinder compound steam engine that used one single-ended boiler powered the single steel screw. Shields Engineering Co. Ltd manufactured the machinery at North Shields. She had one deck, three bulkheads, a 13.1-m quarterdeck, a 2.7-m bridge deck and 5.8-m forecastle.

From 1919, she was registered in Wexford and owned by James J. Stafford of Paul Quay, Wexford until at least 1921.

Chalrton, Oscar and Young owned her at the time of loss and Captain Daniel McLennan was the master.

Final voyage

At 0250 hrs on 12 March 1929, the *Lunesdale,* with Captain Daniel McLennon in charge, sank following a collision with the 1667-ton SS *Melrose* (1906 – George Gibson and Co., Leith) in thick fog, 7 miles S by E of Longstone lighthouse. Four men were drowned, including the master, but the *Melrose* picked up three others. The *Lunesdale* was on passage from Sunderland for Banff with a cargo of coal. A number of boats, including the Holy Island lifeboat, put to sea to search for the men, but after a fruitless search returned to base in the afternoon. The *Melrose* had a slight leak in the forepeak but carried on with her voyage to Kirkpatrick. The crewmen lost were:

Lambert, G., MM of Hull

Mayne, H., MM of Avoch

McLennan, Daniel, Master MM of Avoch

Reid, W., MM of Avoch

The survivors were:

Reid, D., Mate MM

Sutherland, J., Seaman MM

Swanson, J., Chief Engineer MM

On 15 March 1940, the steamer *Melrose* was mined and sunk near Ostend.

LCR 1929, p. 8 (f); LR 1927–1928, no.27921 (L); *The Times,* Wednesday, 13 March 1929, p.18.

Wrecksite

The wreck, believed to be that of the *Lunesdale,* is orientated in a SSE to NNW direction with and the bows to the NNW. It lies on a seabed of firm sand and gravel in a general depth of 70 m (LAT). It is upright, reasonably intact, with the aft superstructure 5.5 m high, but partially collapsed. The deck machinery, davits and jibs are completely intact, if a little bent, and a section of short broken mast, up forward towards the bows, is still in place, with the rest lying broken up across the deck. There is a large hole where the funnel once stood, giving access to to the inside of the bridge structure and holds, which still contain part of the cargo of coal, although a section of hold is now split open.

Baltanglia, Ex *Langfond,* Ex *Laatefos*

Date of loss: 23 January 1940
Wreck: ✵ ✵ ✵ ✵ ✵
Depth: 59 m
Reference: 55 32'.925 N 001 28'.207 W
Location: 5.00 nm E of Beadnell Point

Norwegian steamer Baltanglia

The *Baltanglia* (Official No.165459) was a steel-hulled 1,532-ton British steamship measuring 77.9 m in length, with a 12-m beam and 6-m draught. Ardrossan Shipbuilding and Dry Dock Co. Ltd, Ardrossan built and completed her as Yard No.319 in October 1921; she was launched as the *Laatefos* on 27 April 1921 for Thor Thoresens Linje Aktieselskapet, Kristiania, Norway; Thor Thoresen was the manager and she was registered in Kristiania. The single screw was powered by a 203-nhp three-cylinder triple expansion steam engine that used two single-ended boilers working at a pressure of 180 psi, with six corrugated furnaces, 9.75-sq. m

(105 sq. ft) of grate surface and 326.83 sq. m (3518 sq. ft) of heating surface, which gave 9.5 knots. The cylinders measured 48.26 cm, 81.28 cm and 132.08 cm with a 91.44-cm stroke (19 in., 32 in. and 52 in. with a 36-in. stroke). J. G. Kincaid and Co. Ltd, Greenock manufactured the engine and ancillary machinery. She was equipped with wireless and had one deck, four bulkheads cemented, water ballast, a 7.31-m poop deck of 63 tons, a 106-ton (300.15-cubic.m) house deck and a 6.40-m forecastle of ten tons. She was classed as 100 A1.

In 1923, Svithun Linjen Aktieselskapet, Stavanger purchased her and renamed her *Langfond.* Sigval Bergesen was the manager.

She was sold to Rederi AB Fredrika, Stockholm, Sweden in 1937 and registered in Stockholm: Official No. 8132.

From 1937, Anglo-Lithuanian Shipping Co. Ltd, London was the registered owner and she was renamed *Baltanglia*; United Baltic Corp. Ltd was the manager. Her designated code recognition signal letters were: GZSJ.

Final voyage

The *Baltanglia* loaded her general cargo at Hommelvik and while still in Norwegian waters joined the 38-ship convoy HN.8 (Norwegian waters – Methil) on 19 January 1940, arriving at Methil without incident on 22 January. From Methil she sailed south, independently and unescorted behind the defensive minefields, for her destinations at the Tyne and Rochester. On 23 January 1940, however, the Kriegsmarine submarine *U 19*, commanded by Kapitänleutnant Joachim Schepke, torpedoed and sank the steamer six miles east of Beadnell in Kriegsmarine quadrant AN5186. On the morning of 23 January 1940, *U 19* broke at high speed through the mine warning area off the Farne Islands and immediately found about 20 unescorted southbound ships, including *Baltanglia* and *Pluto*; both these ships had arrived in Methil with convoy HN.8. Schepke later observed minesweepers in that area and on 25 January, a similar group of northbound ships came into sight, of which *Everene* and *Gudveig* were torpedoed. These ships were en route to Methil to join a convoy bound for Norway.

Captain G. Thomas of the *Baltanglia* said that they had left Methil at midnight and at 0710 hrs were abeam of the Longstone buoy. He stated that the Norwegian steamer *Pluto* was ahead of him by about a mile and that there were a number of other ships more or less in line. The captain said he heard an explosion and noticed the *Pluto* beginning to sink by the stern. He was making arrangements to rescue the crew when another ship, in a better position to pick up the lifeboats, dashed past him. Captain Thomas then told the man at the helm to go back on the course, full speed ahead, but just three minutes later, at 0843 hrs (CT) his ship 'detonated a mine', the force of which knocked him unconscious for about half a minute. He asserted that the *Pluto* sank in six minutes, and that they were only about three quarters of a mile astern of her when she 'struck the mine'. He stated that his vessel was about 315° from her position where the *Pluto* struck a mine.

Baltanglia's crew abandoned their ship in two boats and local fishermen from nearby Seahouses towed them in, tidal conditions at Seahouses having prevented the RNLI lifeboat from launching.

Authorities later questioned the mine theory and records released after the war confirmed that torpedoes from Schepke's little *U 19* had sunk the two ships.

LCWLR 1939–1945. p.37; Starke/Schell.

Wrecksite

The wreck, probably that of *Baltanglia*, is orientated in an almost N to S direction. It lies on a seabed of muddy sand and black shells in a general depth of 59 m (LAT). The wreck is intact and upright with midships superstructure still in place and standing almost 8 m high, although much of it consists of steel girders and box-like structures. The cargo appears to consist of stacked tiles of a rubber-like material. Good numbers of fish have been observed so it will make an excellent boat-angling venue. The wreck was identified in 2008 when the bell, inscribed *Laatefos*, was recovered.

Pluto, Ex *Røvær*

Date of loss: 23 January 1940
Wreck: ✮ ✮ ✮ ✮
Depth: 67 m
Reference: 55 33'.963 N 001 26'.787 W
Location: 5.94 nm ENE of Beadnell Point

The *Pluto* was a steel-hulled 1598-ton Norwegian steam cargo ship measuring 74.98 m in length, with an 11.50-m beam and a 4.7-m draught. Laxevaags Maskin and Jernskibsbyg, Bergen in Norway built and completed her as Yard No.126 in August 1918; she was launched as the *Røvær* on 6 July 1918 for Dampsk. Aktieselskapet John K. Haalands Rederi, Haugesund, Norway; John K. Haaland was the manager. The single steel screw was powered by a 138-nhp three-cylinder triple expansion steam engine that used two single-ended boilers, which gave nine knots. The cylinders measured 45.72 cm, 73.66 cm and 124.46 cm with an 83.83-cm stroke (18 in., 29 in. and 49 in. with a 33-in. stroke). Laxerags Mark and Jernskibs in Bergen manufactured the engine and ancillary machinery. She had one deck, four bulkheads cemented, a 40-ton (113.26-cubic.m) forecastle, a 12-ton (33.98-cubic.m) bridge deck, a 109-ton (308.65-cubic.m) quarterdeck, a 39-ton (110.43-cubic.m) poop deck and a 68-ton (192.55-cubic.m) house deck.

Above: Pluto, *ex Røvær*

Below: Pluto, *circa 1927*

She was classed as 100 A1. The designated code recognition signal letters were: MSGW.

In 1923, she was renamed *Pluto* by Dampskipsselskapet Aktieselskapet 'Pluto', Haugesund, who purchased her and B. Stolt-Nielsen and Co. was the manager.

She was later equipped with electric lights, wireless and direction finder.

From 1926, Dampskipsselskapet Aktieselskapet Facto was the registered owner and B. Stolt-Nielsen and Co. was the manager until 1927.

B. Stolt-Nielsen and Sønner Aktieselskapet became the manager from 1927. The designated code recognition signal letters were: LDEX.

Final voyage

The Kriegsmarine U-boat *U 19*, commanded by Kapitänleutnant Joachim Schepke *Rittterkreuz* torpedoed and sank the *Pluto* in Kriegsmarine quadrant AN5186 on 23 January 1940. The *Pluto* had sailed from Bergen as part of the 38-ship convoy HN.8 (Norwegian waters – Methil) and arrived at Methil on 22 January 1940. She then left Methil in ballast at midnight and was travelling south independently for Middlesbrough, although there were about twenty other vessels travelling south and unescorted not far away from her near the Farne Islands.

On 24 January 1940, Captain G. Thomas of *Baltanglia* stated in an interview:

> We sailed from Methil bound to the Tyne on 3 January (this should probably be the 23rd) with a general cargo of 1930 tons. Radio telephone was fitted and the ship was unarmed. The colour of my hull superstructure was grey. We were flying no ensign at the time of the explosion and our confidential books were all thrown over the side in a weighted canvas bag. The crew numbered 27 including myself and we carried no passengers.
>
> We left Methil at midnight and at ten minutes past 7 a.m. we were abeam of the Longstone Buoy. We then had to go two miles further south, then down on to the last true course and through the swept channel. There was a Norwegian steamer, the *Pluto*, ahead of me by about a mile, and ahead of him there were several other steamers more or less in line. I heard an explosion and then noticed the *Pluto* start to sink by the stern. I hauled over to port and came full astern, made a starboard cant to get a lee of his boats when I found another steamer dashing past me in a better position to pick his boats up. I then told the man at the wheel to go back on the course full speed ahead and three minutes afterwards, at 7.50 a.m., we struck a mine. The force of the explosion knocked me unconscious for perhaps half a minute.
>
> The *Pluto* sank in six minutes, and we were only about three quarters of a mile astern of her when the mine hit her. We were about 315° from her position where she struck a mine.

Captain Thomas then described the damage to his own ship, adding that they abandoned her in two lifeboats which were towed in by local fishermen from Seahouses. They had tried to launch a lifeboat but had been unable to do so on account of the tide. Another unconfirmed report stated that a Finnish steamer picked up the crew and took them to Seahouses. Authorities later questioned the mine theory, and believed there was evidence the explosions had been caused by a torpedo. Records released after the war did indeed confirm that torpedoes from *U 19* had sunk both *Pluto* and *Baltanglia*.

Norwegian Maritime Declarations 1914–1918; LCWLR 1939–1945, p.37.

Wrecksite

The wreck believed to be the *Pluto* is orientated in a NNE to SSW direction. It lies on a seabed of muddy sand and black shells in a general depth of 67 m (LAT). The wreck is mostly intact, but appears to be inverted and rather collapsed, covering an area 69 m long and 12 m across, with the highest structure about 8 m off the seabed; on both sides of the main wreckage are debris fields. There are also another three wrecks in fairly close proximity, so this should make an excellent boat-angling venue.

Stamfordham

Date of loss: 4 August 1916

Wreck: ✶ ✶ ✶ ✶

Depth: 65 m

Reference: 55 33'.885 N 001 26'.980 W

Location: 7.29 nm SW of Longstone Lighthouse

Silhoutte of the SS Stamfordham

The *Stamfordham* (Official No. 106650) was a 921-ton steel-hulled cargo steam vessel measuring 64 m in length, with a 9.16-m beam and a 4.04-m registered depth and 4.87-m moulded depth. Wood, Skinner and Co. Ltd at Bill Quay near Newcastle built and completed as Yard No. 78 in November 1898; she was launched on 27 October 1898 for T. and W. Smith at Newcastle. The single screw was powered by a 99-rhp, three-cylinder triple expansion steam engine that used one single-ended boiler. North East Marine Engineering Co. Ltd at Newcastle manufactured the machinery. The cylinders measured 43.18 cm, 71.12 cm and 116.84 cm with a 76.2-cm stroke (17 in., 28 in. and 46 in. with a 30-in. stroke). She had one iron deck and web frames, four bulkheads and a 31.39-m quarterdeck, a 2.74-m bridge deck and 7.62-m forecastle.

In 1905, Stamfordham S.S. Co. Ltd was the registered owner and T. and W. Smith was the manager.

From 1907, Harries Brothers and Co., Newcastle (Swansea) was the registered owner.

Final voyage

On 4 August 1916, the *Stamfordham*, with Captain T.J. Rees in charge, was captured by Commander Werner Fürbringer in the KDM submarine SM *UB 39*, eight miles SW of Longstone light. The crew was forced to abandon ship before she was sunk by gunfire. The steamer was en route from Kirkwall to Seaham in ballast and none of the crew was lost.

Starke/Schell; LCWLR 1914–1918, p. 50; LR 1914–1915, no.1833 (S); BVLS 1914–1918 p. 21; BMS 1914–1918, p.118.

Wrecksite

This wreck, probably that of the *Stamfordham*, is orientated in an ESE to WNW direction. It lies on a firm seabed of gravel and sand in a general depth of 65 m (LAT). The wreck is quite substantial, upright and intact, with her bows to the ESE and standing almost 8 m high amidships. The partially collapsed bridge/wheelhouse superstructure is there, covered in a profusion of soft corals. Many of the vessel's decks, companionways, doors, air ducts and lifeboat davits are in good condition, making this an exciting wreck to explore. When weather conditions permit, this wreck will also make an excellent boat-angling venue.

Kopanes, Ex Dargle, Ex Jericho, Ex Sir John Jellicoe

Date of loss: 19 April 1941
Wreck: ✷ ✷ ✷ ✷
Depth: 67 m
Reference: 55 33.873 N 001 26.681 W
Location: 6 nm E by N of Beadnell Point

Shadow sketch of HMT Kopanes

The *Kopanes* (Official No.136245) was a steel-hulled 351-ton British steam trawler measuring 43.9 m in length, with a 7.3-m beam. Cook, Welton and Gemmell at Beverley built and completed her as Yard No. 309 in March 1914; she was launched as *Sir John Jellicoe* on 22 September 1914 for the Imperial Steam Fishing Co. Ltd, Hull, who registered her in Hull as H.310 on 18 December 1914. The single steel screw was powered by a 100-nhp three-cylinder triple expansion steam engine that used one single-ended boiler working at a pressure of 200 psi, with three plain furnaces, 4.45 sq.m (48 sq.ft) of grate surface and 143.07 sq.m (1540 sq.ft) of heating surface, which gave 11 knots. The cylinders measured 33.02 cm, 57.15 cm and 93.98 cm with a 60.96-cm stroke (13 in., 22½ in. and 37 in. with a 24-in. stroke). Amos and Smith Ltd at Hull manufactured the machinery. She had one deck and was classed as 100 A1. The designated code recognition signal letters were: MFZT.

In May 1915, the Admiralty requisitioned her as Minesweeper No. FY.1577 and renamed her *Jericho*; she was then equipped with two AC and employed on anti-Zeppelin patrols in the North Sea.

On 20 November 1918, the boat was acquired by D Line Steam Fishing Co. Ltd, renamed *Dargle* and registered in Grimsby as GY.1170.

W. Garrat, Grimsby was the registered owner in 1928.

In 1932 she was sold to T. Fisher of Grimsby.

J. Little, Grimsby was the registered owner in 1933.

In December 1933 she was sold to the Kopanes Steam Fishing Co. Ltd, Grimsby and renamed *Kopanes*, with J. G. Little the manager.

When war broke out in 1939, she was requisitioned again and converted into an Admiralty Auxiliary Patrol Vessel (GY.1170) and equipped with one bow-mounted 12-pounder deck gun, wireless, direction finder and an echo-sounding device.

Final patrol

On 19 April 1941, HMT *Kopanes* was on patrol off Northumberland when German aircraft attacked and sank her with machine gun fire and bombs near to the 20G buoy, north of Coquet Island and six nm E of Beadnell. There were no casualties.

LCWLR 1939–1945, p. 226; SRN Vol. 2, p. 200; Cook, Welton and Gemmell, 1883–1963.

Wrecksite

The wreck, which has been identified by divers, is orientated in an E to W direction and lies on a seabed of sand, gravel and shells in a general depth of 67 m (LAT). It is standing upright, almost 7 m high, with some top structural damage to the bridge/wheelhouse area. There is a debris field all around the wreck and it is believed that part of the vessel may be missing. It is covered in a myriad of plumose anemones and masses of soft corals, but is also ensnared with monofilament and trawl nets. Many large fish, including some very large cod, have been reported around and over the wrecksite so she will make an excellent boat-angling venue.

Somali

Date of loss: 27 March 1941
Wreck: ✶ ✶ ✶
Depth: 28 m
Reference: 55 34'.134 N 001 36'.097 W
Location: 1.25 nm NE of Beadnell

The *Somali* (Official No.161938) was a steel-hulled 6890-ton British steam cargo ship measuring 139.9 m in length, with an 18.59-m beam and a 9.14-m draught. Harland and Wolff Ltd at Govan, Glasgow built and completed her as Yard No.898 on 18 December 1930; she was launched on 9 October 1930 for Peninsular and Orient Steam Navigation Co. (P & O), Glasgow (London). The single screw was powered by a 1384-nhp four-cylinder quadruple expansion steam engine fitted with low pressure/exhaust turbines, with D.R. gearing and hydraulic cooling to a pressure of 230 psi that used five single-ended boilers and gave 15 knots. The cylinders measured 77.47 cm, 111.26 cm, 161.29 cm and 231.14 cm with a 152.4-cm stroke (30.5 in., 44 in., 63.5 in. and 91 in. with a 60-in. stroke). J. G. Kinaird and Co. Ltd manufactured the engine and ancillary machinery at Greenock. She had a cruiser stern, two decks and a shelter deck, seven bulkheads part-cemented and a 10.97-m forecastle, along with four insulated cargo chambers with a capacity of 1,936.87-cubic.m (68,400-cubic.ft). She also had wireless, DF and electric lighting and one Carb Anhy refrigerating machine with two compressors manufactured by J. and E. Hall Ltd. The *Somali* also had a cellular double bottom covering 36.13 sq.m (389 sq.ft).

When war broke out, the ship was equipped for defence with one stern-mounted 12-pounder (5.44-kilo shells) deck gun.

Final voyage

The *Somali* left London in the northbound convoy FN.442 (Southend – Methil) during March 1941, acting as the Commodore ship for a convoy that had assembled in the Pool of London. The convoy consisted of 23 ships, mainly colliers, and travelled at seven knots. The *Somali* was on the first part of a voyage to Hong Kong, carrying two DEMS gunners, a crew of 77 and 9,000 tons of general mixed cargo, including horses, fuses, cosmetics, ointments, medical supplies, canisters of celluloid films, shaving kits, salt cellars, bicycles, heavy lorry tyres, several 4×4s, shoes, large amounts of hay, straw and fodder, batteries, gas masks, fire extinguishers, coin for Hong Kong banks, paint, oil, explosives, drums of copper cable, mercury, hundreds of tons of white metal-bearing ingots and 100 tons of toy lead soldiers. It was rumoured that part of the cargo of white metal ingots contained radioactive materials and were destined for India.

On the afternoon of 25 March, she was just north of Blyth in Northumberland when suddenly, out of the heavily cloud-laden sky, a squadron of German Heinkel III bombers came in for the attack, strafing the ship and scoring three direct bomb hits. At least one exploded in the hay-filled no. 3 hold, causing a raging inferno and leaving the ship very badly damaged. The two naval DEMS gunners put up a good effort with the old deck gun, but the Heinkels slipped back into the cloud cover, presumably untouched. A large sea-going tug, *Sea Giant*, was called to accompany the *Somali* on her voyage northwards while the crew fought desperately to get the fire under control, but by 2200 hrs on the following evening, when the vessels were seven miles SE of North Sunderland Point, the fire gained ground. With worsening weather, most of the crew were taken on board the escorting armed trawler HMT *Pelican*. In the early hours of 27 March, the flame and smoke from the fire had been observed from the shore and lifeboats from Holy Island, North Sunderland and

Above: SS Somali

Below: SS Somali *exploding*

Boulmer were launched and went to her aid, with the North Sunderland lifeboat *W.R.A.* being launched at 0155 hrs. On arrival, however, they discovered that the crew and passengers had already been taken on board the *Pelican*. The coxswains of the three lifeboats were each asked if they would put two crew members on board the steamer to help connect a tow line and this they did, returning to their lifeboats once the job had been carried out. The tow with the *Sea Giant* got underway at 0930 hrs and the two ships headed for the shelter of the Farne Islands, where they waited while the Holy Island lifeboat returned to her station.

The salvage vessel *Iron Axe* arrived on the scene and the salvage officer and two seamen were put on board the still-burning steamer by the Boulmer lifeboat *Clarissa Langdon* (a Liverpool class motorised lifeboat). The tug began to tow the damaged ship south with the intention of trying to save her by beaching her. At midday, the *Clarissa Langdon* took off the salvage vessel's officer and returned him to the *Iron Axe*, to which it was proposed to transfer the tow, while the two lifeboats remained on standby in case any assistance was required. They were at this stage some one and a half miles off Beadnell village. The *Clarissa Langdon* began to approach the *Somali* and begin the transfer, but when she was about 60 m from the steamer, an almighty explosion, thought to be the magazine going off, occurred in the bow section of the *Somali*. The force of the blast was so tremendous that it blew the bow section completely off and columns of smoke and pieces of debris were sent thousands of feet into the sky. The shock waves even caused structural damage in local houses and premises around the Beadnell area and many windows were shattered even in Seahouses, nearly five miles to the NW. The explosion lifted the lifeboat clear out of the water, knocking the boat's crew flat on the bottom, their caps were blown off, never to be seen again and it was reported that the blast even emptied some of their jacket pockets. Pieces of metal up to half a metre long then began to rain down on the two lifeboats and both were damaged in the fallout. Several of the lifeboatmen were injured, with the bowman of the *Clarissa Langdon* receiving a severe gash to his head. The *Somali's* stern end and centre section remained afloat with the two salvage men on board, but the bows went down to the bottom. Fearing for the men's safety, Coxswain Campbell on the *Clarissa Langdon* took his boat in through the mass of black smoke and fumes and rescued the two men, who slid down a rope into the sea before the lifeboat was brought clear at full speed, but the lifeboat's screw was fouled by some floating wreckage and the *W.R.A.* had to come in and tow her out of the danger area. When the screw was cleared, the two lifeboats made for Seahouses, where the two seamen were landed at North Sunderland harbour at 1320 hrs.

The ship had a secret cargo compartment near to the bows and it was widely rumoured that she was carrying explosives, which may explain why the blast was so great, ripping her in two at the bow section.

One person died on the *Somali,* possibly when the vessel was bombed.

For his excellent service, Coxswain James Campbell was awarded the RNLI's bronze medal on 17 April 1941, while his crew and Coxswain Dawson of the *W.R.A.* each received additional monetary awards.

LCWLR 1939–1945 p.210; BVLS 1939–1945, p.19; Starke/Schell; *The History of the Seahouses Lifeboats* by J. Morris.

Wrecksite

The wreck of the *Somali* must rate as one of the most popular wreck dives off the northeast coast of England. Local dive charter-boat skippers usually buoy the wreck in three places: close to the boilers, near the starboard side of the hull remains and close to the stern end, although these are sometimes broken away by storms in the early months of spring. The wreck lies on a hard rocky seabed surrounded by numerous large reefs in a general depth of 28 m (LAT). When first discovered in the 1960s, she was fairly substantial, upright with most of her hull complete and standing 9 m high, her aft gun intact and deck fittings still in place. Unfortunately, although the remains of the ship still make an excellent dive, often with 15 m visibility, a considerable amount of salvage work has been carried out over the last twenty years and the wreck is just a shadow of its former self, being somewhat flattened now and dispersed around the seabed. The highest part is probably around 5– 6 m. The remains of large drums of cement lie beneath the bulkheads near where the buoy is tied off at the starboard side of the three boilers, while at the port side is a gap and a further two boilers. Close by are the four huge cylinders, which are probably the highest part of the wreck, and the rest of its engine, pistons, rods and crankshaft, now exposed, where with a little care it is possible to swim through. Moving back towards the stern end, more cargo is visible, with large quantities of cement, piles of truck tyres with the cargo winch lying amongst them, empty rotting gas cylinders and even a large drum reel of heavy copper cable. The old 12-pounder deck gun and gun-mounting structure rest on the seabed next to a pair of bollards, with an anchor and spare screw not far away, although the screw has a section of broken mast lying across and slightly obscuring it. There are still large lumps of copper pipe and brass rods protruding out of the jumbled mass of iron, and steel and white metal ingots, looking like dirty white chocolate bars, can still be found. A word of warning, though: the shipwreck belongs to Stan Hall of Beadnell, who generally does not mind divers taking small trinkets, but the cargo belongs to someone else. Ocean Diving Services used to own the cargo until it was taken over by Novocastrian Diving Salvage Company who lost a valuable remotely operated vehicle (ROV) from the site in 1991. The present owner of the cargo rights is unknown, and there has been no evidence to support rumours which circulated in 1998 that a large gold ingot had been found on the wreck.

The bow section remains a mystery, but there are plenty of reports of divers finding it by chance while on drift dives in the area. It is reputed to lie about 300 m away from the main wrecksite, but whether to the north or south is unclear. Tales of unopened boxes strewn around the seabed are very unlikely to be true. Other reports – that the broken remains of the bow section are draped in steel cables or wires with high numbers of shoaling fish around them – sound more likely. Interestingly, the bow section was said to contain the ship's safe, either hidden in a secret compartment or in the forecastle, and the fact that it has never been located adds spice to the search for this section of the ship.

The tidal run is fairly strong and it is difficult to dive at anything but slack water. It is usually fairly easy to locate at weekends during the summer months because large numbers of diving boats, including the large charter boats from Seahouses, gather on the surface, the water teeming with divers. The best time to dive the wreck is on a neap tide and at low slack water, which is between 1.5 and 1.75 of an hour after low water at Seahouses.

San Bernardo, Ex Bellasco

Date of Loss: 10 August 1916
Wreck: ✷ ✷ ✷ ✷
Depth: 72 m
Reference: 55 34'.660 N 001 14'.025 W
Location: 13.35 nm SE of Longstone and 13.25 nm ENE of Beadnell Point

The *San Bernardo* (Official No. 105992) was a steel-hulled 3,803-ton steam cargo vessel measuring 106.8 m in length with a 13.84-m beam and a 7.82-m draught. David and William Henderson and Co. Ltd, Meadowside, Glasgow built and completed her as Yard No. 389 in May 1896; she was launched as the *Bellasco* on 2 March 1896 for Bellasco S.S. Co. Ltd, Glasgow, and Bell Brothers and McLelland was the manager. The single screw was powered by a 302-nhp three-cylinder triple expansion steam engine that used three boilers. The cylinders measured 60.96 cm, 101.6 cm and 167.64 cm with a 121.92-cm stroke (24 in., 40 in. and 66 in. with a 48-in. stroke). Shipbuilders D.and W. Henderson and Co. manufactured the machinery.

Bell Bros. and Co was the manager in 1908.

From 1916, Palmerston S.S. Co. Ltd, Glasgow (London) was the registered owner and renamed her *San Bernardo*; Edye and Co. became the manager.

Final voyage

The *San Bernardo* left Norway on 8 August 1916 and was SE of the Longstone at 1140 hrs on 10 August when a submarine was sighted two miles distant, with two flags flying. The ship's master quickly turned and made off at full speed as soon as he realised it was an enemy boat. The submarine was in fact the KDM U-boat SM *UB 19*, commanded by Kapitänleutnant Walter Gustav Becker of the Flandern Flotilla. *UB 19* immediately opened fire with its deck gun and the fourth shell struck the ship's bridge. The steamer was then brought to a halt and her crew of 30 abandoned ship, but as they did so, the submarine approached one of the boats and captured its crew. Seven of the crew, including the master, were forced to accompany two German sailors back onboard the *San Bernardo* and the Germans placed explosive charges below her decks while the seven men were allowed to collect personal valuables and some food. All the men returned to the lifeboat and got clear of the ship before the explosives went off, but only two of them detonated. The U-boat commander questioned the men before allowing them to proceed on their way. They rowed in a westerly direction for a while before the 154-ton steam trawler *Magnus* (1896) picked them up at 0330 hrs on 11 August and landed them at North Shields quay at 0930 hrs. The *San Bernardo*, which had been in ballast and en route from Tyssedal, Norway to South Shields, sank about 17 miles SE of the Longstone.

ADM 137/2960; Starke/Schell; LCWLR 1914–1918, p. 52; BVLS 1914–1918, p. 21; BMS 1914–1918, p. 71; LR 1915–1916, no.43 (B) and no.137 (S) Supplement.

Wrecksite

The wreck, which is probably that of the steamer, is orientated in a SE to NW direction. It lies on a rather firm seabed of fine sand, mud, black shells, stones and rock in a general depth of 72 m (LAT). The wreck is at least 6 m high, collapsed and well broken up and covers an area 87 m long and 25 m wide, with widely-scattered debris. The echo sounder showed an abundance of fish over the wrecksite, so it should make an excellent boat-angling venue.

John G. Watson

Date of loss: 20 May 1930
Wreck: ★ ★ ★ ★
Depth: 77 m
Reference: 55 35'.810 N 001 20'.215 W
Location: 9.59 nm ESE of Longstone Lighthouse

Silhouette of the 235 ton trawler
John G. Watson

The *John G. Watson* (Official No. 137384) was a 235-ton steam trawler measuring 37.33 m in length, with a 6.75-m beam and a 3.73-m draught. Hall, Russell and Sons Ltd at Aberdeen built and completed her as Yard No. 588 in September 1916; she was launched on 30 August 1916 for Richard Irvin and Sons Ltd at North Shields, who also owned her at the time of loss. Port reg: SN.305. The single steel screw was powered by a 78-rhp, three-cylinder triple expansion steam engine that used one single-ended boiler. The cylinders measured 30.38 cm, 50.8 cm and 86.36 cm with a 60.96-cm stroke (12 in., 20 in. and 34 in. with a 24-in.stroke). Hall, Russell and Sons Ltd manufactured the machinery. The vessel had one deck and water ballast.

After she was completed, the boat was immediately requisitioned and converted to Admiralty Minesweeper No. 3322 and armed with one six-pounder AA gun. Later she was converted to an Armed Escort Vessel and in 1919 returned to the owners, R. Irvin and Sons Ltd, North Shields.

From May 1930, J.A. Doig was the registered owner.

Final voyage

On 20 May 1930, the trawler was being towed from Aberdeen to Grimsby for repairs when she sprang a leak and sank about five miles off Longstone lighthouse. No one was lost or injured.

LCR 1930 p. 5 (G); LR 1929–1930 no.08267 (J); *The Times*, Thursday 22 May 1930, p. 13.

Wrecksite

The wreck, which is probably that of this trawler, is orientated in a roughly SE to NW direction. It lies on a firm seabed of broken shells, sand, gravel and stones in a general depth of 77 m (LAT). The remains appear intact and upright, but it is collapsed and broken, with the highest part standing about 4 m high. It covers an area 37 m long and 11 m wide.

Tioga

Date of loss: 1 Nov 1943

Wreck: ✷ ✷ ✷ ✷

Depth: 63 m

Reference: 55 35'.903 N 001 25'.063 W

Location: 7.4 nm ENE of Beadnall Point

The *Tioga* (Official No. 132668) was a steel-hulled 742-ton British steam

SS Tioga in port, circa 1925

tanker measuring 54.78 m in length, with a 9.47-m beam and a 3.86-m draught. Greenock and Grangemouth Dockyard Co. Ltd, Grangemouth built and completed her as Yard No. 342 in February 1912; she was launched on 20 December 1911 for the Anglo-American Oil Co. Ltd, London, who owned her at the time of loss; R.A. Garder was the manager. The single screw was powered by an aft-positioned 110-nhp three-cylinder triple expansion steam engine that used one single-ended boiler working at a pressure of 180 psi, with three corrugated furnaces, 5.29 sq.m (57 sq.ft) of grate surface and 204.38 sq.m (2,200 sq.ft) of heating surface. The cylinders measured 35.56 cm, 58.42 cm and 93.98 cm with a 60.96-cm stroke (14 in., 23 in. and 37 in. with a 24-in.stroke). Richardsons, Westgarth and Co. Ltd at Middlesbrough manufactured the machinery. She had one part-steel deck and web frames, nine bulkheads cemented along with a 5.38-m cellular double base weighing 66 tons, a 3.35-m deep-tank fore of 35 tons, an eight-ton (22.65-cubic.m) forepeak tank and a seven-ton (19.82-cubic.m) aft-peak tank. The superstructure consisted of a 19.8-m poop deck, a 4.6-m bridge deck and an 8.53-m forecastle. Lloyd's classed her 100 A1.

The designated code recognition signal letters were: MDRF.

Final voyage

The *Tioga* had joined the northbound 35-ship convoy FN.1165 (Southend – Methil) at Middlesbrough on 1 November 1943 and sailed in ballast on passage for Grangemouth. Later that same day, she was seriously damaged following a collision with the 5,305-ton steamer *Pundit* (1919 – Asiatic Steam Navigation Co. Ltd, London) at position 55 40′ N 01 30′ W. The *Tioga* was taken in tow but began listing badly and was in danger of sinking, so her crew were taken on board an escort vessel. On 3 November, after she had continued to drift for many hours, Royal Navy warships escorting the convoy sank her with gunfire.

LCR 1943 p. 8 (f); Starke/Schell; Miramar Ship Index; LR no.762 (T).

Wrecksite

The wreck is orientated in a N to S direction and lies on a seabed of hard sand and gravel in a general depth of 63 m (LAT). It is very substantial, standing upright and lying at a slight angle, but broken off into three sections, from just past the bows and to the fore of the bridge structure at the stern end, with the highest point of 8 m being at the stern. The wreck is rather broken up, but some of the bridge superstructure, decking, handrails, doors and deck machinery are still in reasonable condition and there are a number of places where access to the inside of the wreck would be possible. The ship's bell, which identified the wreck, has been recovered. The wreck is covered in silt and shoals of large fish swarm all around the superstructure, making it a great boat-angling venue.

Athelduke

Date of loss: 16 April 1945
Wreck: ✫ ✫ ✫ ✫ ✫
Depth: 55 m
Reference: 55 36'.384 N 001 27'.298 W
Other half: 55 36'.333 N 001 28'.400 W
Location: 5.12 nm SE of Longstone lighthouse and 5.94 nm NE of Beadnell Point

The *Athelduke* (Official No. 161081) was a steel-hulled 8,966-ton British motor tanker measuring 144.78 m in length, with a 19.26-m beam. Robert Duncan and Co. Ltd, Port Glasgow built and completed her as Yard No.388 in January 1929; she was launched on 16 November 1928 for United Molasses Co. Ltd, Liverpool. Two aft-positioned 4S.C.S.A 12-cylinder oil engines that developed 709-nhp powered the two huge bronze screws and gave a service speed of 10.5 knots; she also used two donkey boilers working at a pressure of 180 psi. J. G. Kincaid and Co. Ltd at Greenock manufactured the aft machinery. She had two steel decks, 16 bulkheads part-cemented, web frames with longitudinal framing, a 36.27-m poop deck, a 10.36- m bridge deck and a 14.63-m forecastle. She also had a 5.58-m deep-tank fore of 701 tons, a 219-ton (620.13-cubic.m) fore-peak tank and a 434-ton (1228.95-cubic.m) aft-peak tank. The ship was licensed for carrying molasses and

MV Athelduke

petroleum in bulk. Lloyd's classed her 100 A1. The designated code recognition signal letters were: GSRP.

From 1940, Athel Line Ltd, Liverpool was the registered owner.

On 17 January 1941, the *Athelduke* detonated a mine near Porthcawl at 51 21' N 03 20' W and although the ship was only damaged, she was beached for repairs.

Final voyage

The *Athelduke* had sailed from Port Everglades, Florida with 12,600 tons of molasses for Salt End at Kingston-upon-Hull. The motor tanker first sailed from Port Everglades to Boston between 18 and 23 March 1945 and then joined the 21-ship convoy BX.152 to Halifax, Nova Scotia. From there she sailed across the Atlantic to Loch Ewe, leaving Halifax on 27 March 1945 as part of convoy CS.171 (Halifax – Liverpool), consisting of 22 ships and 15 escorts. From Loch Ewe she connected with the nine-ship convoy WN.685 to Methil, before joining the southbound 20-ship convoy FS.1784 (Methil – Southend) to make the final leg of her voyage to Hull. However at 1732 hrs (CT) on 16 April 1945, *U 1274*, commanded by Oberlt.z. S. Hans-Hermann Fitting attacked the *Athelduke* with two torpedoes within an interval of about three seconds, 5.75 miles SE of Longstone in the Outer Farne Islands. The first torpedo detonated on the port side of the cross bunker tank and the second one on the port side of no. 10 cargo tank. The bunkers took fire and clouds of smoke rose in the air. The vessel immediately began to settle at a very fast rate by the stern and by the time the members of the crew were making their way amidships, the poop was awash, the water extinguishing the bunker fire.

The master, Captain Joseph Errett, realising the immediate danger, gave the order to abandon ship in the two midship boats. The ship's complement embarked in the two boats, with the exception of William Alexander McKenzie, the senior fourth engineer, who was on watch at the time and had presumably been killed. No one had seen anything of Mr McKenzie, not even the senior second engineer, who had been in the engine room at the time, although he was on the middle platform and had managed to escape with scalds and burns. There was no panic amongst the crew and everybody abandoned ship in an orderly manner, although the chief officer, Mr G. W. Williams was left on board, floating off on a raft and picked up by one of the boats. The mess room boy, Thomas Wilson, had been trapped in his room below decks aft by the inrushing water and had attempted to escape via a porthole, but had become jammed in it. Mr H. Speed, the senior third engineer, had been proceeding to the boat station when he heard the boy's cries. He immediately leant over the side whilst sitting in the waterway on the poop deck and, getting his feet on the boy's chest, took hold of his arms and hauled him out of the porthole and back on deck, undoubtedly saving his life. A few seconds more and the water would have reached the porthole, drowning him.

The ship sank stern first in three minutes and, owing to the reserve buoyancy contained in the forward ballast tanks, the forward hold up front, and the cofferdam and forepeak, she remained for some time with her stern on the seabed and her forecastle above the surface. The forecastle eventually sank shortly before daylight the following morning, by which time she had remained afloat for about 12 hours. It is understood that the bulkheads in the after cargo tanks and in the cross bunker collapsed with two explosions, and divers later discovered that the ship broke in two and now lies in two separate sections on the seabed.

The 5,224-ton British steamship *King Neptune* (1928 – Messrs Dodd, Thompson and Co. Ltd, Cardiff) rescued the master, 41 crew and four DEMS gunners and landed them at Grimsby at about 1800 hrs on 17 April. The master, Captain Errett, highly commended Mr Speed and on 16 April 1945 he was presented with the Lloyd's War Medal for Bravery at Sea.

Following the sinking, the aging 1,325-ton destroyer HMS *Viceroy* relentlessly pursued *U 1274* and sank her with depth charges, 7.5 nm ESE of Longstone; all of the crew of 44 were lost.

ADM 199/232; ADM 199/2148; CWGC; LCWLR 1939–1945, p. 804; BVLS 1939–1945, p. 71; Report by Mr F.H. Formby, Marine Superintendant, 20 April 1945, via Ms Pamela Armstrong; ADM 199/1047; ADM 199/1046; T1022 Roll 3900.

Wrecksite

The wreck is orientated in a NW to SE direction and lies on a seabed of firm sand and stone in a general depth of 55 m (LAT). The wreck is in two huge sections, one 19 m high and the other 11 m high, with about 200 metres between them, and is now showing signs of collapsing in on itself. As would be expected of a tanker of such big proportions, the bulk of the wreck consists mainly of two huge steel plate hulks with the decks covered in dozens of metres of large steel pipes and tubes running the length of it. There are two bridge-type sections, one at the stern end and another about one quarter of the way forward from the stern, where the bridge/wheelhouse are located. The two sections of the wreck are absolutely enormous and would take literally dozens of dives to inspect properly. The giant 6 m bronze screws, weighing many tons, are still attached to the wreck, next to a massive rudder and surrounded by the overhanging steel structure of the ship's stern end, which is an awesome and eerie sight. Trawl nets draped over some of the huge superstructure hang like giant cobwebs. The wrecks will make excellent boat-angling venues too, thanks to an abundance of large fish, especially cod, ling, pollack and conger, sheltering in and around the remains.

Ascot, Paddle Minesweeper

Date of loss: 10 November 1918

Wreck: ✹ ✹ ✹ ✹

Depth: 56 m

Reference: 55 37.924 N 001 29.860 W

Location: 6.34 nm NE of Beadnell Point and 3.83nm ESE of Longstone Lighthouse

The *Ascot* was a steel-hulled 810-ton Racecourse Class paddle steamer, designed and developed as a purpose-built minesweeper. Ailsa Shipbuilding Co. Ltd, Troon built and completed her as Yard No. 297 on 11 April 1916; she was launched for the Admiralty on 26 January 1916. Two inclined diagonal compound steam engines developing 1400 ihp (cylindrical return tube) that used four boilers powered her two 8.83-m side paddles (17.67 m at the paddles) and gave 14.5 knots. She carried 156 tons of coal and measured 74.86 m in length, with an 8.83-m beam and a 2.01-m draught. The *Ascot* was fitted with a derrick and winch to load and unload the small Sopwith Pup seaplane which she carried, plus an armament of one 7.6-cm (3-in.) bow gun and two aft-mounted 0.91-kilo guns (two-pounders) and one 2.72-kilo (six-pounder) gun, also mounted aft.

The *Ascot* was one of a flotilla of 32 Racecourse-design paddle vessels laid down by the Admiralty in 1915. They served a useful purpose with their shallow draught, being able to venture into shallow water where other ships were unable to go. The danger of mines getting under the paddle wheels meant, though, that no more of this design were built, with those of the class that survived World War One being sold out of service.

HMPS Ascot

Final voyage

On 10 November 1918, the KDM submarine SM *UB 67*, commanded by Oblt.z. S.Hellmuth von Dömming, torpedoed and sank HMPS *Ascot*. There were no survivors from her crew of 53 (six officers, including three Mercantile Marine Officers and 47 other ranks). *UB 67* fired two torpedoes and one of them detonated in the boiler room, breaking her in two and apparently destroying the boats, leaving the crew with no chance of surviving the very rough sea. No attempt at rescue was made by the U-boat crew because it was considered to be too close to land. The position given by *UB 67*'s KTB was 'the lower left corner of grid square 2247K', which is roughly 55 37' N 01 29' W.

The following day the armistice was signed and all hostilities ceased, making the crew the last victims of submarine warfare in World War One.

The crewmen that perished on the *Ascot* were:

Bevan, William George, 205220, Leading Seaman RN

Boulton, Harry, 317TS, 21 yrs, Leading Trimmer RNR

Coneely, Peter, 8257A, 20 yrs, Seaman RNR

Connelly, Percy Janes, J/82042, 18 yrs, Ord. Seaman RNR

Cooper, William, 1345, 23 yrs, Seaman RNR

Coultas, William, 2367ST, 23 yrs, Leading Trimmer RNR

Cross, Cecil James Joseph, 18 yrs, K32192, Stoker 2nd Class RN

Dalton, Harry, 281TS, 26 yrs, Trimmer RNR

Davis, Patrick, 3693A, 27 yrs, Seaman RNR

Dobbs, George Henry, 209.TS, Trimmer RNR

Duggan, David Edward, Third Engineer, MMR

Edmunds, Samuel George, 13865DA, Deck Hand RNR

Gardner, Charles Edward Mafeking, Stoker 2nd Class RN

Grubb, Wilfred Charles, J/33855, 19 yrs, Ord. Seaman RN

Hill, Charles, K/52369, Stoker 2nd Class RN

Horril, Edward Latham, 136091, 48 yrs, PO 1st Class RN

Irvine, James, 238L, Seaman RNR

Irwin, Robert Frederick, 37 yrs, Steward MMR

Jaffa, Leslie Charles Mersey, Z/1798, 29 yrs, Teleg. RN

Jones, Edward W., Signalman RNR

Jones, Matthew George, 2677ST Trimmer RNR

Judge, James, 2650ST Trimmer RNR

Juhle, Alexander Baxter, 3837TS 22 yrs, Ldg. Trimr RNR

Kersey, Robert, 10266DA, Deck Hand RNR

Keutenius, James William, 3034ST, Ldg Trimmer RNR

Kirman, George W., 20 yrs, Junior Engineer MMR

Kirton, Harold Ernest, Signalman RNVR

Lamb, David Bathie, 6881TS, 22 yrs, Trimmer RNR

Leabon. Archie Gordon, 18271DA, Second Hand RNR

Long, Arthur James, 20446DA, 18 yrs, Deck Hand RNR

MacDonald, Donald, 25 yrs, Lieutenant RNR

MacKay, Alexander, 15475DA, 20 yrs, Deck Hand RNR

McLean, Alexander Murray, 3082SD 21 yrs, Deck Hd. RNR

McLeod, James Fowler, Cook MMR

Munn, John William Clyde, Z/4540, 21 yrs, Teleg. RNVR

Osborne, James Walter, 7051TS, 32 yrs, Trimmer RNR

Parrott, Charles Fennell, 19906DA 35 yrs, Deck Hand RNR

Paterson, James Knox, 30 yrs, Engineer Lieutenant RNR

Paul, Thomas Samuel, 723TS, 36 yrs, Trimmer RNR

Pender, Patrick 2656ST, 28 yrs, Trimmer RNR

Postlethwaite, John Matthew, SS/325, 32 yrs, Able Sn. RN

Price, James 2678, ST Trimmer RNR

Redding, Herbert, 858TS, 35 yrs, Trimmer RNR

Reynolds, Arthur, 7447TS, Trimmer RNR

Richards, Francis Arthur, 2232ST, 37 yrs, Ldg Trimr RNR

Robson, James, 6084TS, 27 yrs, Trimmer RNR

Smith, Baden, J/79220, 18 yrs, Ordinary Seaman RN

Tocher, John, 2776ST, Leading Trimmer RNR

Wallen, John William, 48 yrs, Lieutenant RNVR

Wheatland, Arthur, 35 yrs, Lieutenant RNVR

Williamson, Robert, 120927 35 yrs, Able Seaman RN

Woolfe, George 6137TS, 21 yrs, Trimmer RNR

Youll, Alfred John, 33 yrs, Assistant Steward MMR

SRN, Vol 1, p. 53; Mine Warfare Vessels, p. 71–72; CWGC; *The Cross of Sacrifice* Volumes II and IV; KTB of SMU *UB 67*.

Wrecksite

The wreck lies on a firm seabed of stone, gravel and sand in a general depth of 56 m (LAT). The wreck of this once graceful ship is broken in two, has totally collapsed down on itself, is well broken up and rather decayed. The main section runs from the bows to just aft of the engine room. The starboard side is virtually collapsed into the sandy bottom, while the port side stands around 4 metres high. Forward of the decks have all gone and it is possible to see sections of the ribs and keelson. The forward sheerwater is still in place and the gun and searchlight are reported to be lying on their sides. The bridge is one of the highest parts of the wreck and is handy to anchor to. When the wreck was first dived, the radio room was still easily recognisable as an open box, and ladders and brass railings were all in place, but this area has been showing signs of collapse. The boiler room is well open just aft of the bridge with both boilers still in place. The area on either side of the paddle boxes is intact, and in good visibility it is possible to see right across the wreck at its widest point. Behind the paddle boxes the wreck peters out, with the stern section nowhere to be seen. Most of the remains of both paddle wheels are still in place: the wood has long gone but the brass parts

are still there. The upper bridge area of the ship has now collapsed in a huge pile but is still recognisable. The ship's bell identified the wreck in the 1990s. Anyone contemplating diving on this wreck should remember that it was a Royal Navy vessel and is classed as a war grave in remembrance of those brave and unfortunate men who died with it, although no human remains have ever been found.

U 1274 **Kriegsmarine U-Boat**

Date of loss: 16 April 1945

Wreck: ✶ ✶ ✶ ✶

Depth: 63 m

Reference: 55 37ʹ.028 N 001 25ʹ.672 W

Location: 6.32 nm ESE of Longstone Lighthouse and 7.58 nm NE of Beadnell Point

U 1274 was a VIIC/41 ocean-going attack boat built by Vulkan Vegesack

Guns on U1274

Werft, Bremen for the German navy. She was ordered on 13 June 1942 within the batch of U 1271–U 1279, and her keel was laid as Yard No. 69 on 21 June 1943. She was launched on 25 January 1944 and commissioned by Oblt.z. S. Fedor Kuscher on 1 March 1944. *Feldpost*: M 50 816.

The VIIC boat became the workhorse submarine of the German navy during World War Two. The official tonnage of the original design, as of 22 March 1941, was 761.89 tons on the surface and 864.69 tons submerged. These figures may change to a very small degree with later modifications: the standard official figures given throughout the war were usually 769 tons and 871 tons. Boats from different yards may also have differed to a certain degree due to small design variations. The overall general dimensions were 67.1 m in length overall, 6.22 m in beam, with a 4.8-m draught and a height of 9.60 m around the conning tower. Two diesel/oil engines powered the two screws, originally designed in bronze, but a shortage of non-ferrous metals led to the use of steel screws during the war. Boats already ordered before the war were fitted either with engines manufactured by Maschinefabrik-Augsburg-Nürnberg (MAN) or by the Germaniawerft (GW). After the start of the war, other companies or yards manufactured these two diesel types under licence. Frontline experience soon showed the more rigid GW construction to be superior and new constructions were gradually fitted with GW-type diesels only. Both types were fitted with superchargers and each developed 1400 hp at 475 revolutions per minute continuous power, while 495 revolutions maximum power for 30 minutes developed 1600 hp, giving a maximum surface speed of 17 knots. The boat had a calculated operational range of 9700 nm at ten knots, or 6500 nm at 12 knots, and carried a maximum fuel/oil capacity of 113 tons. For running submerged, two 62-cell lead/acid batteries/accumulators, usually manufactured by Accumulatoren-Fabrik-Aktiengesellschaft (AFA), powered the two electric motors which developed 375 hp at 295 revolutions and gave her a maximum speed of 7.6 knots.

The four electric motor manufacturers were:

AEG (Allgemeine Elektrizitäts-Gesellschaft)
BBC (Brown, Boveri and Cie.)
GL u. Co (Garbe, Lohmeyer and Co)
SSW (Siemens-Schuckert-Werke)

These companies all produced motors of a very similar design, sometimes under licence (GL). Using battery power, the boat had a calculated operational range underwater of 80 nm at a steady four knots.

The VIIC was designed with five torpedo tubes, four at the bow and one at the stern.

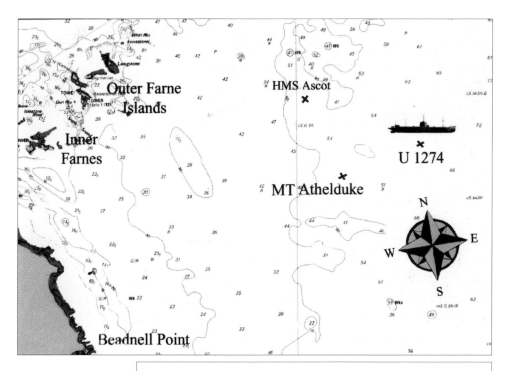

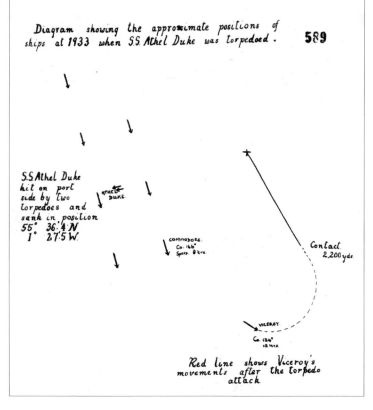

Above: Chart showing position of U1274 and Athelduke

Right: Sketch of the chase of U1274 by Viceroy's command

Above: The control centre of U1274

Below left: The diesel engine room of U1274

Below right: The stern compartment

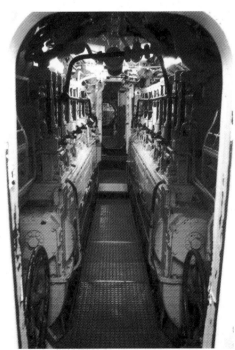

Fourteen torpedoes were carried until the summer of 1943, with two of them in the upper deck reserve containers. These were subsequently removed to save weight and because it became too dangerous to reload them in North Atlantic waters. In 1944 the number was reduced to ten to increase living space in the bow room when the boats stayed submerged for long periods.

From autumn 1944, on boats operating in the Atlantic or in British coastal waters, the ten torpedoes usually consisted of five T5 and five LuT, often stowed as follows:

> T5: one in forward tube, three in forward bilges and one in aft tube.
>
> Five LuT stowed: three in forward tube, one in forward bilges and one in aft bilges.

Mines were only carried on special order and in exchange for torpedoes rather than in addition to them. The figures for mines offered in reference books are theoretical numbers and have little to do with operational realities. There were three different types of U-boat mines, delivered through the torpedo tubes:

> TMA: moored floating mines, designed for, but never actually used on U-boats.
>
> TMB: small ground mines with various fuses and an explosive charge of 1,276 lb (578.7 kg).
>
> TMC: large ground mines with an explosive charge of 2,200 lb (997.9 kg).

The exchange ratios of mines/torpedoes were:

> One torpedo – three TMB
>
> One torpedo – two TMC

Initially, the VIIC gun specifications consisted of one 88 mm (3.46 in.) deck gun, plus 220 rounds and one 20-mm (0.79-in.) AA flak gun, plus 4,380 rounds of ammunition. In the summer of 1943, the deck gun was removed from Atlantic boats. The single gun bandstand aft of the bridge (model 0) was modified in early 1943 by adding a second, lower bandstand with another single 20-mm gun (this was then called 'conning tower modification II'). The Type I modification (two 13.2-mm twin machinegun mounts on the upper bandstand and a single 20-mm mount on the lower bandstand) was abandoned when tests showed that the machine guns were not powerful enough. From May 1943, 'modification IV' was introduced, meaning two single 20-mm mounts on the widened upper bandstand and a quadruple 20-mm mount on the enlarged lower bandstand.

Submarine mines exploding

After 20-mm twin mounts became available in July 1943, they replaced the single mounts. From October 1943, the 37-mm mount replaced the quadruple mounts. This represented the final variation of the Type IV conning tower modification. Later in the war, 37-mm twin mounts were tested experimentally on a few boats, but the snort had by then already reduced the threat from aircraft. Apart from these standard AA modifications on Atlantic boats, further experimental modifications were carried out on other boats but never became a standard form. Modifications were made to all frontline or working-up boats regardless of their date of commission and, during yard layovers, boats were continually upgraded to the latest version.

The operational diving depth of a VIIC boat was 100 m (328 ft), with a maximum depth of 165 m (541.33 ft) and a crush depth of 200 m (656 ft). A crash dive to 20 m took an average of 30 seconds.

The VIIC/41 boat was the same in almost all respects as the VIIC but was designed with a stronger pressure hull, which gave the boat an operational diving depth of 120 m (394 ft) and a crush depth of 250 m (820 ft). Both the VIIC and VIIC/41 boats carried between 44 and 52 crewmen. With increased AA armament in 1943–1944, crew numbers were at their highest. Following the introduction of the Schnorchel the crews were often reduced to 46–50 men. Each Type VII U-boat carried 36 *Unteroffiziere* and ratings, generally two *Unteroffiziere* to every three ratings. Apart from the officers, the crew of a U-boat was divided between technical personnel and seamen. The technical division comprised specialist personnel;

diesel machinists, electricians, radio operators and torpedo mechanics. There were four senior NCOs.

The above technical details of the VIIC and VIIC/41 U-boats are the copyright and courtesy of Dr. Axel Niestlé of Dabendorf, Germany, a naval historian, author and a researcher.

Having completed training in the Baltic Sea, *U 1274* formally joined 5.U-Flottille on 1 March 1945 at Kiel for frontline operations. For her first voyage, *U 1274* left Kiel on 24 March 1945 and sailed to Horten (59 22'. 29 N 10 33'.19 E) near Oslo in Norway, arriving there on the 27th.

Final patrol

U 1274 left Horten on 1 April 1945 bound for Kristiansand South, leaving there on 5 April. The next day, she was ordered to patrol off the east coast, in the area from Fife Ness to Flamborough Head between grid squares AN 5110 and AN 5860. Passing through the east coast mine barrier would have presented no problem, as there were gaps, of which the Germans were aware, between Stonehaven and Arbroath (Gap A), off Blyth (Gap B) and off Flamborough Head (Gap C). There were in any event no deep anti-submarine fields in the barrier for the length of *U 1274*'s patrol area and so she could have safely crossed at any point by diving beneath the mines.

At 1732 hrs (CT) on 16 April 1945, Fitting attacked the 8966-ton British motor tanker *Athelduke* (1928 – Athel Line Ltd, Liverpool) with two torpedoes, 5.75 miles SE of Longstone in the Outer Farne Islands off Northumberland. The *Athelduke* was part of the 20-ship convoy FS.1784 (Methil – Southend) and was on passage from Port Everglades, Florida for Salt End (Kingston-upon-Hull) via Loch Ewe with 12,600 tons of molasses. The torpedoes detonated in the port-quarter, killing 23 year old William Alexander McKenzie, the fourth engineer officer. The 5,224-ton British steamship *King Neptune* (1928 – King Line, Ltd,

On 1 March 1944, *U 1274* was assigned as a training boat to 8.U-Flotilla in Danzig with Oblt.z.S. Fedor Kuscher as commander.

Fedor Kuscher was born in Trebus on 19 January 1919 and began his naval career in 1939. He served as Watch Officer with 34th Minesweeping Flotilla, 13th VP-Boat Flotilla and 22nd Minesweeping Flotilla before commencing U-boat training in March 1943. Kuscher was promoted to Oblt.z.S. (R) on 1 January 1944.

In early July 1944, Kuscher and the whole crew transferred onto the new Type XXI boat *U 3515* and *U 1274* was taken over by a fresh crew under Oblt.z.S. Hans-Hermann Fitting.

Fitting was born on 27 May 1920 in Stargard, Pomerania and began his naval career in 1939, doing his officer training between September 1939 and August 1940. He served with 23rd and 25th U-Flottille between May 1941 and March 1943 and was promoted to Oblt.z.S. on 1 October 1943

251

London) rescued the master, Captain Joseph Errett, 41 crew and four DEMS gunners. Following the sinking, the ageing 1,325-ton destroyer HMS *Viceroy* relentlessly pursued *U 1274*, the former World War One warship attacking the U-boat with depth charges 7.5 nm ESE of the Longstone.

Log of HMS *Viceroy*:

> Convoy FS.84 consisted of seven ships formed in two columns, three small ships being in the port column and four larger ships in the starboard. Course: 1.66 degs. Speed: 8 knots.
>
> *Weather: wind light. Visibility good: 10 miles*

Above: HMS Viceroy

Below: Vessel sinking after being attacked by a U-boat

HMS *Viceroy* was carrying out a broad zig-zag across the front of the convoy at twelve knots, and the other escort, HMS *Woolston*, was zig-zagging on the seaward quarter. MT *Athelduke*, the second ship in the starboard column, was hit aft on the port side by two torpedoes. At this time, *Viceroy* was about one mile ahead of the Commodore and on his port bow, steering 126 degs.

Speed was increased to 18 knots and course altered to port. Three minutes later a good echo was picked up at 2,200 yards, bearing 350 degs. Speed was reduced. The contact was classified as submarine with moderate high doppler and, at 1942½ hrs, an attack was carried out using 100- foot settings.

Range was opened and a second attack carried out ten minutes later using the same settings. This produced traces of oil.

The third attack was broken off during the later stages of the rim, the operator picking up hydrophone effect from *Woolston* and losing contact and by this time the contact appeared to have no movement and was thought to have bottomed. The third attack was carried out at 2017, speed 15 knots, using 250-foot settings. The first charge of this pattern produced a distinctly prolonged explosion. The attack produced a small but steady flow of oil, a sample of which has been collected.

Viceroy's fourth and last attack was carried out at 2113 hrs.

SS *Athelduke* sank slowly in position 55 36′ 04 N, 01 27′ 05 W. The bows remained visible, bearing 249 degrees, 3,200 yards from the contact. The bearing was checked each time the ship passed over the contact in the last three attacks.

The 30th Escort Group arrived in the area, and HMS *Launceston Castle* carried out a Squid attack on the contact at about 2157. *Viceroy* then set course to rejoin the convoy. On returning to this wreck on 24 April, Viceroy again attacked and evidence, including a bottle of brandy made in Heilbron, was recovered.

Surface evidence, 24 April:

German uniform, jacket trousers, pulped body parts, one crate German brandy, German currency notes, one German badge, leather wallet with German notes, leave passes, pages from German books.

Lt. Manners recommended for DSC. ASDIC op PO Mardin recommended for a decoration.

ADM 199/232; ADM 199/2148; AUD 810/45; NARA: Series T-1022, Roll 3900, PG31752; CWGC; U-Boot-Ehrenmal Möltenort.

The bottle of brandy recovered was later presented to Winston Churchill. The crewmen that died in *U 1274* were:

Balke, Hans, Masch.Mt.

von Barlowen, Alexander, Leutnant z.S.

Barnick, Klaus, Oblt.z.S.

Bellman, Werner, Masch.Gfr.

Berek Ernst, Lt.Ing

Bier, Gerhardt, Mech.Gfr.

Blank, Harry, Masch.Mt.

Bojar Helmut, Bts.Mt.

Brehmer, Martin, Masch.Mt.

Briese, Otto, Ob.Masch.

Ebdorn, Friedrich, Flk.Ob.Gfr.

Ettinger, Jacob, Flk.Ob.Gfr.

Fitting, Hans, Oblt.z.S. (Commander)

Fuchs, Werner, Mech.Mt.

Goldner, Erich, Masch.Gfr.

Grube, Ludwig, Mtr.Gfr.

Gurther, Heinrich, Masch.Gfr.

Holz, Bruno, Bts.Mt.

Kirchenhuber, Rdph, Flk.Ogfr.

Kirchmeier, Helmut, Flk.Ogfr.

Koppenhagen, Heinz, Masch.Gfr.

Langheinrich, Karl-Heinz, Masch Gfr

Lankamp, Heinz, Mtr.

Leschke, Walter, Mtr.

Ludwig, Fritz, Ob.Stm.

Lutjen, Heinrich, Masch.Gfr.

Miede, Heinrich, Leutnant z.S.

Persicke, Reinhard, Fk.Ogfr.

Pillowski, Rudi, Mtr.

Potten, Hans, Masch.Gfr.

Schneider, Gottfried, Mtr.Gfr.

Schennegge, Heinz, Mtr.

Schwarzbach, Martin, Masch.Gfr.

Schweiselsen, Fritz, Flk.Ob.Gfr.

Stadele, Georg, Mt.Gfr.

Stenker, Gottfried, Masch.Gfr.

Stroble, Peter, Mtr.Gfr.

Tanzmann, Richard, Ob.Masch.

Tobe, Kurt, Masch.Gfr.

Warnicke, Karl, Masch.Mt.

Weiss, Richard, San.Mt.

Wende, Waldemar, Flk.Mt.

Zielke, Fritz, Mech.Gf

Wrecksite

The wreck of *U 1274* is reported to be standing upright on a clean, well-swept sand and stone seabed in a general depth of 63 m (LAT). It is still totally intact except for the stern end, which is very smashed up, apparently where a number of the depth charges exploded on or close to the boat. The hatches are still sealed and the twin steel screws are there, with the maker's marks embossed on them. The hull and conning tower have a covering of soft corals but the conning tower is also draped with a trawl net. Anyone visiting this wreck should remember that it is a war grave and that entering the boat would be both wrong and a criminal offence.

Gudveig, ex Robert Mærsk

Date of loss: 25 January 1940

Wreck: ✶ ✶ ✶ ✶

Depth: 90 m

Reference: 55 37'.296 N 001 15'.580 W

Location: 11.92 nm ESE of Longstone Lighthouse

The *Gudveig* was a steel-hulled 1307-ton Norwegian steam cargo ship measuring 73.60 m in length, with an 11.04-m beam and a 4.95-m draught. Odense Staalskibsvft., Odense built and completed her as Yard No. 2 on 20 May 1920 and she was launched as *Robert Mærsk* on 20 December 1919 for Aktieselskabet Dampskibsselskabet Svendborg, in Svendborg, Denmark; P. M. Møller was the manager. A. P. Møller became the manager in 1925.

From 1935, Dampskipsselskapet Aktieselskapet Gudvin at Oslo in Norway was the registered owner and she was renamed *Gudveig*; H. Gjerpen was the manager.

The single steel screw was powered by a 106-nhp three-cylinder triple expansion steam engine that used one boiler and gave 9.5 knots. The cylinders measured 41.91 cm, 68.58 cm and 111.76 cm with a 76.2-cm stroke (16½ in., 27 in. and 44 in. with a 30-in.stroke). Flydk and Skbsv at Kjbnhavns in Norway manufactured the engine and ancillary machinery. She had one deck. The designated code recognition signal letters were: LJAR.

Final voyage

On 25 January 1940, the German submarine *U 19*, commanded by Kapitänleutnant Joachim Schepke, torpedoed and sank the *Gudveig* at 2130 hrs (CT). On the morning of 23 January, *U 19* had broken through the mine warning area off the Farne Islands at high speed and immediately found about 20 unescorted southbound ships from the Methil convoy HN.8. Of these, she sank the *Baltanglia* and the *Pluto*. After observing minesweepers in the area on 25 January, Schepke waited and later torpedoed the *Everene* and *Gudveig*, both of which were in another unescorted group, heading north for Methil to join a convoy bound for Norway.

The *Gudveig* had sailed from Bergen and on 9 January 1940 had joined the 38-ship convoy HN.7, sailing from Norwegian waters to Methil, arriving on 13 January. The *Gudveig* then travelled down to the Tyne where she loaded up with coal, intending to sail back to Bergen independently, but she sank in Kriegsmarine quadrant AN5186. Of her crew of 18, ten Norwegians and one Latvian were lost, three of the survivors being picked up by the 3782-ton Norwegian steamer *Dole* (1912 – Mrs. Z. Heinrichsons, Riga) and four by the 1114-ton Norwegian steamer *Vim* (1913 – AS Victor Müllers Rederi, Bergen). All the survivors were landed at Methil.

Six of the Norwegian crewmen that died on the *Gudveig* were:

Andriansen, Bredo, Steward
Andersen, Ellis, Able Seaman
Andersen, Rudolf, Chief Engineer
Beir, Augen, Second Engineer
Bjerke, Henry Olav, Seaman
Johannessen, Jens Aage, Mate

LCWLR 1939–1945, p. 38; LR 1938–1939, no.75344 (G).

Wrecksite

The wreck, possibly that of the Norwegian steamer, is orientated in a NE to SW direction. It lies on a seabed of fine sand in a general depth of 90 m (LAT). The wreck appears to be intact and is upright, with the superstructure still visible. It covers an area of 61 m in length by 16 m across and stands 6 m high. This should make an excellent boat-angling venue, as large numbers of fish can be detected on the echo sounder. If it is the *Gudveig*, the bell will be inscribed: *Robert Mærsk 1920*.

Assuan, Ex *Ptarmigan*, Ex *Glanton*, Ex *Glanton Firth*

Date of loss: 17 October 1943

Wreck: ★ ★ ★ ★ ★

Depth: 75 m

Reference: 55 38'.155 N 001 19'.810 W

Location: 9.48 nm E by S of Longstone Lighthouse

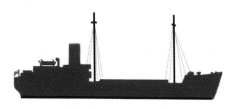

Silhouette of the 499 ton aft cargo steamer Assuan

The *Assuan* (Official No. 142859) was a steel-hulled 499-ton British steam cargo vessel measuring 49.17 m in length, with a 7.67-m beam and a 2.92-m draught. Ardrossan Dry Dock and Shipbuilding Co. Ltd at Ardrossan built and completed her as Yard No. 307 in February 1920; she was launched as the *Glanton Firth* in January 1920 for Cheviot Coasters Ltd, Newcastle; G. T. Gillie and Co. was the manager. The single steel screw was powered by an aft-positioned 51-rhp, three-cylinder triple expansion steam engine that used one cylindrical multitubular steel boiler loaded to a pressure of 180 psi and manufactured by Messrs. J. G. Kincaid and Co. Ltd at Greenock in 1920, with three corrugated furnaces, 4.55 sq.m (49 sq.ft) of grate surface and 140.28 sq, m (1510 sq.ft) of heating surface. The cylinders measured 33.92 cm, 53.34 cm and 88.36 cm with a 60.96-cm stroke (13 in., 21 in. and 34 in. with a 24-in.stroke). Messrs Aitchison Blair Ltd at Clydebank, Glasgow manufactured the engine and ancillary machinery. She had one deck, a well deck, three bulkheads cemented and a 29.98-m raised quarterdeck, a 2.7-m bridge deck and 6.4-m forecastle. She had some cellular double-bottom fore and her main compartments comprised a forepeak, chain locker, crew space and a store room, a 26.21-m long cargo hold divided in the centre by a wooden bulkhead, the engine room, boiler room, a coal bunker and an after-peak. She was classed as 100 A1. The designated code recognition signal letters were: MJWC.

In 1920, she was renamed *Glanton* by the same owners.

General Steam Navigation Co. Ltd, in London purchased and renamed her *Ptarmigan* in 1921. From 16 January 1939, Gordonia Freighters Ltd, London was the registered owner and she was renamed *Assuan*; Mr. William Gillespie Gordon was the manager. The normal crew was ten, including the master, but two DEMS gunners were also carried, making a total of twelve.

Final voyage

At about 1130 hrs on 17 October 1943, the *Assuan* left the loading berth at Lambton and Hetton Staiths at Sunderland for passage to Stromness with a cargo of coal and coke. The cargo included 426 tons and 10 cwt of Lambton house coal and 53 tons and 17 cwt of Lambton large coke nuts. 283.9 tons of coal were stowed in no. 2 hold, 142.6 tons of coal were stowed in no. 1 hold, forward partly on top of the coke, which was stowed at the after end of no.1 hold. The coke was improperly loaded underneath the coal and she sailed with a 5–6° list to port, with a considerable amount of water in one of the ballast tanks. As the vessel proceeded out to sea she had the wind, a fresh to strong breeze, about abeam on the starboard side. The list thereafter steadily increased and at about 1330 hrs water was entering the firemen's forecastle on the port side on the upper deck. The list continued to increase and at about 1400 hrs, several men left the forecastle and climbed aft along the starboard side of the ship towards the boats aft. The port lifeboat and rafts had been washed away and the men were unable to move the starboard boat, so they jumped into the water. According to the evidence, all the crew except the master were seen in the water at this time. After an interval, seven of the men swam back to the ship, which by this time had turned completely over, keel uppermost, and climbed on to the bottom. One of the boats then floated alongside and four survivors scrambled on board. Shortly afterwards the vessel sank, E by S of the Longstone lighthouse.

At around 1615 hrs (BST) the force of the wind had increased and by about 1700 hrs had reached its maximum force in a gust of a moderate gale at moderating and veering.

Her crew had consisted of 12 men – the master, the mate, the two engineers, two able seamen, two deck hands, two firemen, one cook and one ordinary seaman. Eight of the men were lost, including the master, mate and both engineers.

LR 1942–1943, no.19752 (A); LCR 1943 p. 6 (b); Starke/Schell; BoT wreck report for *Assuan*, 1946, no.7941.

Wrecksite

The wreck is orientated in an ESE to WNW direction and lies on a seabed of firm sand and gravel in a general depth of 75 m (LAT). It is upright, completely intact, standing 6.5 m high at the stern end with the bows to the ESE, and covered in a profusion of soft corals. The bridge structure at the stern is slightly collapsed but, apart from the mast, everything else is in reasonable condition. The wreck covers an area 50 m long by 11 m wide. If the bell is located, it should be inscribed: *Glanton Firth 1920*. This is an excellent if extremely deep wrecksite and will make a very good boat-angling venue.

Farne Diving Services

Farne Diving Services was established by Stan Hall in 1982 and is now run by his son Lee. We operate from April until mid-November and cater for all levels of divers.

We operate two charter vessels, *Farne Diver* and *Farne Diver 2*, around the Farne Islands offering seal, scenic and wreck diving. Both vessels are fully insured and operated by experienced skippers who have MCA/RYA licences and a vast knowledge of the Farne Islands' dive sites.

www.farnedivingservices.com

We have accommodation consisting of 15 twin and double en-suite rooms

Contact Lee Hall on 01665720615 or 07534988445

Email: leehalldiving1@aol.com

Auckland Castle

Date of loss: 24 August 1918
Wreck: ★ ★ ★
Depth: 53 m
Reference: 55 38'.777 N 001 30'.202 W
Location: 3.58 nm E of Longstone Lighthouse, Outer Farne Islands

Auckland Castle

The *Auckland Castle* (Official No. 86358) was a 1084-ton riveted iron-hulled steam cargo ship measuring 68.58 m in length, with a 9.77-m beam and a 4.87-m draught. S. P. Austin and Son at Wear Dock, Sunderland built and completed her as Yard No.143 in August 1883; she was launched on 21 August 1883 for Mordey and Carney at Newport. The single iron screw was powered by a 99-hp, two-cylinder compound steam engine that used one boiler. G. Clark of Sunderland manufactured the engine and ancillary machinery. She had one deck, a well deck, four bulkheads and a superstructure consisting of a 26.8-m quarterdeck, a 14.6-m bridge deck and a 7.9-m forecastle.

Mordey, Jones and Co. at Newport in Monmouthshire was the registered owner in 1890.

From 1910, Auckland Castle Steam Ship Co. Ltd was the registered owner and Mordey, Jones and Co. was the manager.

Final voyage

On 24 August 1918, the defensively-armed *Auckland Castle* with (commanded by Captain D. Evans) was approaching the Farne Islands when she was hit by two torpedoes, fired without warning by the KDM minelaying submarine SM *UC 59*, commanded by Oberlt.z.S. Walter Strasser. The steamer had left Hartlepool on 23 August with 1,133 tons of coal, bound for Moss in Norway. She sank in just three minutes, according to the chief officer, taking with her 12 of the crew, including the master, and confidential papers. The six survivors from her crew of eighteen were picked up by an escort vessel and landed at Granton later that day.

The crewmen who died were:

> Barker, Joseph, 28 yrs, Fireman and Trimmer MM
>
> Chesney, Stephen, 22 yrs, Seaman MM
>
> Evans, D., Master MM
>
> Moore, Thomas McDonald, 25 yrs, Sailor MM
>
> O'Donnell, M., 51 yrs, Able Seaman MM
>
> Palmer, Sydney Harry, 23 yrs, Assistant Engineer MM
>
> Poole, James, 70 yrs, Chief Engineer MM
>
> Ryan, H., 29 yrs, Fireman and Trimmer MM
>
> Reed, Sydney, 36 yrs, Fireman and Trimmer MM
>
> Turner, William Thomas, 27 yrs, Steward MM
>
> Upsan, Walter, 35 yrs, Able Seaman MM
>
> Vaagbo, Johan, 17 yrs, Sailor MM

ADM 137/2964; LCWLR 1914–1918, p. 231; BVLS 1914–1918, p. 96; CWGC; *The Cross of Sacrifice* Vol.V.

Wrecksite

The wreck is orientated in a SSE to NNW direction. It sits in a half-metre scour on a well-swept seabed of sand, gravel and shells in a general depth of 53 m (LAT). It stands 5.7 m high but is upside down, with the screw and rudder still attached and pointing skywards. The hull, which is covered in a myriad of soft corals, has now begun to crumble down and is showing signs of serious deterioration. Most of the bridge/wheelhouse structure is smashed up underneath the upturned hull, although broken sections of it are also strewn around on the brittle starfish-covered seabed. Further examination is required to ascertain whether the bow section is also upside down, because only the stern to amidships section has been dived on.

This, like many of the wrecks in this vicinity, has a good few trawl nets draped over it. Many large cod have been observed around the perimeter of the wreck, so she will make a useful addition to the boat-angling venues.

Merwede

Date of loss: 26 January 1918
Wreck: ✹ ✹ ✹
Depth: 49 m
Reference: 55 38′.899 N 001 28′.891 W
Location: 4.31 nm E of Longstone Lighthouse and 7.44 nm NE of Beadnell Point

The *Merwede* was a steel-hulled 744-ton Netherlands steam cargo vessel measuring 54.86 m in length with an 8.53-m beam and a 3.86-m draught. De Groot and Van Vliet, Slikkerveer built and completed her as Yard No. 67 in October 1917 for N.V. Scheepsexploitatie Mij. 'Navis', Sliedrecht, Netherlands, who was the owner at the time of loss; H. K. Nederlof was the manager. The single steel screw was powered by an aft-positioned 83-nhp three-cylinder triple expansion steam engine that used one single-ended boiler and gave ten knots. The cylinders measured 38.1 cm, 63.5 cm and 101.6 cm with a 68.58-cm stroke (15 in., 25 in. and 40 in. with a 27-in. stroke). Y.V. van Capellen manufactured the engine and ancillary machinery at Bolnes in the Netherlands. She had one deck.

Final voyage

On 26 January 1918, the *Merwede* detonated a German-laid mine and sank in just six minutes, 5 miles E of Longstone Lighthouse. She had been on passage from Leith for Rotterdam with a cargo of coal.

LCWLR 1914–1918, p. 197; ANCL 1914–1918, p. 68; Starke/Schell.

Wrecksite

The wreck, known locally as 'Gordon's Wreck', is orientated in a SSE to NNW direction and sits in a 2-metre scour with the bows to the north. It lies on a seabed of gravel and sand in a general depth of 49 m (LAT). The wreck appears intact, but is upside down and in two halves with a debris field between the two parts. It stands about 5 m high at the bow section and slopes down gradually into the seabed towards the stern. The superstructure has collapsed underneath the hull and there is a small section where access would probably be possible. A boiler has been observed towards the stern and the whole wreck is a myriad of soft corals. Tidal streams are fairly strong and very few fish have been noted.

Otago, Ex *Germania*, Ex *Ivanhoe*, Ex *Carib*

Date of loss: 10 June 1915
Wreck: ✹ ✹

Depth: 84 m

Reference: 55 40'.560 N 000 54'.816 W

Location: 23.69 nm E by ¾ N of Longstone Lighthouse

The *Otago* (Official No. 4344) was an iron-hulled 1437-ton Swedish steam cargo ship measuring 73.5 m in length, with a 10.23-m beam and a 4.97-m draught. Richardson, Duck and Co. at Thornaby, Stockton built and completed her as Yard No. 291 in October 1882; she was launched as the *Carib* (Official No. 84642) on 28 September 1882 for Anderson, Anderson and Co. at Stockton. The single iron screw was powered by a 145-nhp two-cylinder compound steam engine that used one double-ended boiler with four plain furnaces and 5.85 sq.m (63 sq.ft) of grate surface. The cylinders measured 73.66 cm and 139.7 cm with an 83.82-cm stroke (29 in. and 55 in. with a 33-in. stroke). T. Richardson and Sons manufactured the machinery at Hartlepool. She had one deck and a well deck.

In 1897, she was renamed *Ivanhoe* by her new owners S.S. Ivanhoe Co. Ltd, Glasgow; Maclay and McIntyre was the manager.

In 1901, the new owners Memeler Dampfschiffs AG, Memel in Germany renamed her *Germania* and R. Schneider was the manager.

In 1904, she was renamed *Otago* (Official No. 4344) by her new registered owners, Handelsb. Sölvesborg Skeppsvarf Karlshamn, Sweden and J. Ingmansson was the manager.

From 1911, J. Ingmansson of Karlshamn, Sweden was the registered owner.

Final voyage

On 10 June 1915, the *Otago* was torpedoed and sunk without warning by Kapitänleutnant Constantin Kolbe in the KDM submarine SM *U 19*, from the III.U-Bootflottille based at Wilhelmshaven. The steamer was voyaging from Hamsund, Sweden to Hull with a cargo of timber and sank about 20 miles E by ¾ N of Longstone light.

Starke/Schell; Lloyd's WWI Losses, p.16.

Wrecksite

The wreck, probably that of the *Otago*, is orientated in a NNE to SSW direction. It lies on a seabed of mud, fine sand and shells in a general depth of 84 m (LAT). The wreck appears to be intact but is collapsed, standing just over 2 m high and covering an area about 58 m long and 20 m wide. Large numbers of fish have been observed on the echo sounder over the top of her remains, which should make for an excellent boat-angling venue. If this is the *Otago*, the bell will almost certainly be inscribed: *Carib 1882*.

Jægersborg, Ex Harrogate

Date of loss: 4 August 1916

Wreck: ✳ ✳ ✳

Depth: 75 m

Reference: 55 41'.727 N 001 20'.966 W

Location: 10.02 nm NE of Longstone Lighthouse

Silhouette of the Danish steamer Jægersborg, ex Harrogate

The *Jægersborg* (Official No. 86958) was an iron-hulled 1797-ton Danish steam cargo ship measuring 81.5 m in length, with a 10.79-m beam and a 5.96-m draught. E. Withy and Co. of West Hartlepool built and completed her as Yard No. 120 in August 1883; she was launched as the 1866-ton *Harrogate* on 6 June 1883 for T. S. Hudson of West Hartlepool. The single iron screw was powered by a 180-hp, two-cylinder compound steam engine that used one boiler. The cylinders measured 83.82 cm and 157.48 cm, with a 99.06-cm stroke (33 in. and 62 in., with a 39-in. stroke). She had one deck, four bulkheads and water ballast.

In 1886, F.I. Hudson was the registered owner and Surtees Jnr was the master.

Late in 1889 the registered owner was Gladstone and Cornforth, West Hartlepool, and Captain Hasland was the master.

In 1896, she was renamed *Jægersborg* by new owners Dampsk. Selsk. af 1896, Copenhagen, Denmark, with C. K. Hansen the manager.

The registered owner from 1901 was Dampsk. Selsk. Neptun and C. K. Hansen was the manager.

Final voyage

On 4 August 1916, the KDM submarine SM *UB 39*, commanded by Werner Fürbringer, captured the *Jægersborg* as she was voyaging, with Captain C.F. Matzen in command, from Narvik to Middlesbrough with magnetic iron ore. The crew was ordered to abandon ship and the steamer was scuttled using explosive charges, 12 miles NE of Longstone Lighthouse.

Starke/Schell; LCWLR 1914–1918, p. 51; LR 1914–1915, no.89 (J); ANCL 1914–1918, p. 60; LR, 1893–1900.

Wrecksite

The wreck, probably that of the Danish steamer, is orientated in an E to W direction. It lies on a seabed of fine sand, broken shells and gravel, in a general depth of 75 m (LAT). The wreck is very broken up and scattered but stands over 8 m high and covers an area 67 m in length and 29 m across. It has not been identified but is in the same area where the ship sank. If it is the *Jægersborg*, the bell will be inscribed: *Harrogate 1883*.

Emma

Date of Loss: 9 December 1914
Wreck: ★ ★ ★ ★
Depth: 61 m
Reference: 55 41'.043 N 001 34'.986 W
Location: 2.51 nm NE of Longstone Lighthouse

The *Emma* was a steel-hulled 2,143-ton cargo steam ship, built and completed as Yard No.446 by W. Gray and Co. Ltd, West Hartlepool in August 1892 and launched as the *Eshcolbrook* (Official No.99143) on 11 July 1892 for J. Forster and Co., Whitby. She measured 87 m in length and had an 11.54-m beam. The single screw was powered by a three-cylinder triple expansion steam engine that used two boilers.

In 1905 the registered owner was Grimsby Steam Shipping Co. Ltd, Grimsby and H. and F. Haagensen was the manager. In 1910 A/S Eshcolbrook, Brevik, Norway was the registered owner and L. Hansen was the manager. In 1913 she had the same owner but T. Christoffersen was the manager. Later in 1913 she was renamed *Emma* (Official No.5516) and the registered owner was Ångfartygs A/B Emma, Gefle, Sweden, while Emil Löfgren was the manager.

Final voyage

The *Emma* stranded on the Knavestone rocks on Wednesday, 9 December 1914 while transporting wood pulp and pig iron from the port of Sundsvall in Sweden to Manchester. Her crew of 20 lowered the boat and three men got into it, but before any more could join them, the boat broke adrift in the heavy seas and quickly floated away. Meanwhile the North Sunderland lifeboat *Forster Fawsett* had been launched at 2345 hrs and set out for the Knavestone. The remaining 17 crewmen were rescued from the stricken steamer and taken back to Seahouses. At 0830 hrs the following morning, the ship's boat was spotted at sea, so the lifeboat was immediately launched again and rescued the three men in it. The *Emma*, though, drifted unseen off the Knavestone and during the next few days was blown away in the very heavy weather and disappeared.

The Times, Monday, 14 December 1914, p. 4; *The History of the Seahouses Lifeboats* by J. Morris.

Wrecksite

The author believes that this wreck is almost certainly that of the *Emma*. It is orientated in a SSE to NNW (145°/326°) direction and lies on a seabed of mud, sand, shell and gravel in a general depth of 61 m (LAT). The wreck is upright, broken and collapsed and now festooned in nets. It covers an area of 96 m in length, is 20 m across and stands 8.5 m high. The bows face to the NNW. If the bell is recovered it should be inscribed *Eshcolbrook 1892*.

Aepos, Torkel, Ex *Uman*

Date of Loss: 25 December 1920

Wreck: ★ ★ ★ ★

Depth: 70 m

Reference: 55 42'.710 N 001 28'.731 W

Location: 5.97 nm NE of Longstone Lighthouse

The *Aepos* was an iron-hulled 630-ton steam cargo vessel measuring 51.86 m in length, with a 7.95-m beam and a 4.13-m draught. W. Lindbergs Warfs and Werkstads A/B, Stockholm, Sweden built and completed her in 1873 as Yard No. 89. She was a 493.75-ton schooner-rigged passenger/cargo steamer and was launched as the *Uman* (Official No. 659) for Umans Ångbåtsbolag, Umeå, Sweden; E. Häggström, Umeå was the manager. The iron four-bladed screw was powered by a 100-nhp two-cylinder compound steam engine that used one boiler.

W. Lindbergs manufactured the engine and ancillary machinery. The designated code recognition signal letters were: HKQG.

In 1876 she was registered to A. Grahn, Umeå.

In 1884 the owner was C. O. Scharins Söner, Umeå.

Umeå Nya Ångfartygs AB, Umeå was the registered owner in 1892.

On 6 June 1893 she was taken over by Umeå Nya Ångfartygs A/B, Stockholm and a new boiler was fitted.

On 4 October 1900 the *Uman* ran aground on Renholmsgrundet, outside Umeå, and was so badly damaged that she sank the following day.

In August 1901 the vessel was salvaged but at such high cost that the owners were forced to relinquish ownership of the vessel to the insurance company, who repaired and rebuilt her as a cargo ship.

On 29 August 1902, she was purchased by Johan Emil Löfgren of Umeå.

She was sold to Carl Georg Bayard of Stockholm on 27 July 1903.

In 1904 Ångfartygs A/B Uman (Hjalmar Blomberg), Stockholm was the owner.

In 1905 she had the same owner but C. G. Bayard was the manager.

In 1916, the vessel was sold to Rederiaktiebolaget Uman in Stockholm

Nils Österman and Co., Stockholm was the registered owner in 1917.

Later in 1917 Claes Birger Below, Stockholm became the registered owner.

On 13 May 1918, Rederi AB Ivar, Stockholm purchased her.

Later that same day, 13 May 1918, she was taken over by Rederi A/B Amazone, Stockholm and renamed *Torkel*. The company had tried to change the name to *Cerigo*, but the Swedish National Board of Trade would not allow it. T. Hillerström, Malmö was the manager.

On 27 March 1920, the *Torkel* was sold to Nicolas Pappalas and Collakis, Chios, Greece for £24,000 and renamed *Aepos*; Nicolas Pappalas was the owner at the time of loss.

Final voyage

On 25 December 1920, the *Aepos* was on passage with a cargo of iron from Rotterdam for Borrowstounness (Bo'ness) in the Firth of Forth, but sprang a leak 25 miles off the Longstone Lighthouse in the Outer Farne Islands. The crew took to the lifeboat and abandoned their vessel, which was left drifting in a westerly direction, 15 miles east of Holy Island. The crew also reached Holy Island later that day.

The Times, Wednesday, 29 December 1920, p. 13; *Svensk kustsjöfart 1840–1940* by C.G. Olsson.

Wrecksite

The wreck, which is probably that of the *Aepos*, is orientated in a SSE to NNW direction with the bows to the NNW. It lies on a firm seabed of gravel, black shells, mud and fine sand in a general depth of 70 m (LAT). The wreck is upright and intact, standing over 6 m high and covering an area 51 m long and 7 m across. If the bell is located it should be inscribed: *Uman 1873*. Large numbers of fish have been observed over the top of the wreck.

Acantha

Date of Loss: 5 April 1915
Wreck: ✷ ✷ ✷
Depth: 79 m
Reference: 55 46'.005 N 001 00'.208 W
Location: 21.79 nm ENE of Longstone Lighthouse

Silhouette of the steam trawler Acantha

The *Acantha* (Official No.137015) was a steel-hulled 322-ton British steam trawler measuring 42.72 m in length, with an 8.22-m beam and a 3.81-m draught. Cochrane and Sons Ltd of Selby built and completed her as Yard No. 621 in December 1914 and launched her on 21 October 1914 for Equitable Steam Fishing Co. Ltd at Grimsby. The single steel screw was powered by an 88-nhp three-cylinder triple expansion steam engine that used one single-ended boiler. The cylinders measured 33.02 cm, 57.15 cm and 83.98 cm with a 66.04-cm stroke (13 in., 22½ in. and 37 in. with a 26-in. stroke). She had one deck, a 23.46-m quarterdeck and 6.09-m forecastle.

Final voyage

On 5 April 1915, the *Acantha* was on a return fishing voyage from Grimsby when she was captured 25 miles E by N of the Longstone by the KDM submarine SM *U 10*, commanded by Kapitänleutnant Fritz Stuhr. The crew was ordered to abandon ship and she was sunk by a torpedo fired on the surface.

The *Times*, however, states that:

> the submarine had been firing at the trawler without warning. The *Acantha* was struck below the water line and began taking in water. The crew took to the boats, but while they were launching the craft on the weather side, several shots were fired, but no one was hit. After the crew had taken to the small boats, the submarine crew continued to fire at them with rifles and several shots hit the sides, making holes in the gunwales. Then the submarine fired a torpedo at the trawler, which sank immediately with a loud explosion. The submarine then went south. Two hours later the *Acantha*'s crew of thirteen hands were picked up by the Swedish steamer *Tord* and landed at Blyth. Captain Pederson, master of the *Acantha*, had reason to believe that the submarine was SM *U 20*; she was painted white with her number painted out.'

German records later showed it, in fact, to have been SM *U 10*.

LCWLR 1914–1918, p.10; Miramar Ship Index.

Wrecksite

The wreck is orientated in a NE to SW (052°/232°) direction and lies on a firm seabed of mud, fine sand and broken shells in a general depth of 79 m (LAT). It is fairly intact but collapsed, standing over 5 m high and covering an area 43 m long and 16 m wide. The wreck should make an interesting boat-angling venue, as there are few reefs nearby to offer shelter to fish.

Florence Dombey, Ex Wyre

Date of loss: 5 May 1933

Wreck: ✯ ✯ ✯ ✯

Depth: 75 m

Reference: 55 44'.030 N 001 33'.026 W

Location: 5.77 nm NNE of Longstone Lighthouse

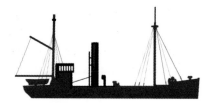

The *Florence Dombey* (Official No. 109673) was a 182-ton British steam trawler measuring 5.17 m in length, with a 6.42-m beam and a 3.47-m draught. Smith's Dock Co. Ltd at North Shields built and completed her as Yard No. 629 in April 1900; she was launched as the *Wyre* on

Silhouette of steam trawler Florence Dombey

17 March 1900 for Wyre Steam Trawling Co. Ltd at Fleetwood (FD.196) and M. Hudson managed her. The single steel screw was powered by a 52-rhp, three-cylinder triple expansion steam engine that used one boiler. The cylinders measured 31.75 cm, 50.8 cm and 81.28 cm with a 57.15-cm stroke (12½ in., 20 in. and 32 in. with a 22½-in. stroke). NE Marine Engineering Co. Ltd manufactured the machinery at Sunderland. She was equipped with wireless and had one deck and three bulkheads. The designated code recognition signal letters were: RQTN.

In 1911, she was sold to M. Hudson and renamed *Florence Dombey*.

The trawler served with the Royal Navy as a boom defence vessel from 1915 to 1917, when she was requisitioned into the Fishery Reserve, then returned to the owner in September 1918. No Admiralty number was issued.

In 1920, she was sold to Aberdeen owner R. Milne (Port Reg. A.264) who owned her at the time of loss.

In 1930, T.T. Irvin Jr was the registered owner.

From 1933, Mrs E. Irvin was the registered owner and T.T. Irvin was the manager.

Final voyage

Carrying a crew of ten, the *Florence Dombey* sailed from Aberdeen under skipper Jack Hague. After a brief stop at Granton, they set course for the Longstone light and the fishing grounds, but the boat foundered on 5 May 1933, about six miles north of the lighthouse. Mr Hague, skipper of the *Florence Dombey*, said that at around 1700 hrs on Friday the chief engineer reported an inrush of water from the main bunker. After opening the hatch to the fish room the crew discovered that sea water had flooded to just a few feet below the deck; the chief engineer then immediately started the pumps. Jack Hague signalled to the 193-ton Aberdeen trawler *Arora* (1903: A Robertson), which was close by, and asked her skipper to stop. Mr Hague then manoeuvred his trawler in towards her, getting virtually alongside. The chief engineer reported that the pumps were not coping and that the water was by that time almost level with the furnaces. Jack Hague was afraid his vessel would sink under their feet, so he gave the order to abandon ship and jump across to the *Arora*.

There was a heavy swell running and they had to watch for their chance to leap at exactly the right moment. The second engineer, who had been in his bunk and was still in his underclothes, launched himself safely aboard the *Arora*. The others, too, scrambled onto the vessel in just the clothes they stood in. The *Arora* landed the eleven men at Anstruther and they all returned to Aberdeen by rail on the Saturday.

LCR 1933, p. 5 (b); IDNS, p. 62; *The Times*, Monday, 8 May, 1933, p. 11; Navires à Vapeur et à Moteur de Moins de 300 tx Chaluties; LR.

Wrecksite

The wreck, most probably that of the *Florence Dombey*, is orientated in an ENE to WSW direction, with the bows to the SW. It lies on a seabed of mud, sand and shell in a general depth of 75 m (LAT). The wreck is upright and intact and stands over 7 m high. Large numbers of fish have been observed over the top of it, which should make it a decent boat-angling venue. If the bell is located, it should be inscribed: *Wyre 1900*.

Maystone, Ex Empire Wapping

Date of loss: 18 October 1949

Wreck: ✵ ✵ ✵ ✵ ✵

Depth: 84 m

Reference: 55 43'.379 N 001 35'.844 W

Location: 4.74 nm N by E of Longstone Lighthouse, Outer Farne Islands

The *Maystone* (Official No.180364) was a steel-hulled 2,025-ton British Icemaid class Empire steam cargo ship measuring 82.9 m in length, with a 12.19-m beam and a 52.3-m draught. Grangemouth Dockyard Co. Ltd at Grangemouth built and completed her as Yard No. 461 in May 1945; she was launched as the *Empire Wapping* on 15 March 1945 for the Ministry of War Transport (MoWT). Grangemouth, and Stone and Rolfe Ltd was the manager. The single screw was powered by an aft-positioned, three-cylinder triple expansion steam engine that used two single-ended boilers. The cylinders measured 43.18 cm, 68.58 cm and 121.92 cm with a 91.44-cm stroke (17 in., 27 in. and 48 in. with a 36-in. stroke). North East Marine Engineering Co. Ltd, Newcastle upon Tyne manufactured the engine and ancillary machinery. She had a cruiser stern, one deck and an aft superstructure consisting of a 49.5-m quarterdeck and 7.9-m forecastle. The designated code recognition signal letters were: GLKD.

The registered owner from 1947 was Thomas Stone Shipping Co. Ltd of Swansea, who renamed her *Maystone*.

Final voyage

Early on the morning of 18 October 1949, the *Maystone* sank during a gale four miles east of the Longstone Lighthouse, following a collision with the new aircraft carrier HMS *Albion*. Four crewmen, the only survivors from her crew of 23, were taken on board the *Albion*. The *Maystone*, which was valued at £105,000, had left Methil late on the previous night bound for Deptford with a cargo of coal. One of the three tugs towing the *Albion* from the Tyne sent out an SOS message and the Holy Island lifeboat was dispatched to the scene. Over a period of eight hours and in very rough seas, she searched an area of about 50 square miles, but returned to harbour without finding any further survivors. Searches by aircraft also proved fruitless.

The men lost were:

Buttlgice, C. M., Fireman MM from Cardiff

Camillieri, F., Fireman MM from Cardiff

Crombie, C., First Mate MM from Stirlingshire

David, J., Chief Engineer MM from Porthcawl

Davidson, J. B., Cook MM from Glasgow

Ethill, J. C., Second Engineer MM from Boldon, Co Durham

Gills, G. C., MM from Glasgow

Haywood, J., Able Seaman MM from Grays, Essex

Houston, W. J., Able Seaman MM from Belfast

Kirkwood, J., Boatswain MM from Grangemouth

Lodrenis, Second Mate MM from Cardiff

McGurk, A., Steward MM from Carrickfergus

Ross, J., Deckhand MM from Co Antrim

Snoddes, H., Catering Boy MM from Belfast

Thomason, J., Able Seaman MM from Gravesend

Vella, P. P., Fireman MM from Cardiff

Wahtris, M., Able Seaman MM

Williams, J. H., Master MM from Penarth

Wilson, J., Catering Boy MM from Belfast

The four survivors were:

Camilleri, A., Donkeyman MM from Malta

Loudon, R., Third Engineer MM from Edinburgh

Williams, Tom, Third Mate MM from near Pontypridd

Aiken, W., Assistant Steward MM from Belfast

HMS *Albion* was holed near the stern but continued on her journey to Rosyth. Later, off Eyemouth, she was carried eastward by the strong gale-force wind, which had veered west. In case the big ship foundered, tugs tried to take her into shallow water. One of the tugs became disabled off St Abb's Head when some wire wrapped around its screw shaft and the *Albion* continued to drift out to sea. During the afternoon, another tug was sent out from Rosyth and the destroyer HMS *St James* was ordered by the Commander and Chief, Home Fleet to render assistance. The *Albion* ended up 10 miles off St Abb's Head before the wind eased and two tugs were able to tow her to the Firth of Forth, where they arrived the next morning.

The *Albion* was a sister ship to HMS *Centaur*, one of the 18, 200-ton Hermes class light fleet aircraft carriers, and was capable of carrying 50 aeroplanes. She had been lying in a berth off Jarrow-on-Tyne for two months prior to the incident, with little work being done on her. In August the previous year, the Admiralty had decided that the job of fitting her out would be resumed; she was to be taken to Rosyth naval yard for dry-docking before returning to Wallsend for final completion.

LCR 1949, p. 9; LR 1948–1949, no.67945 (M); BoT Wreck Report 1949; *The Times*, Wednesday, 19 October 1949, p. 4.

Wrecksite

The original co-ordinates were kindly supplied in 1998 by the late Ian Douglas, skipper/owner of Sovereign Divers at Seahouses. The wreck, believed to be the *Maystone*, is orientated in a S to N direction. It lies on a firm seabed of shell, sand and stone, in a general depth of 84 m (LAT). It is intact but on its side and stands 7 m high, with much of her bridge structures still intact and covered in a profusion of soft corals. Adjacent to the hull is a large debris field. Most of her navigational equipment should still be in place, probably along with the ship's bell. To the author's knowledge this has never been recovered but will be inscribed: *Empire Wapping 1945*. The wreck will certainly make an excellent boat-angling venue.

Isabella Fowlie

Date of loss: 10 July 1941

Wreck: ✶ ✶ ✶ ✶

Depth: 71 m

Reference: 55 44′.694 N 001 31′.715 W

Location: 6.62 nm NE of Longstone Lighthouse

Silhouette of the trawler Isabella Fowlie

The *Isabella Fowlie* (Official No. 129371) was

a steel-hulled 196-ton British steam trawler measuring 35.1 m in length, with a 6.73-m beam and a 3.58-m draught. Hall, Russell and Co. of Aberdeen built and completed as Yard No. 501 in November 1911; she was launched on 8 November 1911 for W. F. Dawson, Aberdeen and registered as A.418. The single steel screw was powered by a 78-rhp three-cylinder triple expansion steam engine that used one single-ended boiler. The cylinders measured 30.48 cm, 50.8 cm and 86.36 cm with an 86.36-cm stroke (12 in., 20 in. and 34 in. with a 34-in. stroke). Hall, Russell and Co. manufactured the machinery.

She had one deck. The designated code recognition signal letters were: GPGM.

In July 1915, the *Isabella Fowlie* was requisitioned and converted to Admiralty Minesweeper No. 473; she was then armed with one 12-pounder gun and one six-pounder AA gun.

While serving on *Isabella Fowlie*, Chief Petty Officer William Alexander McHardy (147548) died (cause unknown) on 20 November 1916.

On 21 October 1918, HMT *Isabella Fowlie* rescued the entire crew of the 2100-ton American steamer *Lake Borgne* (1918 – Naval Overseas Transportation Service, USA), which sank after striking a rock close to Mathieu Point near Brest (48 26′. N 04 50′.40 W); she was in convoy and transporting coal from Penzance to Roscanval in France. The ship was based at Cardiff and had been making runs from Cardiff and Belfast to French ports.

The trawler was returned to its owner in 1920. Later that year, J. Graham and Sons at Hartlepool was the registered owner.

The owner at the time of loss was Hartness Steam Fishing Co. Ltd, Hartlepool, Port Reg. D.677; J. Graham and Sons was the manager.

Final voyage

On 10 July 1941, the *Isabella Fowlie* had left Hartlepool for a fishing voyage when aircraft of the Luftwaffe bombed her, reportedly 7 miles ENE of Longstone Lighthouse; three of her crew of nine were lost, including:

Roders, Henry, 60 yrs, Cook MM
Smith, Thomas Richard, 54 yrs, Chief Engineer MM

LCWLR 1939–1945, p. 277; BVLS 1939–1945, p. 59; LR 1940–1941, no. 59304 (I); CWGC.

Wrecksite

The wreck, probably that of the *Isabella Fowlie*, sits in a half-metre scour at the stern and bows and is orientated in an E to W direction. It lies on a seabed of sand, mud and shells in a general depth of 71 m (LAT). The wreck is upright and intact with the bows facing west. The highest section stands 4.5 m from the seabed and the wreck covers an area 41 m long and 9 m across. High numbers of fish were observed on the echo sounder, so the site should make a decent boat-angling venue.

Aulton, Ex *Ardenza*, Ex *Melford*, Ex *Gipsy*

Date of loss: 23 March 1918

Wreck: ✷ ✷ ✷

Depth: 60 m

Reference: 55'.857 N 001 45'.339 W

Location: 3.77 nm NNE of Emmanuel Head, Holy Island

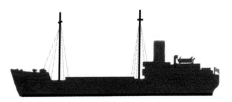

Silhouette of what the Aulton *may have looked like*

The *Aulton* (Official No. 102003) was a steel-hulled 634-ton British steam cargo vessel measuring 55.67 m in length, with an 8.43-m beam and 3.37-m draught. Richard Williamson and Son, Workington built and completed her as Yard No. 162 in October 1899; she was launched as the *Gipsy* on 7 September 1899 for Waterford S.S. Co. Ltd, Limerick. The single screw was powered by an aft-positioned 85-nhp three-cylinder triple expansion steam engine that used one boiler. Ross and Duncan at Glasgow manufactured the engine and ancillary machinery. She had one deck, a well deck, three bulkheads, a 28.6-m quarterdeck, a 3.3-m bridge deck and a 6.7-m forecastle.

In 1901, she was sold to Limerick S.S. Co. Ltd, Limerick.

J. Stewart and Co. Glasgow purchased her in 1911.

In 1912, she was renamed *Melford* by Ford Shipping Co. Ltd, Glasgow who purchased her. Mann, MacNeal and Co. was the manager.

T. C. Steven, Glasgow purchased and renamed her *Ardenza* in 1914.

From 1915, Adam Brothers Ltd, Aberdeen (Newcastle) was the registered owner and she was renamed *Aulton*.

The steamer was then armed for defence in 1915/1916 with a deck-mounted 12-pounder (5.44-kilo) gun.

Final voyage

At 0620 hrs on 23 March 1918, the submerged KDM submarine SMU *UB 83*, commanded by Kapitänleutnant Günther Krause, torpedoed and sank the *Aulton*, 9 miles SE by E ½ E of Berwick Harbour. The steamer, with Captain W. Wright in charge, had left Seaham Harbour at 2203 hrs the night before for passage to Aberdeen with 650 tons of coal. The torpedo detonated in the no.2 hold and two of her crew of 15 were killed instantly; the survivors quickly abandoned ship. The *Aulton* sank five minutes after the explosion and took the ship's confidential papers down with her. The surviving crew were picked up by a patrol vessel shortly afterwards and landed at Berwick. The two crewmen that died were:

Buyers, Alexander Bisset, 22 yrs, Fireman MM
Young, Alexander, 30 yrs, Cook MM

ADM 137/2964; LCWLR 1914–1918, p. 208; BVLS 1914–1918, p. 85; CWGC.

Wrecksite

The wreck is orientated in a NE to SW direction, with the bows to the SW. It lies on a seabed of mud, sand and shells in a general depth of 60 m (LAT). The wreck is upright and almost intact, but with a trail of debris extending 10 m from the stern. The wreckage stands 7.1 m high and covers an area 46 m in length by 8 m wide. The bell, if and when it is located, will almost certainly be inscribed: *Gypsy 1899*. Quite a lot of fish have been observed on a depth sounder so it should make a good boat-angling venue, although nets cover much of the upper sections.

Bowling, Ex Clydemhor

Date of loss: missing since 19 November 1939
Wreck: ✲ ✲ ✲ ✲ ✲
Depth: 67 m
Reference: 55 43'.644 N 001 29'.060 W
Location: 5.56 nm NE of Longstone Lighthouse

The *Bowling* (Official No. 129523) was a steel-hulled 793-ton British steam cargo vessel measuring 60.7 m in length, with a 9.2-m beam and a 3.4-m draught. John Fullerton and Co. at Paisley built and completed her as Yard No. 216 in October 1910; she was launched as the *Clydemhor* on 8 September 1910 for Clydeside S.S. Co. Ltd, Glasgow and J. B. Couper was the manager. A single screw was powered by an aft-positioned 150-nhp three-cylinder triple expansion steam engine that used two single-ended boilers working at a pressure of 170 psi with four plain furnaces, 7.24 sq.m (78 sq.ft) of grate surface and 250.46 sq.m (2696 sq.ft) of heating surface, giving ten knots. The cylinders measured 43.18 cm, 69.85 cm and 114.3 cm with an 83.82-cm stroke (17 in., 27½ in. and 45 in. with a 33-in. stroke). Ross and Duncan in Glasgow manufactured the engine and ancillary machinery. She had water ballast, one steel deck, three bulkheads cemented, a 36.88-m quarterdeck and a 10.97-m forecastle. She also had some cellular double bottom fore of 186 tons and a 79-ton fore-peak tank. Lloyd's classed her 100 A1. The designated code recognition signal letters were: HRSJ.

In 1913, the new owners, Rankine Line, Ltd, Glasgow, renamed her *Bowling*.

From September 1914 to February 1919 the Admiralty requisitioned her as an ammunition carrier.

From 1920, George Gibson and Co. Ltd, Glasgow (Leith) was the registered owner and fitted her with electric lighting. The designated code recognition signal letters were: MDKN.

Final voyage

Under the command of Captain James Scott, the *Bowling* sailed from Leith on 19 November 1939 and was posted as missing while carrying a general cargo on a voyage from Bo'ness to Antwerp. However, at 2328 hrs (CT) that same day, the *Bowling* was torpedoed and sunk by the Kriegsmarine submarine *U 13*, commanded by Kapitänleutnant Heinz Scheringer, at Kriegsmarine quadrant AN 5183, about six miles NE of Longstone in the Outer Farne Islands. None of the crew of thirteen survived.

Kptlt. Scheringer reported hitting a 'darkened tanker' carrying a full cargo of about 2,000 tons What he took to be a tanker was, in fact, the SS *Bowling*, which was hit with one torpedo, causing a massive explosion in the fore-section. The ship broke in two and sank within 40 seconds. The 13 crewmen lost were:

Cameron, Alexander, Second Officer MM
Gilfallan, Peter, Fireman MM
Hutchison, James, Second Engineer MM
McDiarmid, Alexander, Ordinary Seaman MM
McTaggart, Walter, Donkeyman MM
Moran, W., Ordinary Seaman MM
O'Brien, John, Able Seaman MM
Scott, James, Master MM
Short, James Ian Swanney, Ordinary Seaman MM
Stark, Donald, Chief Engineer MM
Watson, William, Chief Officer MM
Young, Alfred, Fireman MM
Young, Thomas Fisher, Steward MM

KTB of *U 13*; Starke/Schell; Miramar Ship Index; CWGC; LR 1930–1939

Wrecksite

The wreck is orientated in a S by E to N by W direction. It lies on a seabed of gravel, pebbles, fine sand, mud and shells in a general depth of 67 m (LAT). The wreck is upright and largely intact, but with about 9 m of the bow section separated from the hull. It stands 5.8 m high and covers an area 46 m in length by 7 m across. Shoals of bib swarm over the wrecksite and large numbers of big cod have also been observed.

Fortuna, HMT Trawler

Date of loss: 3 April 1941

Wreck: ★ ★ ★ ☆

Depth: 44 m

Reference: 55 45'.957 N 001 48'.367 W

Location: 4.68 nm N of Snipe Point, Holy Island

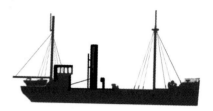

Silhouette of what HMT Fortuna would have looked like

The *Fortuna* (Official No. 123567) was a steel-hulled 259-ton steam trawler completed as Yard No.108 on 8 May 1906 by Cook, Welton and Gemmell at Beverley. She was launched on 14 March 1906 for Alec L. Black at Grimsby and registered as Grimsby trawler GY.140. She measured 39.85 m in length, with a 6.70-m beam and a 3.55-m draught. The single steel screw was powered by a 70-rhp (63-nhp) three-cylinder triple expansion steam engine that used one single boiler, two corrugated furnaces, 33 sq.ft of ground surface and 115 sq. ft of heat surface that gave her 10.75 knots. The cylinders measured 31.75 cm, 55.88 cm and 88.9 cm with a 60.96-cm stroke (12.5 in., 22 in. and 35 in. with a 24-in. stroke). C.D. Holmes and Company manufactured the machinery at Hull. She had one deck, four bulkheads cemented and a 20.72-m quarterdeck. The boat was also fitted with wireless and an echo sounding device. The designated code recognition signal letters were: MCLD.

On 16 June 1909 she was sold to South Western Steam Fishing Company Ltd, Grimsby.

On 5 May 1913, Thomas W. Baskcomb of Grimsby purchased the boat.

On 27 September 1915, Spurn Steam Trawling Company, Grimsby bought her.

On 29 November 1916 she was sold to George F. Sleight of Grimsby.

The Admiralty requisitioned her into the Fishery Reserve in 1917 with Port Registration GY.1048 and she was armed with one three-pounder; she was returned to the owner in 1919.

On 28 November 1933, Dobson Ship Repair Company Ltd of Grimsby acquired the vessel.

On 11 June 1940, the Admiralty requisitioned her for a second time, but as an auxiliary patrol vessel (APV) and she was armed with one forward-facing six-pounder; Port Registration GY.140.

Final patrol

On 3 April 1941, HM Trawler *Fortuna* was on patrol off Berwick when aircraft of the Luftwaffe bombed and sank her; all of her 15 crew were lost with the boat.

The crewmen lost were:

Bruce, Adam H. M., Seaman RNPS

Charlton, William T. M., Temporary Skipper RNR

Feeney, Edward V., Stoker RNPS

Foote, Samuel E., Second Hand RNPS

Glyde, Lawrence E., Seaman RNPS

Hall, George O., Stoker RNPS

Harris, Ernest E., Ordinary Seaman RNPS

Jones, Henry, Ordinary Seaman RNPS

Nicholson, William E., Engineman RNPS

Phillips, Sidney, Stoker RNPS

Robson, Edward, Engineman RNR

Smith, William J., Seaman RNPS

Whyte, Gilbert, Seaman RNPS

Winsor, Stanley G., Seaman RNPS

Wright, Josiah V., Seaman RNPS

CWGC; *RN Trawlers Pt. 2* by Toghill.

Wrecksite

The wreck is orientated in a SE to NW (135º/315º) direction. It lies on a seabed of mud, fine sand and gravel in a general depth of 44 m (LAT). The wreck is intact and upright, standing 5.8 m high and covers an area of 42 m in length by 7 m across. The ship's bell was recovered a few years ago by a diver from Seahouses, and identified the wreck as that of HMT *Fortuna*. Fifteen men of the Royal Naval Patrol Service (RNPS) and Royal Navy Reserve (RNR) died on the vessel so the wreck is a war grave and should be respected as such. Large numbers of fish are attracted to the wrecksite, which should make an excellent boat-angling venue.

Venus, Ex Fri, Ex Sif, Ex Serantes

Date of loss: 14 April 1917

Wreck: ✷ ✷ ✷

Depth: 52 m

Reference: 55 48'.101 N 001 51'.711 W

Location: 4.70 nm NE of Berwick

Sketch of the Venus, *ex* Sif

The *Venus* was a steel-hulled 715-ton Norwegian steam cargo vessel measuring 63.72 m in length, with an 8.68-m beam and a 4.11-m draught. A. Simey and Co. (John and Luke Crown) at Monkwearmouth, Sunderland built and completed her as Yard No. 40; she was launched as the schooner-rigged *Serantes* on 17 October 1872 for Johnson and Co., Newcastle upon Tyne. The single screw was powered by an aft-positioned 95-nhp two-cylinder compound steam engine that used one boiler. The cylinders measured 63.5 cm and 121.92 cm with a 76.2-cm stroke (25 in. and 48 in. with a 30-in.stroke). John Stewart in London manufactured the engine and ancillary machinery. She had one calked deck and four bulkheads. The designated code recognition signal letters were: JVFB.

In 1876, C.L. Lapricht, Newcastle upon Tyne was the registered owner.

In 1877, the registered owner was T. W. Bulman, Newcastle.

Nelson, Donkin and Co. Newcastle owned her in 1879.

T.W. Bulman, Newcastle was the registered owner in 1886.

In 1887, H.C.F. Hartman, Goole, purchased her.

Jacob R. Olsen, Bergen, Norway, with others, renamed her *Sif* after acquiring the vessel in October 1889.

She was sold to Aktieselskapet B. Stolt-Nielsen, Haugesund, Norway in October 1898 and renamed *Fri*.

In 1899, B. Stolt-Nielsen with others, Haugesund, Norway, owned the *Sif* (Official No. 624).

In 1900, the *Sif* (designated code recognition signal letters: JVBF) was owned by J. R. Olsen of Bergen.

She was sold to E. B. Aaby, Drammen, Norway in March 1906 and renamed *Venus*.

In 1912, Aktieselskapet Dampskipsselskapet 'Venus', Porsgrunn, Norway owned the vessel; Nils Olsen was the manager. The engine was then changed to a 102-nhp three-cylinder triple expansion steam engine.

Aktieselskapet Dampskipsselskapet 'Venus', Porsgrunn, Norway owned the *Venus* in 1913, but Fred. Th. Beergh was the manager.

In October 1915, Aktieselskapet Vigdis, Skien, Norway acquired her and C.B. Nilesen was the manager.

In December 1915, Aktieselskapet Prompt, Holmestrand, Norway was the registered owner and A.Steen and A. Rafen was the manager.

In 1916, Aktieselskapet 'Prompt', Axel Steen and Niels Rafen, Holmestrand was the registered owner.

From June 1916, Aktieselskapet 'Venus', Kristiania, Norway was the owner and Ole Sørensen was the manager.

Final voyage

On 14 April 1917 the *Venus*, with Captain Fr. Fredriksen in charge, was carrying a cargo of coal from Blyth to Drammen when she detonated a German mine. The mine had been laid on 15 March 1917 by the KDM submarine SM *UC 50*, commanded by Kapitänleutnant Rudolf Seuffer. The steamer sank very quickly, sucking down a number of the crew who were attempting to launch the lifeboats. Some of the men managed to get back up to the surface and stayed afloat by clinging to bits of wreckage. Unfortunately, only two men of the crew of 16 were still alive by the time a fishing boat appeared. The survivors were taken back to hospital in Berwick. The 14 men who died were:

Abrahamsen, Jacob, Sailor, Harstad
Andersen, Martin, Cook, Tønsberg
Anderson, Axel, Stoker, Sweden
Fredriksen, Fr., Master, Hvaler, Fredrikstad
Friberg, Joh, Second Engineer, Kristiania
Hansen, Hans M., Stoker, Kristiania
Hanssen, Peder, Stoker, Kristiania
Johannesen, Eugen, First Mate, Fredrikstad
Johannesen, Kristen, Sailor, Tjøme
Johannesen, Pefer, First Cook, Tønsberg

Johannesen, Rolf, Sailor, Drammen

Marthinsen, Sigurd, Sailor, Drammen

Reif, David, Stoker, Sweden

Wahlqvist, P., First Engineer, Kristiania

Sjøforklaringer over norske skibes krigsforlis 1914–1919; ANCL 1914–1918, p.105; Starke/ Schell; LCWLR 1914–1918, p.117; LR 1915–1916, no.227 (V); Record of American and Foreign Shipping, 1857–1900.

Wrecksite

The wreck sits in a half-metre scour and is orientated in a NNE to SSW (012°/192°) direction. It lies on a seabed of mud, fine sand and shells in a general depth of 55 m (LAT). The wreck is upright and reasonably intact, with the bows to the NNE, and stands 6.9 m high. It covers an area of 50 m in length by 8 m wide and there is a debris field extending 12 m from the bows. Soft corals are well established on the highest parts of wreck. Shoals of fish – especially bib, cod and the occasional big ling – are attracted to the wreck, making it a worthy boat-angling venue. In 2005, divers from Seahouses recovered the ship's bell, which identified the wreck.

Genoa, Ex Centurion

Date of loss: after 15 January 1912

Wreck: ✮ ✮ ✮ ✮

Depth: 68 m

Reference: 55 49'.033 N 001 50'.783 W

Location: 5.62 nm ENE of Berwick Lighthouse

The *Genoa* (Official No.97525) was a steel-hulled 1,942-ton British spur deck-type steam cargo ship measuring 84.25 m in length, with an 11.58-m beam and 4.88-m depth, with a moulded depth of 7.21 m. John Blumer and Co. at North Dock, Sunderland built and completed her as Yard No.100 on 22 April 1890; she was launched as the schooner-rigged *Centurion* on 8 February 1890 for A. Robson and J. Blumer at Sunderland. The single steel screw was powered by a 170-nhp three-cylinder triple expansion steam engine that used two single-ended boilers, six ribbed furnaces and gave 9.5 knots. The cylinders measured 53.34 cm, 83.82 cm and 134.16 cm with a 106.68-cm stroke (21 in., 33 in. and 54 in. with a 42-in. stroke). Alley and McLellan manufactured the engine and ancillary machinery in Glasgow. She had four bulkheads, water ballast and web frames.The designated code recognition signal letters were: LRBJ. The vessel was valued at £10,000.

In 1898 the ship was registered to Robson and Spencer at Sunderland and the master from 1896 to at least 1900 was Captain Beal.

She was renamed *Genoa* in 1900 when sold to Messrs Bailey and Leetham Ltd at Hull. Messrs Thomas Wilson, Sons and Co. Ltd at Hull became the registered owners in 1903. The ship had been used for the Mediterranean trade but the last two voyages had been to Baltic ports.

Final voyage

On 8 January 1912, the *Genoa*, under the command of Captain Westcott, sailed from Hull on passage to Blyth, where she took on a cargo of coal. Two Blyth men, Able Seamen H. Olsen and J. Dillon both left the ship at Blyth and were replaced by W. Allen and J. Marchland. With her cargo on board, the steamer left the port on 15 January for the six-day voyage to Riga. Nothing more was ever heard or seen of the vessel until, about two weeks later, lifebuoys marked 'Genoa, Hull', lifebelts marked 'T.W.S. and Co. Ltd' and some hatches were reportedly washed up along the coast between Berwick-upon-Tweed and Holy Island.. Just after the ship had sailed, a dense fog had enveloped the English and Scottish eastern coasts, followed soon after by southeasterly and then easterly gale-force winds. The company presumed that she had been overwhelmed in mountainous seas off Berwick and posted her as missing on 6 March 1912. The master, Captain Westcott, was an experienced mariner and had been in charge of the ship for six years. The crewmen lost were:

Allen, W., Able Seaman MM, Montserrat

Anderson, C., Carpenter MM, Gothenburg

Ankin, W., Boatswain MM, Croydon

Brameld, C., Assistant Steward MM, Hull

Cousins, L., Able Seaman MM, Hull

Daley, W., Fireman MM, Hull

Drury, T., Steward MM, Barton

Dunley, Second Officer, MM

Fawcett, J.L., Third Engineer MM, Hull

Garner, T.G., Donkeyman MM, Sutton Bridge

Goodwin, A., Able Seaman MM, Hull

Haller, E., Fireman MM, Hull

Johnson, C., Cook MM, Hull

Marchland, J., Able Seaman MM, Blyth

Newman, J., Fireman MM, Wisbech

Rawson, F.R., Second Engineer MM, Liverpool

Shaw, W.J., Second Mate MM from Hull

Stark, R., First Engineer MM, Glasgow

Stevens, H., Sailor MM, Poole

Westcott, Master MM

Wilkinson, C., Fireman MM, Hull

Wrigley, J., Fireman MM

Able Seaman Cousins replaced a man who left the ship at Hull.

Able Seaman Stevens was a former RN sailor on HMS *Russel* and the cook, C. Johnson, was a former RN sailor on HMS *Enchantress*.

The Times, Tuesday, 30 January 1912, p. 6; Starke/Schell; BoT Wreck Return *Genoa* 1912; *The Times*, Monday, 29 April 1912, p. 22.

Wrecksite

The wreck is orientated in an ENE to WSW direction. It lies on a firm seabed of mud, fine sand and black shells in a general depth of 68 m (LAT). The wreck appears to be upright and intact, with the bows to the SW and covered in various nets, many of which float up over the top of it. Plenty of fish appear to shoal over the top of the wreck, but the risk of losing tackle will not endear it to the boat-angling fraternity. The bell, if or when located, should be inscribed: *Centurion 1890.*

ABBREVIATIONS

100 A1 and 90 A	These indicate the character of a vessel as assessed by the surveyor
ANCL	Allied, Neutral and Central Merchant Shipping Losses of World War One
A/S	Aksjeselskap – the Norwegian term for limited company or joint stock company. Formally referred to as Aktieselskapat
BEM	British Empire Medal
BISCO	The British Iron and Steel Corporation. After World War Two, BISCO was the forerunner in buying up ships to scrap in UK breaker's yards and most of such established yards broke up ships on behalf of BISCO. This went on until at least the 1960s, with many, although not all, ships destined for scrapping owned by BISCO. BISCO actually owned the metal and paid a fee to the scrapyards for their service
BMS	British Merchant Ships sunk by U-boats in the 1914–1918 War (see bibliography, Tennant, A.J.)
BoT	Board of Trade wreck returns, Annual Parliamentary Returns, 1855–1920, contained in state papers
BVLS	British Vessels Lost at Sea – 1914–18 published by HMSO, 1919 and British Vessels Lost at Sea – 1939–45 published by HMSO, 1947
CT	Continental Time
CWGC	Commonwealth War Graves Commission
dampskip	Norwegian term for 'steamship'
DF	direction finding equipment
DoT	Department of Transport
DSM	Distinguished Service Medal
DSO	Distinguished Service Order
HMS	His Majesty's Ship
HMT	His Majesty's Trawler
hp	horsepower
ihp	indicated horsepower
Kapitänleutnant (Kplt.)	Lieutenant, usually the commander
KDM	Kaiserliche Deutsche Marine (Imperial German Navy)
KTB	Kriegstagebuch (ship's log)
LAT	Lowest Astronomical Tide

Lt.z.S.	Leutnant zur See (sub-lieutenant)
MAN	diesel engines manufactured by Maschinefabrik-Augsburg-Nürnberg
MM	Mercantile Marine (Merchant Marine) or Military Medal
MoWT	Ministry of War Transport
NAP	Naval Auxiliary Personnel (Merchant Navy)
NARA	US National Archives and Records Administration
nhp	nominal horsepower
nm	nautical miles (approx. 6,076 ft or 1,851.96 metres)
Oblt.z.S.	Oberleutnant zur See (lieutenant)
PRO	Public Records Office, London
qf	quick firing
Q-ships	Armed Special Service vessels disguised as merchant ships and often crewed by Royal Naval Reserve personnel
RFA	Royal Fleet Auxiliary
rhp	reciprocating horsepower
Ritterkreuz	The Knight's Cross of the Iron Cross, awarded for military distinction in the service of Germany in World War Two
RHIB	rigid hulled inflatable boat
ROV	remotely-operated vehicle, used to search the seabed
selskap	Norwegian term for 'company'
shp	shaft horsepower
SMS	Seiner Majestät Schiff (His Majesty's Ship)
SMU	Seiner Majestät Unterseeboot (His Majesty's Submarine)
SS	steamship
VC	Victoria Cross, Britain's highest award for bravery

BIBLIOGRAPHY AND SOURCES

American Lloyd's Register of American and Foreign Shipping, 1857–1900.

Lloyd's Confidential Index.

Lloyd's War Losses.

Lloyd's Marine Collection:
- Lloyd's Register of British and Foreign Shipping
- Lloyd's Shipping Index
- Lloyd's Weekly Casualty Reports
- Lloyd's Register Wreck Returns
- Lloyd's War Losses, First and Second World Wars
- Lloyd's Loss and Casualty Books

Lloyd's Register of Shipping.

Miramar Ship Index.

Starke/Schell Registers 1870–1991 by Wm. A. Schell in association with Tony Starke.

The Times archives.

Bendert, H. 2001. *Die UC-Boote der Kaiserlichen Marine 1914–1918*, Verlag Mittler, E.S. Mittler & Sohn GmbH, Hamburg, Berlin, Bonn.

Busch, R and Röll, H.J. 1999. *German U-Boat Commanders of World War Two.* Greenhill Books, London, Naval Institute Press Annapolis, Maryland.

Corbett and Newbolt. 1920. *History of the Great War: Naval Operations* (five volumes). Longmans.

Hocking, C. 1969. *Dictionary of Disasters at Sea during the Age of Steam, including Sailing Ships and Ships of War Lost in Action, 1824–1962.* Lloyd's Register, London.

Jarvis, S.D. and Jarvis D.B. 1993. *The Cross of Sacrifice Vol. 1: Officers who died in the service of British, Indian and East African Regiments and Corps, 1914–1919.* Roberts Medals Ltd, Reading.

Jarvis, S. and Jarvis, D.B. 1993. *The Cross of Sacrifice Vol. 2: Officers who died in the service of the Royal Navy, Royal Navy Reserve, Royal Navy Volunteer Reserve, Royal Marines, Royal Naval Air Service and Royal Air Force, 1914–1919.* Roberts Medals Ltd, Reading.

Jarvis, S. and Jarvis, D.B. 1996. *The Cross of Sacrifice Vol. 4: Non-commissioned officers, men and women of the United Kingdom, Commonwealth and Empire who died in the service of the Royal*

Navy, Royal Marines, Royal Naval Air Service, Royal Flying Corp and the Royal Air Force, 1914–1921, including the Commonwealth navies and air forces. Roberts Medals Ltd., Reading.

Jarvis, S. 2000. The Cross of Sacrifice Vol. 5: The officers, men and women of the merchant navy and mercantile fleet auxiliary 1914–1918. The Naval and Military Press Ltd., Uckfield.

Krigsforliste Norske Skip 3 September 1939–8 Mai 1945 (Norwegian Losses from 3 September 1939–8 May 1945). 1949. Grondahl & Son for the Sjofartskontoret, Oslo.

Lloyd's of London. 1990. Lloyd's War Losses: Casualties of the First World War. Lloyd's of London Press Ltd.

Lloyd's of London, 1989. Lloyd's War Losses: The Second World War (two volumes). Lloyd's of London Press Ltd.

Morris, J., 1995. The History of the Seahouses Lifeboats. Royal National Lifeboat Institution.

Sjøforklaringer over Norske skibes Krigsforlis 1914–1918, Kristiania (Maritime Accident Statements for Norwegian Ships Sunk in Wartime 1914–1918, Kristiania). Volume I–III 1917, Volume IV–V 1918. Office of Maritime Affairs, Oslo, Norway.

Sjøforklaringer for 2.verdenskrig (Maritime Inquiries for The Second World War). Maritime declarations (Merchant Navy only) kept in the National Archive.

Stephens, P. 1988. British Vessels Lost at Sea 1914–1918. HMSO.

Stephens, P. 1988. British Vessels Lost at Sea 1939–1940. HMSO.

Svenska handelsflottans krigsförluster åren 1914–1920 (Swedish Merchant Navy war losses, 1914–1920) 1921. Redogörelse av Kommerskollegium, Stockholm (Report by the National Board. Stockholm).

Tennent, A.J. 1990. British Merchant Ships sunk by U-boats in the 1914–1918 War. Starling Press, Newport.

Thompson, M. 1999. Cook, Welton and Gemmell: Shipbuilders of Hull and Beverley 1883–1963, Hutton Press, Beverley.

Toghill, G. 2003. Royal Navy Trawlers Part One: Admiralty Vessels. Maritime Books, Cornwall.

Toghill, G. 2004. Royal Navy Trawlers Part Two: Requisitioned Trawlers. Maritime Books, Cornwall.

Våre Falne (Our Fallen). The biographies (four volumes) of all Norwegians killed or lost at sea or on land, including those who served on RNoN or Allied vessels. Published by the Norwegian government.

Young, R. 2002. Shipwrecks of the North East Coast, two volumes. Tempus Publishing Ltd, Stroud.

Young, R. and Armstrong, P. 2006. Silent Warriors: Submarine Wrecks of the United Kingdom, Vol.1. Tempus Publishing Ltd, Stroud.

Websites used

http://www.aberdeenships.com
http://www.plimsoll.org/WrecksAndAccidents/wreckreports/default.asp
http://www.plimsollshipdata.org
http://library.mysticseaport.org/initiative/VMSearch2.cfm
http://infotrac.london.galegroup.com/itweb/somelib
http://www.clydesite.co.uk
http://www.warsailors.com

http://www.uboat.net

http://www.cwgc.org

http://www.royal-naval-reserve.co.uk

http://ubootwaffe.net/quadrant.cgi

http://www.deutsche-marinesoldaten.de/lebenslaeufe/liste-ritterkreuztraeger-t-z.htm

http://www.2worldwar2.com/knights-cross.htm

www.uboat-memorial.org

http://www.aberdeenships.com/browse.asp

http://www.grantontrawlers.com/

http://uboat-memorial.org/en/index.htm

http://www.ubootehrenmal.de/en/index.htm